Psychoanalysis, Class and Politics

The effects of an increasingly polarized, insecure and threatening world mean that the ideologically enforced split between the political order and personal life is becoming difficult to sustain. This book explores the impact of the social and political domains on individual experience.

The contributions included in this volume describe how issues of class and politics, and the intense emotions they engender, emerge in the clinical setting and how psychotherapists can respectfully address them rather than deny their significance. They demonstrate how clinicians need to take into account the complex convergences between psychic and social reality in order to help their patients understand and more effectively deal with the anxiety, fear, insecurity and anger caused by the complex relations of class and power that affect their lives. This examination of the psychodynamics of terror and aggression and the unconscious defenses employed to deny reality offers powerful insights into the microscopic unconscious ways that ideology is enacted and lived.

Psychoanalysis, Class and Politics will be of interest to all mental health professionals interested in improving their understanding of the ideological factors that impede or facilitate critical and engaged citizenship. It has a valuable contribution to make to the psychoanalytic enterprise, as well as to related scholarly and professional disciplines and public intellectual discourse.

Lynne Layton is Assistant Clinical Professor of Psychology in the Department of Psychiatry at Harvard Medical School and is in clinical practice in Brookline, Massachusetts.

Nancy Caro Hollander is Professor Emeritus at California State University and a member of the Psychoanalytic Center of California and is in clinical practice in Los Angeles, California.

Susan Gutwill is Faculty and Supervisor at the Women's Therapy Centre Institute, New York, and is in private practice in Highland Park, New Jersey.

Psychoanalysis, Class and Politics

Encounters in the clinical setting

Edited by Lynne Layton, Nancy Caro Hollander and Susan Gutwill

Routledge
Taylor & Francis Group
LONDON AND NEW YORK

First published 2006
by Routledge
2 Park Square, Milton Park, Abingdon, Oxon OX14 4RN

Simultaneously published in the USA and Canada
by Routledge
52 Vanderbilt Avenue, New York, NY 10017

Routledge is an imprint of the Taylor & Francis Group, an informa business

Typeset in Times by Garfield Morgan, Rhayader, Powys, UK
Paperback cover design by Code 5 Design Associates Ltd

British Library Cataloguing in Publication Data
A catalogue record for this book is available from the British Library

Library of Congress Cataloging in Publication Data
Psychoanalysis, class, and politics : encounters in the clinical setting / edited by Lynne Layton, Nancy Caro Hollander, and Susan Gutwill.
p. cm.
Includes bibliographical references and index.
ISBN 0-415-37940-7 (hbk : alk. paper) – ISBN 0-415-37941-5 (pbk : alk. paper)
1. Psychoanalysis. 2. Social problems. 3. Political psychology.
I. Layton, Lynne, 1950– . II. Hollander, Nancy Caro, 1939– .
III. Gutwill, Susan.
[DNLM: 1. Psychoanalytic Therapy–methods. 2. Mental Disorders–etiology. 3. Social Problems–psychology. 4. Psychoanalytic Theory.
5. Politics. WM 460.6 P97325 2006]
RC506.P75 2006
616.89'17–dc22

2005023323

ISBN 13: 978-0-415-37940-3 (hbk)

Contents

Contributors

Neil Altman is co-editor of *Psychoanalytic Dialogues: A Journal of Relational Perspectives* and Associate Clinical Professor in the Postdoctoral Program in Psychotherapy and Psychoanalysis at New York University. He is author of *The Analyst in the Inner City: Race, Class, and Culture through a Psychoanalytic Lens* and co-author of *Relational Child Psychotherapy*.

Jessica Benjamin is a Faculty Member and Supervisor in the Postdoctoral Program in Psychotherapy and Psychoanalysis at New York University and is in private practice in New York. She is the author of *Bonds of Love: Psychoanalysis, Feminism, and the Problem of Domination*.

Muriel Dimen is Adjunct Clinical Professor of Psychology, Postdoctoral Program in Psychotherapy and Psychoanalysis, New York University. Incoming Editor (2006) of *Studies in Gender and Sexuality* and Associate Editor of *Psychoanalytic Dialogues*, her most recent book is *Sexuality, Intimacy, Power*; she has co-edited, among other collections, *Gender in Psychoanalytic Space* with Virginia Goldner. She practices and supervises in Manhattan.

Amanda Hirsch Geffner is Co-editor and Interview Editor of *Psychoanalytic Perspectives: A Journal of Integration and Innovation.* She sees children and adults in private practice in Manhattan and in the Bronx. She also practices EMDR.

Susan Gutwill is Faculty and Supervisor of the Women's Therapy Centre Institute in New York and maintains a private practice in Highland Park, NJ. She is co-author of *Eating Problems: A Feminist Psychoanalytic Treatment Model* and on the boards of Psychoanalysis for Social Responsibility and Psychotherapists for Social Responsibility.

Nancy Caro Hollander is Professor Emeritus of Latin American history at California State University, a Member and Faculty at the Psychoanalytic Center of California and is in private practice in Los Angeles. President of Section IX, Psychoanalysis for Social Responsibility, Division 39 of the APA, she has authored many articles on the psychological meanings and sequelae of authoritarian cultures and radical social movements. Her latest book is *Love in a Time of Hate: Liberation Psychology in Latin America*.

Theodore J. Jacobs is Clinical Professor of Psychiatry at the Albert Einstein College of Medicine. He is also Training and Supervising Analyst at the New York Institute and the New York University Psychoanalytic Institute. He is author of *The Use of the Self: Countertransference and Communication in the Analytic Situation*.

Maureen Katz is an adolescent and adult psychoanalyst on the clinical faculty at UCSF and San Francisco Psychoanalytic Institute, and consults for Survivors International, treating torture survivors, and for the Rosa Parks Elementary School-based mental health program in Berkeley, CA. Her current writings focus on ideology, culture and society and their impact on internal psychic states.

Lynne Layton teaches psychoanalysis and culture at Harvard University and the Massachusetts Institute for Psychoanalysis. She is editor of *Psychoanalysis, Culture & Society* and the author of *Who's That Girl? Who's That Boy? Clinical Practice Meets Postmodern Gender Theory*. She is co-editor of *Narcissism and the Text: Essays in Literature and the Psychology of Self*, and of *Bringing the Plague: Toward a Postmodern Psychoanalysis*.

Rachael Peltz is the past president of Section IX, Psychoanalysis for Social Responsibility, Division 39, APA. She is a training and supervising analyst and on the faculty at the Psychoanalytic Institute of Northern California. Author of "My father's flags: psychoanalytic perspectives on being an American from the streets and the consulting room" (*Psychotherapy and Politics International* 2, 3, 2004), she practices psychotherapy and psychoanalysis in Berkeley, CA.

Andrew Samuels is Professor of Analytical Psychology, University of Essex and Training Analyst of the Society of Analytical Psychology, London. He works internationally as a political consultant and is co-founder of Psychotherapists and Counselors for Social Responsibility. His books include *Jung and the Post-Jungians*; *A Critical Dictionary of Jungian Analysis*; *The Father*; *The Plural Psyche*; *Psychopathology*; *The Political Psyche*; and the award-winning *Politics on the Couch: Citizenship and the Internal Life*.

Paul L. Wachtel is CUNY Distinguished Professor in clinical psychology at City College and the CUNY Graduate Center. On the faculty of the Postdoctoral Program in Psychoanalysis and Psychotherapy at New

York University, he is the author of *Race in the Mind of America: Breaking the Vicious Circle between Blacks and Whites*; *The Poverty of Affluence: A Psychological Portrait of the American Way of Life*; and *Psychoanalysis, Behavior Therapy, and the Relational World.*

Gary Walls is an Associate Professor of Clinical Psychology at the Chicago School for Professional Psychology and is affiliated with its Center for Multicultural and Diversity Studies. He is an advanced candidate at the Chicago Center for Psychoanalysis and in private practice.

Cleonie White is a graduate of the William Alanson White Institute, where she is a supervisor of psychotherapy and a member of the faculty of the Intensive Psychoanalytic Psychotherapy Program. Dr White maintains a private practice in New York.

Acknowledgments

This project emerged in part from our participation in Psychoanalysis for Social Responsibility, Section IX of Division 39 (The Division of Psychoanalysis) of the American Psychological Association. For almost a decade, this Section has offered its members an intellectual venue to develop our ideas about the convergence of psychic and social reality. Many of us have presented our work in our Section-sponsored panels at Division 39's annual meetings. Since 9/11, we have had the opportunity with our colleagues to think together about the psychological impact on individual and group experience of the deepening political and economic crises in our society and in the world. As professionals and activists, we have been able to share and reflect together on how the social/political world affects our daily practice. The dominant institutions and ideologies in the USA have become cause for increasing concern, and we have been privileged to find in Section IX the possibility through our many dialogues and activities to elaborate our intellectual and emotional responses, to learn from one another, to remember history and to oppose violence in its many forms. Each of us is grateful to our patients/clients for the opportunity to co-create a potential space in which we are all enlightened.

Nancy Hollander and Susan Gutwill especially thank Lynne Layton for the breadth of her scholarship, intellectual collegiality and for her leadership and attention to detail in the process of stewarding this project through to fruition.

All of us are grateful for the intelligence and commitment to social justice of the contributors to this volume. To Andrew Samuels we offer a special "thank you" for his thoughtful, groundbreaking, down-to-earth and yet spiritual work in the area of politics and psychotherapy, as well as for his help in publishing this volume. We join him in his commitment to the work to heal and repair the world.

Susan Gutwill is profoundly grateful for Nancy Hollander's intellectual, personal, and political sisterhood for these many years, for the loving, technical and co-parenting support of David Stone and for the Women's

Therapy Centre Institute for bringing together feminism, politics and psychoanalysis in our work in both public and professional venues.

Nancy Hollander is deeply appreciative of Susan Gutwill's partnership in our shared explorations of how to integrate intellectual, clinical, personal and political aspects of life and of Stephen Portuges' loving embrace of our decades-long emotional, intellectual and political journey together. To my Latin American colleagues, I am forever grateful for your inspiration in modeling psychoanalytic activism and commitment to social change, even in the darkest of times.

Lynne Layton is endlessly grateful to her family, many friends, and to Oliver Buckley for their good sense, warm hearts, and comradeship in these troubled times. I am grateful, too, to my wonderful colleagues in the Association for the Psychoanalysis of Culture & Society, which, like Section IX, provides another of those all too rare "potential spaces" where I can think with smart and caring activist/scholars about social injustice and psychic reality. To Simon Clarke, my co-editor of *Psychoanalysis, Culture & Society*, a special thanks.

Permission to reprint the following is gratefully acknowledged. We particularly wish to thank the National Institute for the Psychotherapies Training Institute and the NIP Professional Association for allowing us to reprint the political roundtable and responses (Chapters 12 through 16) from their new publication, *Psychoanalytic Perspectives: A Journal of Integration and Innovation*.

- Chapter 1: Working Directly with Political, Social, and Cultural Material in the Therapy Session. Permission from Brunner-Routledge to reprint a revised version from Robert Withers (ed.), *Controversies in Analytical Psychology* (2003).
- Chapter 2: Money, Love, and Hate: Contradiction and Paradox in Psychoanalysis. Permission from The Analytic Press to reprint an excerpted version of *Psychoanalytic Dialogues* 4(1): 69–100 (1994). Copyright © The Analytic Press.
- Chapter 3: That Place Gives Me the Heebie Jeebies. Permission from Lawrence & Wishart to reprint *International Journal of Critical Psychology* 10 (Psycho-Social Research): 36–50 (2004).
- Chapter 4: The Manic Society. Permission from The Analytic Press to reprint *Psychoanalytic Dialogues* 15(3): 347–366 (2005). Copyright © The Analytic Press.
- Chapter 12: Is Politics the Last Taboo in Psychoanalysis? A Roundtable Discussion with Neil Altman, Jessica Benjamin, Ted Jacobs, and Paul Wachtel. Moderated by Amanda Hirsch Geffner. Permission from the National Institute for the Psychotherapies Training Institute and

the NIP Professional Association to reprint *Psychoanalytic Perspectives: A Journal of Integration and Innovation* 2(1): 5–37 (Fall 2004).

- Chapter 13: Response to Roundtable: Something's Gone Missing. Permission from the National Institute for the Psychotherapies Training Institute and the NIP Professional Association to reprint *Psychoanalytic Perspectives: A Journal of Integration and Innovation* 2(1): 57–64 (Fall 2004).
- Chapter 14: Response to Roundtable: Politics and/or/in/for Psychoanalysis. Permission from the National Institute for the Psychotherapies Training Institute and the NIP Professional Association to reprint *Psychoanalytic Perspectives: A Journal of Integration and Innovation* 2(1): 39–47 (Fall 2004).
- Chapter 15: Response to Roundtable: What Dare We (Not) Do? Psychoanalysis: A Voice in Politics? Permission from the National Institute for the Psychotherapies Training Institute and the NIP Professional Association to reprint *Psychoanalytic Perspectives: A Journal of Integration and Innovation* 2(1): 49–55 (Fall 2004).
- Chapter 16: Political Identity: A Personal Postscript. Permission from the National Institute for the Psychotherapies Training Institute and the NIP Professional Association to reprint *Psychoanalytic Perspectives: A Journal of Integration and Innovation* 2(1): 65–73 (Fall 2004).

Introduction

Lynne Layton, Nancy Caro Hollander and Susan Gutwill

This book offers a rich compilation of essays that represent a radical departure from contemporary mainstream psychoanalysis. It was conceived within the context of our specific historical moment, for in this post-September 11th world, the apparently hard and fast boundaries between the political order and personal life have been increasingly difficult to maintain, or to put it another way, harder to deny or disavow. How this political climate, characterized by increasing threat, violence, polarization and unpredictability, is felt personally and how the personal psychic reality makes its way into the political process are relevant to the psychotherapeutic enterprise, to scholars and to critical intellectuals alike.

Our entrée into this subject is as psychoanalysts concerned about how events in the social domain are making their way into the clinical setting with more regularity and how they are entering into the transference/countertransference relationship. All of the book's contributors have had a keen interest for some time in what we view as the last taboo in the psychoanalytic field: namely, how to theorize the complex relationship between psychoanalysis, class, and politics and deal with its manifestations in the clinical setting. Mental health professionals are increasingly challenged to consider the place of class and politics in conscious and unconscious life. Even more significant questions are raised by instances in which we find a lack of any apparent concern on the part of patient or therapist about the impact of the troubled social and political environment. As Slavoj Žižek charged in a dialogue with psychoanalytic social theorists Judith Butler and Ernesto Laclau (2000), even in left postmodern theory the traditional singular focus on class has been eclipsed by the interest in other forms of oppression. Žižek argued that when class and capitalism are excluded categories of analysis, their omission allows for the successful functioning of mainstream political thought. By this he means to say that those left academic theorists (and we could add left psychoanalytic practitioners) who write as though capitalism is natural and here to stay are not effective in helping us understand its obscured dynamics of class and power.

This trend among the academic left has been entrenched within the psychoanalytic profession in the USA. Since most traditional training settings provide no way to think about how class and politics enter treatment, therapists have little chance to reflect together or develop strategies to deal with the mutual interaction of psychic and social reality. Moreover, according to the research of Andrew Samuels (1993), many therapists worry that if they were to deal seriously with political issues with their patients they would be violating an ethical standard of "psychoanalytic neutrality." Samuels' research also indicates that many clinicians report that they do not know or understand enough about the social and political world to deal with patient material that either alludes to or denies it. The articles in this book explore a variety of themes related to class and politics and how the underlying dynamics of power are meant to be mystified and confusing even to the most well-educated citizens. These articles offer multiple ways to think about the ideological underpinnings of what psychoanalyst and sociologist Earl Hopper calls the "social unconscious" (2003). They suggest how clinicians can work respectfully to reflect on their own and their patients' responses to an increasingly traumatogenic sociopolitical order.

This book, then, represents a radical psychoanalytic appreciation of the interpenetration of subjectivity and the sociopolitical order. It addresses the dramatic shift in this culture and consequently in the psychological experience of living in the United States in the post-9/11 era. September 11 marks the moment at which the American people could no longer feel invulnerable to the devastating forces of violence and destruction throughout the world that appear to be beyond control. The tragedy of 9/11 itself – the deaths, the disappeared, the grieving families, the fear shared by an entire population – was unprecedented in the most powerful country in the world. However, in addition to its impact on Americans, 9/11 has also had complicated effects on other countries and on the latent complexities of global politics that became manifest when the US invaded and occupied Iraq. In fact, the militarized response of the US government has outraged and frightened people throughout the world. And in spite of domestic opposition, 9/11 has revealed how too many US citizens uncritically identify with the government's policies and its ideological justifications, both of which represent but the latest chapter in well over a century's claims to a "Manifest Destiny" to control the internal politics and resources of other countries. And, paradoxically, despite the enormous military budget and the sacrifice of civil liberties demanded by "homeland security," people in the USA know that we are not safer. Indeed, we may be less safe because US strategy has paradoxically produced increasing numbers of people throughout the world who resent what they believe to be the country's motivation to shore up its hegemonic position militarily and economically. Moreover, the state's policies have produced a redistribution of wealth within the United States upward to a small elite, which enjoys increasing profits and influence at the expense of working Americans who suffer rising unemployment, lower wages, loss of health care, deteriorating school systems and impoverishment. Superimposed upon these threatening political and economic trends is a governmental and media discourse primarily designed to deny, mystify and distort critical consciousness about this experience.

A traumatogenic environment is constituted when individual and group physical safety, social security and symbolic capacities are all simultaneously assaulted. Psychoanalysis, which is devoted to analyzing what it means to people when their experience is traumatic and then rendered unnameable and unspeakable, can illuminate this phenomenon as it occurs in the relationship between the individual and society. Further, psychoanalysts and their colleagues among psychodynamic and trauma theorists are in a particularly important position with respect to elaborating the anxieties, fears and defenses engendered by such traumatic experience. Our profession can appreciate the profound need to attach to others, including the larger society, and we can analyze what happens when the social order fails to provide a holding environment, which then leaves individuals and groups vulnerable to destructive and antisocial behaviors. In this context, we can explicate the psychodynamics of aggression as well as the unconscious defenses utilized to deny truth and reality.

This book's psychoanalytic authors explore these and related issues. As such, the book takes its place in the long tradition within a psychoanalysis that has been committed to understanding the fundamental and inescapable role played by the sociosymbolic order in the construction of subjectivity. Class and politics were central to the thought and practice of many of the first generation of psychoanalysts. For example, the Berlin Polyclinic and the Vienna Ambulatorium (see Danto 1998, 1999), free clinics set up in the 1920s with Freud's blessing, expressed not only their founders' commitment to bring psychoanalysis to the masses, but also their conviction that social forms of oppression caused by capitalism needed to be altered to secure a decent standard of mental health for the popular classes.

The creative intellectual and political movements that grew in Europe during the interwar years, among them a socially conscious psychoanalysis (in the work, for example, of Wilhelm Reich (1972)), were devastated by the rise of Nazism. With the emigration of several of the most radical analysts to the United States, including Edith Jacobson and Otto Fenichel, the left wing of clinical psychoanalysis was eclipsed (see Jacoby 1983). Many factors were responsible for the dilution of this radical tradition, including censorship by the International Psychoanalytic Association, which was too often willing to insure the survival of psychoanalysis by compromising with the demands of right-wing regimes (Roazen 2003). In the United States, émigrés anxious about their status in their new homeland adopted a defensive self-censorship in response to the Cold War and McCarthyism (Jacoby

1983). They situated themselves within the prevailing medical model that had eschewed the cultural and humanistic tradition within psychoanalysis. In this historical period, US psychoanalysis tended to be practiced through the ideological lens of resolving psychic conflict via adaptation to the existing social structures and prevailing cultural values of a consumer society.

Interestingly, the United States has been unique in its isolation from the dialogue between critical social theory and psychoanalysis. Such interchange fared better in the United Kingdom, Continental Europe and Latin America, where a rich radical cultural discourse, vital working-class politics, and psychoanalytic theory and practice enjoyed an easier cross-fertilization. In some countries, most notably France and Argentina, a left psychoanalysis emerged that was identified with revolutionary struggles against social as well as psychological repression. In the United States, it was only the "cultural" school, represented by culture critic/analysts Erich Fromm (1941, 1962), Harry Stack Sullivan (1965), Karen Horney (1937) and Clara Thompson (1964), that maintained the link with a socially critical psychoanalysis. It was not until the 1970s that a larger group of psychoanalysts in the USA began again to think critically about class and politics. Even then, most psychoanalytic thinking in this area, including that of the critical social theorists Herbert Marcuse (1955, 1966) and Horkheimer and Adorno (1973), or Christopher Lasch's (1979) more widely disseminated theory of capitalism as a culture of narcissism, was produced outside of clinical circles and had little effect on clinical theory or practice.

At the same time, however, a new generation of clinicians – social workers and psychologists as well as psychoanalysts – not necessarily steeped in radical psychoanalytic theory and sometimes even opposed to it, were influenced by the civil rights movement, the anti-war movement, the war on poverty and other liberation movements such as feminism and gay rights. They became active in a variety of community mental health initiatives, some of which were akin to the early Berlin and Vienna models of free or very low cost treatment. Particularly important was a growing interest in trauma; Judith Lewis Herman (1992), who was central in the formation of a new generation of theorists, developed paradigms for understanding the psychosocial dynamics and treatment for posttraumatic stress disorder caused by war and incest and explicated the social context of the production of psychic pain and mental disorders.

The politics of the 1960s, 1970s, and beyond were often formulated around attaining rights and recognition for groups excluded from the benefits of full citizenship in a social order viewed as oppressive to women, people of color, gays and lesbians. The feminist movement, with its understanding that the "personal is political," privileged the development of a psychotherapeutic practice that embraced the social context of pain and suffering. By the mid-1970s many feminists, including Dorothy Dinnerstein (1976), Nancy Chodorow (1978), and Jessica Benjamin (1988), were critically rethinking the patriarchal aspects of psychoanalytic theory and practice. Their rich theorizing about how gendered arrangements are internalized and reproduced in the unconscious of both male and female contributed significantly to changing the face of contemporary psychoanalysis.

This new generation of feminist psychoanalytic thinkers, whose work exposed many facets of social and psychological hierarchies, led the way toward a democratization of clinical practice as well as theory. However, an additional frontier had yet to be explored, that of subjectivity and its relationship to class and the social order. Although the important work of Joel Kovel (1981, 1988), Richard Lichtman (1982) and Victor Wolfenstein (1993) sought to develop various aspects of the Freud/Marx dialogue, the interface between radical social theory and psychoanalysis remained much more developed in other parts of the world.

This book strives to put both class and politics back in the center of clinical thinking in the United States. The editors and contributors feel that the marginalization of class and politics from mainstream analytic thinking in the USA is itself a profoundly political phenomenon. As several of the authors in this volume argue, the split between the psychic and the social that informs most American discourses, including psychoanalysis, is a false dichotomy that serves an individualist and capitalist *status quo*. It is a split that too often discourages critical awareness and sustains psychic pain.

We are living in a particularly fertile historical moment that demands of us and offers us the opportunity as well once again to address this dichotomy in an effort to challenge the split. This book represents a collaborative effort to take up this challenge within the context of clinical work. Mental health professionals are increasingly faced with patients who speak of their individual feelings of despair, cynicism and confusion. When patients express their anxieties about concerns related to politics and class, how do we take them up? How do we address fears about global warming? How do we explore concerns about the Iraq War? What do we say about potential terrorist attacks with weapons of mass destruction? How do we take up the real problems of unemployment, underemployment or lack of medical care? How do we understand patients' distrust or naïve acceptance of the media's presentation of political and social reality? On the other hand, what do we make of it when the external world is absent – when patients do not mention the Iraq War, or major weather events that signify effects of global warming, or controversial political struggles? What is our role when patients do not think about participating in civic life, either because of disinterest or the inability to imagine lively political engagement that might change current conditions? What happens when the patient and therapist have similar political perspectives or are at different poles of a polarized society? How do we challenge an official professional ethic of neutrality that requires us to evade and deny the personal impact of the sociosymbolic order? Is this neutrality or collusion with our patients' denial? How do we respect psychological boundaries while venturing into the political aspect of personal experience without being polemical? This book elaborates ways of thinking about and dealing with, in the clinical encounter itself, the relationship between psychic and social reality. It thus offers psychotherapists (as well as their patients) an important reflective space.

Since many of the book's essays center squarely on the clinical encounter, non-clinicians have the opportunity to learn more about the application of psychoanalytic theory to the therapeutic endeavor, including the psychodynamic experience of resistance and change. Because clinicians are privy to the microscopic ways that unconscious process reveals itself, non-clinicians interested in psychoanalytic cultural studies or psychoanalytic social theory will discover here compelling examples of the way ideologies are enacted and lived.

The contributors to this book explore themes related to psychoanalysis, politics and class from a variety of psychoanalytic perspectives, including Object Relations, neo-Freudian, Jungian and Post-Jungian, Kleinian, Lacanian, and Relational. They provide an exciting kaleidoscope of perspectives on our shared emotional experience of the current period's ominous political landscape.

We begin the book with essays by Andrew Samuels, the foremost spokesperson and researcher on the use of politics in the clinical setting (see, for example, *The Political Psyche* (1993)), and by Muriel Dimen, whose 1994 essay on love and money in clinical work, which we reprint here, opened a space for discussion of the taboo subject of class. In "Working directly with political, social, and cultural material in the therapy session," Samuels summarizes the results of his research with therapists of several countries and several analytic paradigms. He asked his subjects to discuss whether or not they talked about politics in their sessions, what kinds of political topics were most often broached, and what was done with this material clinically. He argues that a person's political developmental history is an important dimension of every psyche and needs to be addressed in treatment.

Muriel Dimen's "Money, love, and hate: contradiction and paradox in psychoanalysis" discusses the contradictions that arise from the fact that clinicians charge for the love and care they provide. Drawing on Barbara Ehrenreich's book, *Fear of Falling* (1989), Dimen examines the anxieties and aspirations of the professional, managerial class to which most analysts belong. With attention focused on the way the therapists' needs affect the treatment, this essay also broke new ground in the relational paradigm's expansion of the meaning of countertransference.

Lynne Layton's "That place gives me the heebie jeebies" is a psychosocial study of the emotions that keep class alliances in place. Layton draws on Bourdieu's idea (1984) that class identities are established by processes that involve the repudiation of the attributes of other classes, and, more particularly, that the various fractions of the bourgeoisie build their identity on "distinction" from the lower classes. The essay includes an empirical study of the emotions members of the professional middle class feel when shopping in low-end vs high-end stores; it also reveals the way the subjects anxiously avoid encounters with whatever connotes poverty.

Rachael Peltz's "The manic society" is a stunning indictment of a society that, in fetishizing free markets, has abdicated its role as facilitating environment for its subjects. For Peltz, the frenzied activity of the US adult population originates with this abandonment; she worries that the parent generation is passing the frenzy onto its children. As her clinical examples show, few are conscious that their symptoms stem as much from this abandonment as from familial distress. In fact, the primary symptom is a manic denial of need for the withheld social support. Tragedies such as September 11 break through the defense and reveal to all the need for the caretaking function of government.

Nancy Caro Hollander and Susan Gutwill's "Despair and hope in a culture of denial" examines the psychological impact on the American population of 9/11 and how psychic defenses mobilized by the trauma of terrorism facilitated the state's initial support for an aggressive agenda in both foreign and domestic policies. Hollander and Gutwill analyze the convergence of hegemonic ideology and unconscious defenses that masked important real class relations in US society and produced a manic identification with state priorities. They suggest these conditions produced despair in the aftermath of 9/11, but also show how, in response to the rise of an oppositional movement, a new potential space was opened up that permitted the emergence of a genuine depressive position experience of hope within significant sectors of the population.

In their companion piece, "Class and splitting in the clinical setting: the ideological dance in the transference and countertransference," Gutwill and Hollander extend their analysis to explore how, in the context of the current traumatogenic environment, political themes appear increasingly in patient material. They discuss the need for psychotherapists to consider patients' concerns with events in the public realm as real rather than simply displacements or symbolic references to unconscious conflicts rooted in family and personal relationships. Specific case examples illustrate analysts' experiences dealing with the passionate feelings mobilized by issues of class and politics in the transference and countertransference relationship.

Lynne Layton's "Attacks on linking: the unconscious pull to dissociate individuals from their social context" explores the way a Western cultural norm that separates the individual from the social is enacted both by the psychoanalytic profession as a whole and by patient and therapist in the clinical encounter. The chapter focuses on a vignette in which a patient discusses her political views and both therapist and patient become anxious about whether or not they are properly doing therapy. Layton suggests that the very norms that cause psychic damage in the first place are often upheld and reinforced in treatment repetition compulsions that involve both patient and therapist.

In "The normative unconscious and the political contexts of change in psychotherapy," Gary Walls continues to explore the ways that we unconsciously live the separation of the psychic and the social, in accord with social norms that dictate that we do so. A clinical vignette illustrates what happens when Walls confronts a patient, who is caught up in depression and blames himself for his misery, with the social reality from which Walls feels he suffers. In a second essay, "Racism, classism, psychosis and self-image in the analysis of a woman," Walls draws on Eng and Han's (2000) notion of racial melancholia and Homi Bhabha's (1984) notion of racial mimicry to discuss his treatment of an African-American woman who had suffered a psychotic break. Rendering psychoanalytic DuBois's (1903) concept of "double consciousness," Walls argues that racism subjects African-Americans to a kind of pathological splitting that accounts for the greater incidence of mental disorders among African-Americans.

Maureen Katz explores the grip on US citizens of three related events as they were framed through the visual symbols intruded upon us by major news media: the attacks on the World Trade Center and Pentagon, the Iraqi beheading of Nicholas Berg, and the torture of Iraqi prisoners by the American military as it was documented at Abu Ghraib. In her aptly titled "The beheading of America: reclaiming our minds," Katz's compelling narrative – which includes her own and her patients' fantasies as well as critical reflections gleaned from Freud, Jay, Žižek and other psychoanalytic historians – takes the reader through the visual imprinting of these events upon our minds. Her essay describes how citizens' capacities to think, reflect, and connect present events to history, capacities necessary to be able to be responsible in our world, are overwhelmed by ideology meant to frighten us into primitive states of mind. Such states support acts of retaliatory sadism and aggression – even when such acts are in opposition to our consciously held humanitarian values.

Nancy Caro Hollander's "Psychoanalysis and the problem of the bystander in times of terror" analyzes the psychopolitical dynamics of life under Argentine state terror during that country's Dirty War (1976–1983) and the factors responsible for the creation of a bystander population. She does so to illuminate aspects of our own experience in another time of terror since 9/11. In her exploration of the reactions of the psychoanalytic community to the military dictatorship's culture of fear, she describes a sector of Argentine psychoanalysts who challenged their institutes' principle of neutrality. These analysts embraced an "ethic of nonneutrality" to provide patients and themselves with a potential space to explore together the severe psychological impingements of living in a terrorist state. The analysis has implications for contemporary psychoanalysis.

The book concludes with a candid and revealing roundtable discussion on politics and psychoanalysis, featuring several of the most important political analytic theorists writing today. The participants include Jessica Benjamin, whose book *The Bonds of Love* (1988) is a classic of feminist psychoanalytic theory, Neil Altman, whose *The Analyst in the Inner City* (1995) was one of the first books to talk about class and clinical work, Paul Wachtel (1983, 1999), whose theory of vicious circles applies to any number of social problems, and Ted Jacobs (1990), an innovator in the field of working with the analyst's subjectivity. Muriel Dimen, Andrew Samuels, Cleonie White, and Amanda Hirsch Geffner are discussants. The roundtable broaches such issues as analytic neutrality in work with people who hold the same and different politics as those of the analyst, what psychoanalysts have to offer in the understanding of current political problems, and whether or not an analyst should be "out" as a political activist.

References

Altman, N. (1995) *The Analyst in the Inner City: Race, Class and Culture through a Psychoanalytic Lens*. Hillsdale, NJ: The Analytic Press.

Benjamin, J. (1988) *The Bonds of Love: Psychoanalysis, Feminism and the Problem of Domination*. New York: Pantheon.

Bhabha, H. K. (1984) Of mimicry and man: the ambivalence of colonial discourse. *October*, 28 (spring):125–133.

Bourdieu, P. (1984) *Distinction*. Cambridge, MA: Harvard University Press.

Butler, J., Laclau, E. and Žižek, S. (2000) *Contingency, Hegemony, Universality: Contemporary Dialogues on the Left*. London: Verso.

Chodorow, N. J. (1978) *The Reproduction of Mothering*. Berkeley: University of California Press.

Danto, E. A. (1998) The Ambulatorium: Freud's free clinic in Vienna. *International Journal of Psychoanalysis*, 79:287–300.

Danto, E. A. (1999) The Berlin polyklinik: psychoanalytic innovation in Weimar Germany. *Journal of the American Psychoanalytic Association*, 47/4:1269–1292.

Dinnerstein, D. (1976) *The Mermaid and the Minotaur: Sexual Arrangements and Human Malaise*. New York: Harper Colophon Books.

Dubois, W. E. B. (1903) *The Souls of Black Folk*. New York: Bantam, 1989.

Ehrenreich, B. (1989) *Fear of Falling: The Inner Life of the Middle Class*. New York: Pantheon.

Eng, D. and Han, S. (2000) A dialogue on racial melancholia. *Psychoanalytic Dialogues*, 10:667–700.

Fromm, E. (1941) *Escape from Freedom*. New York: Farrar & Reinhart.

Fromm, E. (1962) *Beyond the Chains of Illusion: My Encounter with Marx and Freud*. New York: Simon and Schuster.

Herman, J. (1992) *Trauma and Recovery*. New York: Basic Books.

Hopper, E. (2003) *The Social Unconscious: Selected Papers of Earl Hopper*. London: Jessica Kingsley Publishers.
Horkheimer, M. and Adorno, T. (1973) *Dialectic of Enlightenment*. London: Allen Lane.
Horney, K. (1937) *The Neurotic Personality of Our Time*. New York: W. W. Norton.
Jacobs, T. J. (1990) *The Use of the Self: Countertransference and Communication in the Analytic Situation*. Madison, CT: International Universities Press.
Jacoby, R. (1983) *The Repression of Psychoanalysis*. New York: Basic Books.
Kovel, J. (1981) *The Age of Desire: Reflections of a Radical Psychoanalyst*. New York: Pantheon.
Kovel, J. (1988) *The Radical Spirit: Essays on Psychoanalysis and Society*. London: Free Association.
Lasch, C. (1979) *The Culture of Narcissism*. New York: W. W. Norton.
Lichtman, R. (1982) *The Production of Desire: The Integration of Psychoanalysis into Marxist Theory*. New York: Macmillan.
Marcuse, H. (1955) *Eros and Civilization: A Philosophical Inquiry into Freud*. Boston: Beacon Press.
Marcuse, H. (1966) *One-Dimensional Man: Studies in Advanced Industrial Society*. Boston: Beacon Press.
Reich, W. (1972) *Sex-Pol: Essays 1929–1934*, L. Baxandall (ed.). New York: Random House.
Roazen, P. (2003) The exclusion of Erich Fromm from the IPA. *Cultural Foundations of Political Psychology*. New Brunswick, NJ: Transaction Publishers, pp. 1–34.
Samuels, A. (1993) *The Political Psyche*. London: Routledge.
Sullivan, H. S. (1965) *Collected Works*. New York: Norton.
Thompson, C. (1964) *Interpersonal Psychoanalysis: The Selected Papers of Clara M. Thompson*, M. R. Green (ed.). New York: Basic Books.
Wachtel, P. (1983) *The Poverty of Affluence*. New York: Free Press.
Wachtel, P. (1999) *Race in the Mind of America: Breaking the Vicious Circle Between Blacks and Whites*. New York: Routledge.
Wolfenstein, V. (1993) *Psychoanalytic Marxism: Groundwork*. New York: Guilford Press.

Chapter 1

Working directly with political, social and cultural material in the therapy session

Andrew Samuels

What shall we do about politics?

I am going to explore how the practice of psychotherapy might become more sensitive to political issues as these affect therapists and their clients. The hope is that therapists and analysts who seek to work directly in a responsible way with the whole person, including the social and political dimensions of the experiences of their clients, may do so with greater confidence and clarity. I believe this detailed work has not really been done yet, though there is by now a major shift in awareness concerning the social, cultural and political aspects of the subject positions of both therapist and client.

In spite of an interest in how these differing subject positions evolve in practice and the consequent recognition that everyone, not just members of sexual, ethnic or economic minorities, belongs to a "culture" and has a subject position, I shall not focus much on the external and internal political dynamics of the therapy encounter itself (see Samuels 2002). Equally, I will say almost nothing about the politics of the profession, though this remains a concern of mine. Instead, I present some ideas about addressing politics in therapy practice. Although these ideas derive from work with individuals, they may be even more pertinent and useful in group analysis and psychotherapy. The group matrix may facilitate the politicization of the practice of therapy rather well (see Brown and Zinkin 1994: *passim*).

In referring to "politics," I have in mind the crucial interplay to which feminism introduced us between formal and institutional economic power and power as expressed on the domestic, private level. One implication of this reading is that power is understood as a process or network as much as a stable factor. Political power is experienced psychologically: in family organization, gender and race relations, and in religious and artistic assumptions as they affect the lives of individuals.

Where the public and the private, the political and the personal, intersect, I think there is a special role for analysis and psychotherapy in relation to political change and transformation. The tragicomic crisis of our *fin de siècle* civilization incites clinicians to challenge the boundaries that are conventionally accepted as existing between the external world and the internal world, between life and reflection, between extroversion and introversion, between doing and being, between politics and psychology, between the political development of the person and the psychological development of the person, between the fantasies of the political world and the politics of the fantasy world. Subjectivity and intersubjectivity have some political roots; they are not as "internal" as they seem.

There is little point in working on the orientation of psychotherapy to the world of politics if its own basic theories and practices remain completely unaltered.

I support the continuing practice of therapy and analysis with individuals and small groups. This is because I do not agree that analysis and therapy inevitably siphon off rage that might more constructively be deployed in relation to social injustices. In fact, I think that it is the reverse that often happens: experiences in therapy act to fine down generalized rage into a more constructive form, hence rendering emotion more accessible for social action. Even when this is not what happens, the potential remains for a move from private therapy to public action – and I propose to discuss that potential in this chapter.

The idea is to develop a portrayal of the clinical setting as a bridge between psychotherapy and politics, rather than as the source of an isolation from politics. Critics of the clinical project of depth psychology (e.g. Hillman and Ventura 1992) have noted the isolation – and this is not a totally wrong observation. But I want us also to see the potential links and to create a truly radical revisioning of clinical work, not a simplistic huffing and puffing aimed at its elimination.

One of the most potent criticisms of therapy and analysis is that the client is encouraged or even required to run away from external concerns – for example, political commitments or actions – and focus exclusively on the "inner world." This, it is argued, makes any statement about therapy engaging the whole person an absolute nonsense. Most textbooks of therapy and analysis continue to accentuate the introspection by making it clear that exploration of outer world issues is simply not done in "proper" therapy and analysis.

Over a period of time – from about 1980 to 1990 – I sensed that this professional consensus, derived from psychoanalysis, was collapsing and that therapists and analysts were indeed beginning to pay more attention to what could be called the political development of their clients (Samuels 1993:134–137). In my own practice I noticed that many clients seemed to be introducing political themes more often than they had before. Talking to colleagues confirmed that this was also going on in their work, so it was not all due to suggestion on my part. We tended to put it down to the fact that, since the mid-1980s, the pace of political change in the world appeared to have quickened. At times, I still felt that the usual formulation – that such material needs to be understood as symbolic of what is going on in the client – worked pretty well. At other times it turned out that the clients had a need to talk about some public issue, maybe to work out what their true feelings and opinions were. But the clients might also have learned that you are not supposed to do that in therapy or analysis. For example, during the first Gulf War there were certainly some clients who used war imagery to tell me something about their inner state. Yet, there were others who were hiding a profound need to talk about the Gulf War behind the flow of regular, ordinary clinical material.

I decided that what was needed was a large-scale investigation, by means of a questionnaire, to see if analysts and therapists were experiencing something similar in significant numbers. I therefore obtained the cooperation of 14 professional organizations with differing theoretical orientations in seven different countries and sent out 2,000 survey forms. I got a return rate of almost exactly one-third (quite high for a cold-calling survey on which the respondents had to spend some time and write fairly lengthy and thoughtful answers).

In the survey, I asked which themes of a list of 15 possibilities were the most frequently introduced by clients. This produced a worldwide league table as follows: (1) gender issues for women, (2) economic issues (e.g. distribution of wealth, poverty, inflation), (3) violence in society, (4=) national politics, and gender issues for men, (4=) racial or ethnic issues, (6) international politics.

There were some striking departures from the order. For instance, the German analysts placed "the environment" at the top of the list as the most frequently introduced issue, while for the British psychoanalysts economic issues came in seventh. This enables us to make all kinds of speculations about whether there is or is not something like a "national psyche" or "collective consciousness," at least as evidenced in the political themes the clients of therapists and analysts bring to their sessions.

I asked the participants how they reacted to, handled or interpreted the material. Seventy-eight per cent of the respondents mentioned that they understood the material as referring in some sense to reality. For many, this was in conjunction with a symbolic interpretation or an exploration of why the client was interested in that particular theme at that particular moment. The replies – thoughtful and extensive – showed considerable struggle by the respondents as they endeavored to mark out their positions.

I went on to ask if the respondent "discussed" politics with his or her clients. Of course, I realized the explosive nature of the question and deliberately did not define what might be covered by the word "discuss." Worldwide, 56 per cent said they did discuss politics and 44 per cent that they did not. American Jungian analysts do the most discussing (72 per cent) and British psychoanalysts the least (33 per cent). However, it is interesting to note that the implication of the one-third "yes" of the British psychoanalysts is that 43 of them admit to discussing politics with clients (one-third of the 129 respondents).

I asked the respondents the obvious question: "Have you ever been/are you politically active?" Sixty-seven per cent said they had been politically active at some time – a figure which, unsurprisingly, dropped to 33 per cent at the present time. My intuitive impression, just from talking to colleagues, that a good many of them had been politically active at some time was borne out. The stereotype of a profession composed of introspective, introverted, self-indulgent types was challenged.

So what might it all mean? In the most down-to-earth terms, it could mean that if a person is contemplating analysis or therapy, and if that person is interested in politics (however defined), it would be as well to explore with a potential therapist or analyst what they are likely to do if one brings political material to the consulting room. For the profession is clearly divided about it. Even if everyone who did not return the survey forms abhors politics in the consulting room, there is still a significant minority of practitioners who do not. This other, hitherto unknown, group of clinicians sees that involvement in and concern for the world is part of growing up, of individuation, and maybe even part of mental health. The split in the therapy profession is at its most destructive when it is between the public, apolitical, hyperclinical face of the profession – something that has quite rightly been criticized – and a much more politically aware, private face of the profession. Many therapists and analysts seem all too aware that they are citizens too, that they have political histories themselves, that they too struggle to find the balance between inner-looking and outer-looking attitudes. As a British psychoanalyst put it when replying to the questionnaire: "We are political animals. Everything we are and do takes place within a political framework. It is impossible to divorce this from the inner world of either our patients or ourselves" (see Samuels (1993:209–266) for a fuller account of the survey).

Politicizing therapy practice

When attempting to link psychoanalysis or psychotherapy with political and social issues, we need to establish a two-way street. In one direction travel men and women of the psyche, bringing what they know of human psychology to bear on the crucial political and social issues of the day, such as leadership, the market economy, nationalism, racial prejudice and environmentalism. Going the other way down this street, we try to get at the hidden politics of personal life as broadly conceived and understood: the politics of early experience in the family, gender politics, and the politics of internal imagery, usually regarded as private. The dynamic that feminism worked upon between the personal and the political is also a dynamic between the psychological and the social. It is so complicated that to reduce it in either one direction (all psyche) or the other direction (all socio-political), or to assert a banal, holistic synthesis that denies differences between these realms, is massively unsatisfactory. There is a very complicated interplay, and this chapter trades off the energy in that interplay. One hope is to develop a new, hybrid language of psychology and politics that will help us to contest conventional notions of what "politics" is and what "the political" might be. The aspirations of so many disparate groups of people worldwide – environmentalists, human rights activists, liberation theologians, feminists, pacifists and peacemakers, ethnopoliticians – for a reinvigorated and resacralized politics would gain the support of the psychological and psychotherapy communities (see Samuels (2001) for a fuller statement of this position).

It is worthwhile focusing on therapy and on clinical work for two main reasons – first, because the results of the survey show that this is a hot issue for practitioners; second, because exploring the politicization of practice might help to answer the awkward question: why has the political world not shown up for its first session with the therapists who are so keen to treat it? Freud, Jung and the great humanistic pioneers such as Maslow and Rogers truly wanted to engage with the institutions and problematics of society. But they, and even more their followers, did this in such an on-high, experience-distant, mechanical fashion, with the secret agenda of proving their own theories correct, that the world has been, quite rightly, suspicious. Objecting to psychological reductionism in relation to the political and social is reasonable – not resistance. But what if clinical experience were factored in? At the very least, there would be a rhetorical utility. For, without their connection to the clinic, to therapy, why should anyone in the world of politics listen to the psychotherapeutic people at all? What do we have to offer if it does not include something from our therapy work? Therapy is certainly not all that we have to offer, but it is the base.

The professional stakes are very high. In certain sectors of humanistic and transpersonal psychology, clinical work is becoming more overtly politicized so that the whole client may be worked with. But this is still very much a minority view in the psychodynamic and psychoanalytic sectors of psychotherapy. Politically speaking, most clinical practice constitutes virgin territory. The stakes are so high because what people like me are trying to do is to change the nature of the field, change the nature of the profession – that which we profess, believe and do. As the survey showed, this attempt is part of a worldwide movement in which the general tendency is to extend the nature of the psychotherapy field so as to embrace the social and political dimensions of experience.

If we do want to treat the whole person, as some of us do, then we have to find detailed ways of making sure that the social and political dimensions of experience are included in the therapy process regularly, reliably, and as a matter of course. We must try to achieve a situation in which the work is political always, already – not unusually, not exceptionally, not only when it is done by mavericks, but when it is done in an everyday way by Everytherapist.

I feel that we are at the earliest stages of this project, and are handicapped by the lack of a much-needed new language. These thoughts and speculations are my best shot. I want to discuss the politicization of therapy practice under the following headings:

1 The therapeutic value of political discussion in the session.
2 Exploring the political myth of the person in therapy.
3 The hidden politics of internal, private imagery.
4 Working out a socialized, transpersonal psychology of community.

However, as the project of creating a responsible way to work directly with political material has developed, I have found it useful at the outset to attempt to deal with, or at least discuss, the objections to what is being proposed. In this way, readers are alerted to my own awareness of the radical and often risky nature of these ideas. Moreover, dealing first with the objections resembles good psychoanalytic technique whereby resistance is analyzed before content. Of course, the objections are not only resistance and I am convinced that an ongoing engagement with objections (and objectors) to the politicization of therapy practice is enhancing for all sides in the debate.

The first objection is that removing the focus of the clinical enterprise away from the internal world and onto the political world constitutes bad clinical practice. The reply to that objection can be equally assertive. Foreclosure on politics, the privileging and valorizing of the internal over the external, may, as we stagger through the first decade of the new century, itself constitute bad clinical practice. From today's perspective, maybe I do want or need to do some bad practice as I change my practice. Those who do not or cannot change their practices may, from tomorrow's point of view, be the ones guilty of bad practice. What is or is not "on" in clinical technique has evolved strikingly over the first psychoanalytic century. These matters are not definitively settled.

The second objection concerns the problem of suggestion and undue influence on the part of the therapist. This is a sensitive issue these days, given the moral panic surrounding psychotherapy stemming from the notion of false memory syndrome. Is there a risk that a politicized therapy practitioner will foist his or her own political ideas, principles, and values onto the vulnerable, open-to-suggestion client? Would not that be a shattering objection to the politicization of therapy? In reply, I would ask if we are really supposed to believe that a practitioner who sticks to the way he or she was trained and keeps the political out of the consulting room is thereby devoid of the sin of ever suggesting anything to the client. Many studies show that an enormous amount of influencing by the therapist of the client goes on, and in fact may be essential for some kind of psychological movement to happen. At times, even Freud equates transference and suggestion, making a defensive point that also serves me well: you cannot suggest something into somebody unless they are ready for it, unless it "tallies" with what is already alive in them. I would use Freud against the objection. Suggestion is going on already. There is no reason to suppose that a politicized practitioner would necessarily be intruding his or her own values more than somebody whose interest was in object-relations, sexuality, aggression, spirituality or the soul.

Of course, there is always a risk of discipleship in the psychotherapy situation, as those who have had training therapy know. But I feel confident in saying that there is today a huge amount of uncritically accepted suggestion in clinical practice and that, from a certain point of view, the more "bounded," "contained" and "disciplined" the behavior of the practitioner, the more suggestion is taking place in his or her practice. I think this is inevitable. The technical rules of analysis are not politically or culturally neutral; they do more than "facilitate" the unfolding of the self. They have themselves cultured depth psychology in a permanent way, and they have themselves done it to a certain extent by suggestion. On the basis of the replies received to the questionnaire on political material that is brought to the consulting room, it is clear that a good deal of rule-breaking goes on in ordinary therapy and analysis – probably much more than is revealed in supervision, wherein words like "discussion" are dirty words. If psychotherapists and analysts are already discussing politics with the client, then it is clear that the hygienic sealing of the consulting room from politics is a virginal fantasy on the part of practitioners.

The third objection concerns what is to be done when the therapist is confronted with somebody with political views he or she finds repulsive. Discussing my ideas at a meeting of the British Association of Psychotherapists, I was once asked: "what would happen if Hitler came into your consulting room?" Well, psychodynamically speaking, I think I have seen quite a few Hitler-types in my consulting room already. Although this point cannot settle the very real worries that working with somebody whose views you find repulsive creates, surely we can agree that, from time to time, every practitioner will meet a version of this problem. Moreover, politics is not the only source of repulsion.

A fourth objection concerns the alleged elitism of what I am proposing. Do I have some kind of fantasy that we are going to send a well-analyzed vanguard of the psychopolitical revolution out into the world? Of course I have had that fantasy from time to time but, in a more moderate vein, and in terms of developing an argument about changing the field, I do not for one minute think that a person who has had psychological analysis or therapy is in some kind of elite vanguard. However, as indicated, I do recognize that there is some strength in this objection, and I try to stay conscious of the problem.

The fifth objection is extremely subtle and hence difficult to deal with. This objector claims that he or she is carrying out a political therapy practice already. Sometimes I feel that this is undoubtedly the case. At other times, when I am told that the mere practice of therapy, or even just the making of interpretations, is a political act, I must demur. Similarly, when it is blandly observed that all of inner life obviously involves the outer world, including politics, and there is no point in going on about it, I feel I need to know about the fate of the outer world in therapy done by such an objector. I think it is a sign of the times that many practitioners do not want to admit to working oblivious to the world of politics. The rules of the game are changing. And, as the survey shows, it is clear that many people are trying to work in a more politically attuned way. But the mere recognition that inner and outer are connected cannot constitute a politicization of practice.

A sixth and final objection concerns the scope and timing of political work in therapy. I am often asked if these ideas are applicable to every client. Of course, they are not. There is a further question in connection with timing and it is certainly important to wait and see where the client is headed. This is easy to say, but I think there may be a smear in the way this objection is sometimes posed, in that the not-so-secret intent is to characterize political work as inappropriate and likely to be done in a clumsy way. Sometimes, a politicized therapist will mis-time or misplace his or her interventions. But therapists often take ideas derived from object-relations or archetypal theory or psychosexuality and make use of them in situations where these ideas turn out to be woefully inappropriate and irrelevant. It happcns all thc timc and it is not mcant as damaging to thc clicnt. Somchow "politics" is singled out as more likely to lead to such an abuse of the client.

While there is little doubt that political action outside the therapy entered into by a client can be defensive or resistant, this is surely not always the case. Sometimes, when working with politically active clients, there has come a move from within the client to withdraw from politics for a while – and this is, of course, respected. Nevertheless, we might perhaps question the psychoanalytic (or maybe the bourgeois) depreciation of action in general and political action in particular. Political action is psychologically valid, positive and creative. Not to act would sometimes constitute a special form of repression – a repression supported by the institutions of therapy and analysis themselves.

The therapeutic value of political discussion

Now I want to move on to the first of my positive proposals concerning the therapeutic value of political discussion in the session. Here, I will bring in the experiences of important practitioners in other fields who sought to politicize the practices of their own fields.

The German dramatist Bertolt Brecht conceived of the idea of a politicized theatre and developed a whole body of practices to go with that notion. Some of his practices, which constitute a sort of Brechtian clinical theory, are relevant to psychotherapy. For example, consider his well-known idea of the alienation effect, or "distanciation effect." Via certain technical theatrical devices, the audience is encouraged to step back and to distance itself from the drama going on onstage in order to apperceive more clearly what the social, political and economic dynamics of the drama are. The intention is that the audience should not only identify emotionally with the characters in the play but should also try to understand and analyze what it is that those characters are doing. Brecht replaces involvement in theatre with what I would call "exvolvement." In psychotherapy practice, it is possible to conceive of a therapeutic situation in which therapist and client get exvolved, without worrying that this could be a transgression of the principle that requires maximum emotional involvement and identification with the issues being processed in the therapy. Brechtian exvolvement serves, in very general terms, as a helpful model for the introduction of political discussion in the session as a therapeutic tool.

Another parallel is even more pertinent, and it concerns certain developments in feminist art practice, in particular what could be described as the framing of the everyday. For example, in 1976 the feminist conceptual artist Mary Kelly produced a work that became notorious, called *Post-Partum Document*. This was a record of her evolving relationship with her son over the first few years of his life. The part that everybody remembers, and on which I will concentrate, is the first room of *Post-Partum Document* in which the only works on show were the feces – and urine-stained nappy (diaper) liners of this little boy, backed by white vellum, well framed and hung on the walls of the Hayward Gallery in London. The condition of the nappy liner showed how ill or healthy the baby (or his bowels) were at any one moment. Kelly could therefore track and comment upon her 'success' as a mother. The irony and political pointedness were deliberate.

A similar art work was created by Care Elwes in 1979, called *Menstruation 2*. Seated on a clear perspex stool in a clear perspex booth in a white, diaphanous dress with no underwear or sanitary towels during the time of her period, she would allow the menstrual blood to flow, staining the garment, all the while dialoguing with an audience that surrounded this booth about what the wider implications of her female bodily processes were, what they meant to her, and about what the audience thought was going on.

Mentioning these art works is not intended to start a discussion about conceptual and feminist art. But these works worked because the ordinary was framed, whether in the traditional frame of a picture or by the frame of the perspex booth in which a bleeding woman stains her garments before spectators and discusses it with them. My argument is that political discussion within the therapy frame will be different from ordinary political discussion in a bar, living room or workplace. Just as menstruation, framed in the way I described, ceases to be menstruation and becomes conceptual art and has an impact in the cultural sphere, so, too, a discussion of politics in a therapy situation that, if transcribed, would look ordinary, takes on a wholly other significance. Contained within the therapy vessel or frame (itself a therapy term), the ordinary becomes something other, and enters the psychological processes of therapist and client in a way that may be profoundly unsettling, possibly clarifying, and occasionally transformative. If we seek to explore the meaning and relevance of the political for ourselves and our clients, then an espousal of political discussion, in which the therapist has to make all the usual therapist's decisions about his or her degree of involvement, openness and about the timing, is one way to proceed. Perhaps it is necessary to try it to see what happens. For a practitioner reading this who already discusses politics with clients, maybe these thoughts will help to theorize what is at present being done on an intuitive or ethical basis.

The political myth of the person

The next proposal concerns what I call the political myth of the person. Is there such a thing as a person's political development? Just as we refer to psychological development generally, or people talk about how they have or have not developed over a lifetime, might there not be a way of approaching politics on the personal level that can make use of the idea of development without getting hooked up on linear, normative and mechanistic notions of development?

How does the political person grow and develop? An individual person lives not only her or his life but also the life of the times. Jung told his students that "when you treat the individual you treat the culture." Persons cannot be seen in isolation from the society and culture that have played a part in forming them – as much feminist thinking has demonstrated.

Once we see that there is a political person who has developed over time, we can start to track the political history of that person – the way the political events of her or his lifetime have impacted on the forming of his or her personality. So we have to consider the politics people have, so to speak, inherited from their family, class, ethnic, religious, and national background, not forgetting the crucial questions of their sex and sexual orientation. Sometimes, people take on their parents' politics; equally often, people reject what their parents stood for. Social class often functions within the unconscious and sometimes I have found that it is the social class issues of the socially mobile client's parents that are truly significant.

But all this is a bit too rational. If there is something inherently political about humans – and most people think there is – then maybe the politics a person has cannot only be explained by social inheritance. Maybe there is an accidental, constitutional, fateful and inexplicable element to think about. Maybe people are just born with different amounts and kinds of political energy in them. If that is so, then there would be implications both for individuals and for our approach to politics. What will happen if a person with a high level of political energy is born to parents with a low level of it (or vice versa)? What if the two parents have vastly different levels from each other? What is the fate of a person with a high level of political energy born into an age and a culture that does not value such a high level, preferring to reward lower levels of political energy? The answers to such questions shape not only a person's political myth but the shape and flavor of the political scene in their times.

The questions can get much more intimate. Did your parents foster or hinder the flowering of your political energy and your political potential? How did you develop the politics you have at this moment? In which direction is your politics moving, and why? I do not think these questions are at present on either a mainstream or an alternative political agenda. Nor are they on the agenda of many therapists or analysts.

My interest is not in what might be called political maturity. No such universal exists, as evaluations by different commentators of the same groups as "terrorists" or "freedom fighters" shows. My interest is in how people got to where they are politically and, above all, in how they themselves think, feel, explain and communicate about how they got to where they are politically – hence my reference to the political myth of the person. From a psychological angle, it often turns out that people are not actually where they thought they were politically, or that they got there by a route they did not know about.

In therapy, we can explore how the client got to where he or she is politically and, above all, how the clients themselves think, feel, explain and communicate about how they got to where they are politically – a subjective narrative of political development.

When a client describes his or her formative or crucial political experiences, an analyst or therapist would listen with the same mix of literal and metaphorical understanding with which he or she would listen to any kind of clinical material – but with the ideas of political myth and political development in mind as permanent heuristic presences. Sometimes, the most productive path to follow would be to accept the client's account of his or her political history; at other times, what the client may have to say may be understood as image, symbol and metaphor; at other times, as defensive and/or distorted; sometimes, it will be a mélange of these ways of understanding; sometimes, a tension or competition may exist between them. In a sense, all of this moves us towards a conception of what could be called the "psychological citizen."

The implications for depth psychology of taking in these ideas about political development could be profound. In 1984 I suggested to my fellow members of the training committee of a psychotherapy organization that we should start to explore with candidates something about their political development – its history, roots, antecedents, patterns, vicissitudes and current situation – just as we looked into sexuality, aggression and spiritual or moral development. At that time, the idea was regarded as a bit way out, but more recently it has evoked a favorable response. Similarly, if political and social factors are part of personality and psychological development, should not analysts and therapists explore those areas in initial interviews with prospective clients?

Incidentally, here, as so often, I have found that what looks like new theory is really only a necessary theorization of cutting-edge practice. In the survey, when I asked the respondents to say something about their own political histories and what had influenced their own political development, they tended to cover the same ground as I have covered in this section of the chapter, though with very wide linguistic, conceptual and hermeneutic variations.

One last point about political myth and political development is that it is crucial to challenge the psychoanalytic assumption that the citizen is always in the baby role *vis-à-vis* the state or its leaders. Elsewhere (Samuels 2001) I have detailed how citizens might make use of analytical methodology to recast themselves as "citizens-as-therapist" who see their role as offering therapy to the political world in which they find themselves. Of course, they are "in" that world – but so, too, is the therapist "in" the therapy with her patient or client.

The hidden politics of private, internal imagery

The image of the parents in bed

My first proposal about the hidden politics of private, internal imagery concerns the primal scene – the image of father and mother together, the image of their intimate relationship, whether in bed or not. I have suggested on several occasions (e.g. Samuels 1989) that primal scene imagery functions as a kind of psychic fingerprint or trademark. Now I want to extend that idea in a political direction, to argue that the kind of image held of the parents' relationship to each other demonstrates, on the intrapsychic level, a person's capacity to sustain conflict constructively in the outer world – a crucial aspect of the person's political capacity. In the image of mother and father in one frame, the scene can be harmonious, disharmonious, one side may dominate the other side, one parent could be damaging the other parent, there will be patterns of exclusion, triumph, defeat, curiosity or total denial. These great and well-known primal scene themes are markedly political. How they work out in the patient tells us something about that patient's involvement and investment in political culture and his or her capacity to survive therein.

I see the primal scene as a self-generated diagnostic monitoring of the person's psycho-political state at any moment. The level of political development is encapsulated in the primal scene image. This is why images and assessments of the parental marriage change so much in the course of therapy or analysis. The parental marriage is not what changes in the majority of instances. Nor is it merely an increase in consciousness on the part of the patient that makes the image change. The image changes because the patient's inner and outer political styles and attitudes are changing. And the specificity of the image communicates what the new styles might be. The parents stand for a process as well as for particular attributes and capacities.

The experience of primal scene imagery may be additionally understood as an individual's attempt to function politically, coupling together into a unified whole his or her diverse psychic elements and agencies without losing their special tone and functioning: a sort of universalism versus multiculturalism on an individual level. What does the image of the copulating parents tell us about the political here-and-now of the client? The image of the parents in bed refers to an unconscious, pluralistic engagement by the client with all manner of sociopolitical phenomena and characteristics, many of which appear to him or her as so unlikely to belong together (to be bedfellows) that they are "opposites," just as mother and father, female and male, passive and active sexual partners are said to be opposites, or "whites" and "blacks," or Israelis and Palestinians, or Catholics and Protestants, or rich and poor are regarded as irreconcilable political opposites.

Thus the question of the image of the parents in bed as a harmonious coming together of conflicting opposites can be worked on in more detail, according to the degree and quality of differentiation a person makes between the images of mother and father. For a primal scene only becomes fertile when the elements are distinguishable.

In plain language, it is not a stuck image of parental togetherness that we see in a fertile primal scene, but something divided and unstuck, hence vital – but also linked, hence politically imaginable. The psyche (society) is trying to express its multifarious and variegated nature (multiculturalism) – and also its oneness and integration (universalism). Primal scene images can perform this pluralistic job perfectly and the message they carry concerns how well the job is going. Via primal scene imagery, the psyche is expressing the patient's pluralistic capacity to cope with the unity and the diversity of the political situation he or she is in. As Aristotle said, "Similars do not a state make."

I do not think that the reproductive heterosexuality of the primal scene should be taken as excluding people of homosexual orientation. Far from it: I am convinced that the fruitfulness signified in the primal scene, and the problems therein, are completely congruent with homosexual experience. I also think that there is a set of cultural and intellectual assumptions that need to be explicated. Why is it that psychological fecundity, variety and liveliness do not yet get theorized in homosexual terms? Why is psychological maturity still envisaged in a form of complementary wholeness that requires heterosexual imagery for it to work at all? Why do we not refer to a conjunction of similars? One could easily defend the thesis that heterosexual primal scene imagery works quite happily for persons of a homosexual orientation by recourse to metaphor, saying that primal scene heterosexuality refers not to the fact of reproduction but to the symbol of diversity, otherness, conflict, potential. Similarly, one could also point out that, since everyone is the result of a heterosexual union, heterosexual symbolism is simply inevitable and not excluding of a homosexual orientation. But I am dubious about these liberal maneuvers because they still leave a question mark in my mind concerning the absence of texts replete with homosexual imagery that would perform the psychological and political functions of primal scene imagery. We might begin a search for the homosexual primal scene. Though this idea may sound controversial, it merely involves a recognition that the primal scene is about processes and functions and not about the actual parents. Hence the proposition that there could be a primal scene couched in gay or lesbian imagery will only cause problems to homophobic members of the psychotherapy world. We know by now how much psychoanalytic theory about homosexuality is little more than dressed-up prejudice, marching in step with the moral majority.

Personal narratives of primal scene imagery, and their working through, demonstrate to a considerable extent a person's capacity to sustain political conflict constructively. This general point about politics becomes more pertinent when applied to the professional politics of the field of depth psychology. Stuck parental imagery fits the field's symptoms of intolerance, fantasies of superiority, and difficulties with hearing the views of others. If depth psychology's primal scene imagery could be prodded into vigorous motion, perhaps by active ideological dialogue, I would feel more optimistic about its future.

One specific reason for choosing to focus on the primal scene is that we are then invited to address the conventional twinning of man with active and woman with passive sexual behavior. This twinning both reflects and, I think, inspires many gender divisions. When individuals access and work on their primal scene imagery, often in fantasy or via the transference in analysis, it is remarkable that the conventional male/active–female/passive divide does not invariably appear. Quite the reverse. In fact, it often seems as if the unconscious "intention" of the sexual imagery associated with the primal scene is to challenge that particular definition of the differences between men and women. The challenge to the sexual *status quo* symbolizes a kind of secret challenge to the political *status quo*.

From the standpoint of gender politics, this discussion of the political relevance of a primal scene enables us to introduce the mother in a transmogrified and politicized form, as an active player in the sexual game and hence, potentially, as an active player in the political game.

Here, I am reminded of the Midrashic story of Lilith. She was, as readers will recall, the first consort of Adam, who was created from the earth at the same time as Adam. She was unwilling to give up her equality and argued with Adam over the position in which they should have intercourse, Lilith insisting on being on top. "Why should I lie beneath you," she argued, "when I am your equal, since both of us were created from dust?" But when Lilith saw that Adam was determined to be on top, she called out the magic name of God, rose into the air, and flew away. Eve was then created. Lilith's later career as an evil she-demon who comes secretly to men in the night (hence responsible for nocturnal emissions) and as a murderer of newborns culminated, after the destruction of the temple, in a relationship with God as a sort of mistress. The importance for us of Lilith's stories is that the woman who demands equality with the man is forced to leave the Garden and gets stigmatized as the personification of evil.

Dream imagery

An Italian client dreamt of a beautiful lake with clear deep water. He said this represented his soul and then immediately associated to the pollution on the Italian Adriatic coast. The image of the lake, and the association to coastal pollution, suggested, in the form of one symbol, the client's unconscious capacity for depth and his present state, of which he was all too conscious – a state of being clogged up by "algae," like the coastal waters of the Adriatic. When disparate psychological themes are thrown together like this, the symbolic image makes a powerful impact on the individual, who cannot ignore it. In this particular instance, the notion that there was possibly a "solution" for the clogging up of his lake/soul potential, and the idea that being clogged was a state he had gradually gotten into over time and was not a witch's curse, together with the vision that depth and clarity and beauty were options open to him, were powerful and liberating thoughts. He made a choice to return to Italy, to tell his father that he was homosexual, and, in his words, to "get more involved," perhaps in environmental politics.

Returning to the dream of the lake, I would like to suggest an alternative reading, couched in more political terms. I think that this re-reading constitutes a further statement about the political properties of private, internal imagery. The images of the dream can be approached via their individual presence, or via their political presence, or via the movement and tension between the two. In the dream of the lake, the tension between the individual and the political presences of the image was prominent and insistent; after all, the client was Italian. What, the client and I asked together, is the role of pollution in the soul, or even in the world? What is the role of pollution in the achievement of psychological depth? Can the soul remain deep and clear while there is pollution in the world, in one's home waters? Did the lake, with intimations of mystery and isolation, clash with the popular, extroverted tourism of the Adriatic? Eventually, the patient's concern moved onto the social level: who owned the lake? Who should have access to such a scarce resource? Who would protect the lake from pollution? These were his associations. From wholly personal issues, such as the way his problems interfered with the flowering of his potential, we moved to political issues, such as the pollution of natural beauty, not only by industry but also by the mass extroversion of tourism. And we also moved back again from the political level to the personal level, including transference analysis. I do not mean to foreclose on other interpretations, but rather to add a more "political" one so that the client's unconsciously taken up political commitments can become clearer.

I think much imagery in therapy performs this particular kind of transcendent or bridging function, transcending and bridging the gap between the apparently individual, private, subjective and the apparently collective, social, political. Much of this chapter argues for the general thesis that there is a constant relationship and articulation between the personal/subjective and the public/political dimensions of life. Can we discriminate these separate dimensions in such a way that eventually we can, on a more conscious level, better bring them together? I think we do find that private, internal imagery carries a public and political charge. Moreover, we need to be better placed to make practical, clinical use of the by now conventional observation that the external world, particularly its social and power relations, has an effect on our subjective experience.

Applying this approach to imagery to a psychological analysis of the politics of the client, we would try to discriminate the individual and the social aspects of an image and see whether they can be brought to an equal level of consciousness. This process would increase the range of choices available to the client, rather than collapse them into a solution. In the example, the question of ownership of the lake at first seemed a distant "political" concern. But gradually the client's social sensitivity came to the fore: he asserted that the lake, like his soul, was not a commodity to be owned by anyone. Then a celebration of his social conscience came to the fore. He addressed the fate of his "Italian-ness" on a personal, individual level. Finally, as the hidden politics of his imagery continued to pulse, he discovered more collective, cultural and political associations to pollution on the Adriatic. I hope it is clear that the public/political and private/subjective dimensions were both thoroughly alive.

This interpretive reworking of the imagery onto a sociopolitical level provides the beginnings of a model by which therapists and clients can track moves between individual and social realms and a means of studying conflicts and harmonies between culture and individual as these appear in the session. For individual and culture are not the crude opposites that many, including Freud, have taken them to be. Both terms enjoy the complex interaction produced by their dynamic relationship; the relationship changes the nature of the original "opposites." The more deep and personal the experience, the more political and public it may turn out to be.

A socialized, transpersonal psychology of community

In contemporary Western politics the buzz word is "community." Aside from the politicians, many clients also speak in therapy of a sense of pulling together that used to exist and is now lost. They feel the loss keenly. For other clients, the idea of community is more proactive, referring to a new kind of egalitarian politics based on their belief in what is shared, held in common, faced together. Communitarian thinking will (hopefully) refresh our ideas both of the state and, for many among this group of clients, of the power dynamics of the therapeutic relationship. It is extraordinary that in the many lucid discussions about community that are taking place, there has been little space for a psychological contribution. Communitarian politics requires an overtly socialized psychology and when we try to create one we find that it will, at some level, have to be a transpersonal psychology. Politics is also a transpersonal activity and, like most transpersonal activities, politics points in what can only be described as a spiritual direction. Psychotherapy is not a religion, though it may be the heir to some aspects of conventional religion. The project of factoring the psychological into the political seems to want to be done in quasi-religious language. Perhaps this is because psychotherapy, politics and religion all share, at some level, in the fantasy of providing therapy for the world. The very word "fantasy" must, I am sure, create problems for some readers. Fantasy is not in itself pathological and there is a necessarily Utopian role for fantasy in political discourse.

Sometimes I see psychotherapy as a new monasticism, meaning that just as the monks and nuns kept culture in Europe alive during the so-called "Dark Ages," so, too, in their often equally rigorous way, the therapists and analysts are keeping something alive in our own age. However, the values that psychotherapy keeps alive are difficult to classify. They do not always have the ring of absolute Truth (though such a possibility is not ruled out); nor are they based on a fixed account of human nature (though that is what is invariably being attempted, time and again). In its discovery of values and value in that which other disciplines might reject, psychotherapy helps to keep something alive in the face of threats ranging from state hegemony, to vicious market forces, to nostalgic longings for a return to a past in which it is assumed that the old certitudes of nation, gender and race would still hold. We sometimes hear calls for a global ethic or a global sense of responsibility to be placed at the heart of political theory and the political process. My question is: how can this be done without some kind of psychological sensitivity and awareness? Such sensitivity and awareness may not be easily measurable by the sturdy tools of empiricism but reveal themselves in dream, in parental and primal scene imagery, in an understanding of a person's own political history, development and myth. Hence, clinical work on oneself coexists with political work in one's society. My working out of a "clinical" model with which to engage political problematics is intended to make every citizen into a potential therapist of the world. An active role for the citizen-as-therapist is highlighted, and nowhere will this be more apparent than in relation to experts (myself included). People's active, generative, inventive, compassionate potential is not being tapped and, as I see it, in order to tap into that kind of energy we need a reinvention of politics inside and outside the therapy session.

References

Brown, D. and Zinkin, L. (1994) *The Psyche and the World: Developments in Group-Analytic Theory*. London: Routledge.

Hillman, J. and Ventura, M. (1992) *We've Had a Hundred Years of Psychotherapy and the World is Getting Worse*. San Francisco: Harper.

Samuels, A. (1989) *The Plural Psyche: Personality, Morality and the Father*. London: Routledge.

Samuels, A. (1993) *The Political Psyche*. London: Routledge.

Samuels, A. (1994) Replies to an international questionnaire on political material brought into the clinical setting by clients of psychotherapists and analysts. *International Review of Sociology*, 3:7–60.

Samuels, A. (1998) Responsibility. In J. Corrigal (ed.), *Development through Diversity: The Therapist's Use of Self*. London: United Kingdom Council for Psychotherapy, pp. 2–23.

Samuels, A. (2001) *Politics on the Couch: Citizenship and the Internal Life*. London: Profile Books; New York: Karnac/Other Press.

Samuels, A. (2002) The hidden politics of healing: foreign dimensions of domestic practice. *American Imago*, 59(4):459–481.

Chapter 2

Money, love, and hate

Contradiction and paradox in psychoanalysis

Muriel Dimen

Taking up the question of money in the spirit of the Marx–Freud tradition (a project already called for by Rendon (1991)) but adding a postmodern spin, I consider money's vicissitudes in the psychoanalytic relationship. Freud may discuss money as a practical (1913) and a psychological matter (e.g., 1908) in separate essays (see Whitson 1989:3), but in light of recent psychoanalytic and social thought, its clinical, political, and theoretical locations are quite proximate. Developments in psychoanalytic theory (i.e., the Kleinian understanding of love and hate, the Winnicottian notion of paradox, the interpersonal assessment of countertransference, and relational arguments about the simultaneity of one-person and two-person psychologies) and developments in social theory (i.e., social constructionism, critical theory, and postmodernism) permit a synthetic and evolving interpretation of money in the psychoanalytic relationship that is clinically relevant, socially located, and theoretically responsible.

Freud's approach to money is, however, rather one-dimensional. Psychosexuality is his guide. Although money has a narcissistic dimension, being "in the first instance . . . a medium for self-preservation and for obtaining power . . . powerful sexual factors are [also] involved in the value set on it" (1913:131). Therefore, money is to be approached with the same matter-of-factness as sex, a modeling that furthers psychoanalysis' educative project. Freud says that his attitude toward money counters the familiar fact: "Money matters are treated by civilized people in the same way as sexual matters – with the same inconsistency, prudishness and hypocrisy" (1913:131). By "voluntarily telling [patients] the price at which he values his time," he shows them that "he himself has cast off false shame on these topics" (1913:131).

As for setting fees and session hours, Freud speaks from "ordinary good sense" (1913:131) – no theory or deep thought required here. He speaks as a practical man of the world who must consider his material existence by charging for all time leased and regularly collecting his debts (1913:131–132). The arrangement of "leasing" one's time, he observes, is "taken as a matter of course for teachers of music or languages in good society" (1913:126). He is faithful to his beliefs: not only his own theory of treatment but what is closely related, his ethics. In contrast to other professionals, he does not take patients without charge or extend courtesy to colleagues' kin, because he wants to prevent resistance to transference and countertransference, and, by straightforwardly acknowledging self-interest, avoid the customary medical pretense to philanthropy (1913:131–132).

The common sense from which Freud reasons is, however, like any system of "folk" knowledge: informed by unexamined presuppositions, it melds expectations and prejudices customary for his class with his personal needs and predilections. As such, it tacitly takes stands on issues only now being theorized in psychoanalysis (e.g., the patient's experience of the analyst's subjectivity (Aron 1991) or the relation between one-person and two-person psychologies (Ghent 1989; Aron and Hirsch 1992)) or social thought (e.g., the economic and political place of the helping professions, the social class of analysts and patients, and the psychology of class (Sennett and Cobb 1972; Ehrenreich 1989)). Such vantage points being absent both from classical theory and from psychoanalytic thought altogether, it is unsurprising that, until recently, few analysts have systematically examined the matter of money. Whatever the other resistances to this topic (see below), the intellectual tools to study it have been missing.

I want here to refurbish the intellectual tool kit by conversing in several languages, not only psychoanalysis but social theory, anthropology, and, less centrally, feminist theory as well. I decode money's unconscious and emotional resonance, as well as its cultural meanings. I track its clinical and theoretical vicissitudes in terms of cultural symbolism and economic change, as well as the class position of psychoanalysts and the psychology of class itself. Through both an examination of Freud's dicta and feelings about money and a clinical example, I render its relational meaning in transference and countertransference.

Money in psychoanalytic question

If Freud and his contemporaries were laconic on this matter, his followers have become exponentially voluble. The bibliographical entries in Krueger's (1986) anthology on psychoanalysis and money are scarce until the 1960s. Then they cluster in the 1970s and blizzard in the 1980s. Finally, in the 1990s, with the economy struggling out of a depression that has bitten into private practice, comes yet another anthology as well as an entire book on the question (Klebanow and Lowenkopf 1991; Herron and Welt 1992).

The snowballing discussion of money has a history, part of which is cultural. Psychoanalysis' "last taboo" fell during an iconoclastic period when the class position of professionals too was subtly but permanently shifting. If in the 1960s (the "we decade") sexuality blossomed and, in the 1970s (the "me decade"), narcissism bloomed, the 1980s and 1990s (the "greed decades") made greed and covetousness culturally common if not socially safe. But, we might ask, safe for whom? Surely not stockbrokers, corporate raiders, or venture capitalists. People who trade in money are to be on good terms with selfishness. Helping professionals are, instead, to value money only for its ability to serve a modest standard of living.

What was surprising in the 1980s and 1990s, then, was the seemingly sudden acquaintance with avarice on the part of professionals and intellectuals (Denby 2004). Psychoanalysts' heightened interest in money, not to mention their greed, had, however, more than a decade behind it, responding to and expressing a long, slow slide in their socioeconomic fortunes. The 1960s were a watershed in a century-long trend; until then, the gap between rich and poor in the United States had steadily decreased. After that, the gap began to yawn. The middle class, the usual source of analysts and analysands, began to shrink; at present, middle-class people can no longer count on owning their homes or sending their children to college without impoverishing themselves (Newman 1988; Ehrenreich 1989). By the same token, the insurance reimbursements that subsidized their psychoanalytic treatment dwindled, bruising both those needing therapeutic help and those making their living from it.

This decline in middle-class fortunes coincided with a boom in the helping professions, which in turn further reduced any given professional's share of the pie. The extension of parity to psychologists and social workers by insurance companies, the growing participation of social workers in the psychoanalytic profession, the proliferation of "media shrinks," and the flood of self-help books – these belong to the expansion of psychotherapy to all levels of the middle class, even to the working class. Part of the democratizing trend in psychoanalysis (Havens 1989:142; Zaphiropoulos 1991:242), this growth also belongs to a cultural shift that might be called the "therapization of America." Analysts' incomes were also reduced by the evolution of a therapy-sensitive culture in which people are knowledgeable about and receptive to psychotherapy, in which consumers assume the right to question and choose among medical authorities, and in which psychotherapy is packaged by managed health care. The more private practitioners compete, the fewer the patients and the lower the fees (Chodoff 1991:254–256; Drellich 1991:159–161; Aron and Hirsch 1992); the more knowledge consumers have, the more they question analysts' authority and resist what have often seemed arbitrarily high fees (see also Herron and Welt (1992:171)).

The disturbance of money

In responding, if only unconsciously, to the widening chasm between rich and poor, however, analysts are merely noticing what has been there all along. Just as we learn from "hysterical misery" about "common unhappiness" (Freud 1895), so, if we look into disrupted economics, we come upon money's complicated quotidian meaning in countertransference. Although economies rise and fall, everyone – clinician and patient alike – wants analysts to be as invulnerable as tenured full professors, even though they actually feel about as secure as part-time adjuncts. Yet analysts have been so uncomfortable with their own feelings of need and greed (Aron and Hirsch 1992:255) that they have tended, like Freud, to treat money as a psychological problem for patients and merely a practical one for themselves (Whitson 1989:3). Indeed, analysts' dystonic relation to their own dependence may constitute the biggest single counterresistance in regard to money (Aron and Hirsch 1992:243; Whitson 1989:3; Herron and Welt 1992:48; Shainess 1991).

As we can see from Freud's by now well-known financial preoccupations, analysts' pecuniary need of their patients is an inevitable thorn in their sides. Throughout his 17-year correspondence with Fliess (Freud 1985), Freud writes periodically about his money-related comforts but mostly about his worries. His uneven cash flow breeds cynicism. For example, he prefers American patients for their hard currency (Gay 1988): "Mrs. M. will be welcome; if she brings money and patience with her, we shall do a nice analysis. If in the process there are some therapeutic gains for her, she too can be pleased" (Freud 1985:107). He objectifies his wellborn, well-to-do patients: "The goldfish (L. von E., an S. by birth and as such a distant relative of my wife) has been caught, but will still enjoy half her freedom until the end of October because she is remaining in the country" (Freud 1985:375). Such mordant humor ought not to gainsay Freud's famous largess toward some of his patients, for example, the Wolf Man (1918). Still Freud's pervasive, if intermittent, focus on money and its ups and downs of anxiety, cynicism, optimism and the like suggests that the rollercoaster of comfort and fear about income so familiar to contemporary analysts is doubly determined: the product of hard times, this anxiety may also be an aggravated variant of a pattern actually inherent to the work not only of psychoanalysts but of most helping professionals.

In the last generation or two, analysts have had a far smoother economic ride than Freud, and those made anxious by money were more likely to be in the beginning stages of practice. For example, at the beginning of the affluent 1980s, when my practice was relatively new and supplemented by an academic position, I made my anxiety known to my supervisor, a very senior and well-known analyst of interpersonal persuasion. His reply was, "You can do your best work only when it's become a matter of indifference to you whether you gain or lose an hour." Although he seemed to be saying that one can work well only when money is out of the picture, I would now put it another way. It's not that money is relevant to analytic work only when times are bad. When times are good, it's relevant by its absence; then, we're like TAPS, which is what the disabled call the rest of us: "temporarily abled persons."

These questions intersect another vital clinical issue, money's representational function in regard to the quotidian analytic tension between safety and danger. If feeling unsafe threatens to impede the analyst's confidence and hence competence, it is also possible to feel too safe (Greenberg 1986). For a variety of reasons, insecurity is intrinsic to the work. For one thing, uncertainty rules the clinical day because psychoanalysts cannot guarantee their method will work. For another, success depends on the day-to-day work of establishing and maintaining a relationship (P. Bromberg, personal communication, 1989). For a third, as suggested by current emphases on the importance of not knowing too precisely where you are in a session, analysts must be able to bear a certain amount of danger (Bion 1980; Eigen 1986), because only in an atmosphere of danger can we hope to come upon the new and/or the forgotten (Stern 1997). The difficulty of sustained recognition of this ordinary unsafety is eased by money's rollercoaster effect, which becomes a convenient, rationalized, and inevitable container for the risks of psychoanalytic process.

While not arguing that the uncertainty of earning a living in capitalist society guarantees the feeling of risk necessary to analytic process, I insist that the anxiety money generates cannot be banished from the consulting room. On the contrary, it is endemic to the particular sort of work analysts do (see, e.g., Chodoff (1986)). Analysts, it turns out, are not alone in their unease about money matters. They share it with everyone else in the "professional–managerial class" (Ehrenreich and Ehrenreich 1979; Ehrenreich 1989), which came into being between 1870 and 1920 (the birth period, note, of psychoanalysis). Professional–managerial work ranges from law and medicine to middle management, from social work and psychotherapy to education, from academe to journalism. It entails what is crudely called mental labor but is better characterized as labor that combines intellect and drive with considerable, although not total, autonomy and self-direction (Ehrenreich 1989:38, 78).

Professional–managerial work is not only a livelihood. It is also a means to power and prestige, and a shaper of personal identity. Because it involves conceptualizing other people's work and lives (Ehrenreich 1989:13), it confers authority and influence. Indeed, it was arguably the chisel that the then-emerging middle class used "to carve out" its own "occupational niche that would be closed both to the poor and to those who were merely rich" (Ehrenreich 1989:78). Finally, by providing the opportunity for creativity and discovery in regard not only to one's work but also to one of its chief instruments, one's self, it enters – indeed, expresses, reflects, and generates – one's identity.

This kind of work renders the professional–managerial class a highly anxious elite (Ehrenreich 1989). Its members know that their power, privilege, and authority can make their clients envy, resent, and hate them (and, analysts would add, idealize them). Also, like their clients, they sometimes suspect that because they do not produce anything visible or tangible, they do nothing real; as such, not only does their work seem worthless, it also cannot meet their own or their clients' idealization. Because their only "capital," so to speak, is "knowledge and skill, or at least the credentials imputing skill and knowledge" (Ehrenreich 1989:15), their high status is insecurely founded. Unlike real, material capital, skill and knowledge cannot be used to hedge inflation, nor can they be bequeathed. They must be renewed by and in each person through hard work, diligence, and self-discipline. Consequently, members of the professional–managerial class, like anyone in any class but the highest, fear the misfortunes that have overnight sent even middle-income people sliding into homelessness and indignity, a fear that Klein and Riviere (1964) liken to that of children who imagine being orphaned or beggared as punishment for their unconscious aggression (p. 109, n1). They fear falling through the economic and moral safety net, hence Ehrenreich's aptly titled *Fear of Falling*. They fear "falling from grace" (Newman 1988), losing their financial status, their elite position of authority, the work they love, and their identity as moral and beneficent. Rooted in the very work of professionals, then, this anxiety about felt fraudulence and looming loss is actually built into the role of analyst in a class-structured society.

Class, countertransference, and alienation

Like all social institutions, class has powerful unconscious resonance. In the most general sense, class refers to the material aspect of society and the way it divides and joins people along a ladder of economic and political power. By definition, class is hierarchical: the relation between classes is determined by their economic and political superiority or inferiority to one another. To put it bluntly, class is about money and its unequal distribution in society. Conversely, money represents the veritable or potential variations in power among individuals and among groups. It indicates not only class differences but those constituting other hierarchies, like race, ethnicity, gender, sexual preference, and so on. Money, in other words, symbolizes the fault lines webbing and cracking a psychological and social reality in which difference is the nucleus of hierarchy (Dimen-Schein 1977:88–92). The hierarchy of privilege organized by class, status distinctions, the unequal amounts of money people have – these trigger not only greed but envy, excite questions of self-esteem, invite Oedipal competitions.

The fault lines of class and other hierarchies show up systematically in transference and countertransference. If, in his most despondent moments, Freud felt greed and cynicism toward his "goldfish," he was unreflectively contemptuous of the middle class and benevolently condescending toward those poorer than he. Addressing the petit bourgeois reluctance to pay for psychoanalysis, Freud argued that the restored health and increased "efficiency and earning capacity" afforded by treatment made therapy less expensive than it appeared. Therefore, he concluded, "We are entitled to say that the patients have made a good bargain. Nothing in life is so expensive as illness – and stupidity" (1913:133).

As for the poor, he opined that the best psychoanalysis could supply was "a practical therapy of . . . the kind which . . . used to be dispensed by the Emperor Joseph II" (1913:133). Known as the "emperor of the beggars" (1780–1790), Joseph, in good Enlightenment fashion, occasionally lived among the poor so as to know firsthand what they needed (C. Fink, personal communication, 1993). It would not, of course, have occurred to emperor or physician what is now assumed, that poor people might actually have been able to articulate at least some of their own needs. Still, while Freud (1913) regrets psychoanalysis' inaccessibility to the impecunious, he acknowledges that "one does occasionally come across deserving people who are helpless from no fault of their own, in whom unpaid treatment does not meet with any of the obstacles [including secondary gain] that I have mentioned and in whom it leads to excellent results" (133). Nevertheless, in his relation to such poor patients as he might have taken on, his paternalism would have had to be analyzed. That it would not have been is a foregone conclusion. As we know from his unconscious sexism, the emotional structure of socioeconomic hierarchy does not appear on his map.

From a psychoanalytic perspective, one might see in Freud's intermittent dyspepsia about his patients a symptom of what has been called the "money neurosis" suffered by the bourgeoisie in Vienna and other European cities in the late nineteenth century (Warner 1991). From a political perspective, one could label it "classism," or class prejudice. If we put psychoanalysis and politics together, however, what we discern in Freud's heart is the social malaise called "alienation." What I mean by alienation is not so much estrangement or disaffection as the cause of these feelings. Hear, for example, the dysphoria of a supervisee who reported thinking, during a difficult session, "I wouldn't be sitting here if I weren't doing it for the money." His guilt, bewilderment, loss, hate, and self-hate proceed from the way money, which permitted him to do his work, nevertheless stole from him its pleasures and meaning. When money is exchanged in a capitalist economy, both buyer and seller – patient and analyst – come to be like commodities, or things, to one another because they enter into relation with each other through the mediation of a third thing (money) that, simultaneously, separates them. As money wedges them apart, so it estranges them from themselves, a distancing that creates anxiety in both (Amar 1956:286; Marx 1964:113; Mészáros 1975:178, 186). This theft of the personal satisfaction you take in work and in your relationship to those with whom you work is alienation, the process by which your labor and its fruit become alien to you because of the very socioeconomic structure that lets them be (Ollman 1976:135).

An occupational hazard of modern life, alienation is core to psychoanalysis. As Khan puts it: "In the nineteenth century two persons dictated the destiny of the twentieth century, Karl Marx and Sigmund Freud. Each . . . diagnosed the sickness of the western Judaeo-Christian cultures: Marx in terms of the alienated person in society; Freud, the person alienated from himself" (1979:9). And, of course, we would add today, "herself." Elsewhere, Khan (1972) calls psychoanalysis the "inevitable result of a long [social] process of the evolution and alienation of the individual" in the West. Freud's genius was "to evaluate the situation and give it a new frame in which [the alienated] could find [their] symbolic, therapeutic speech and expression" (1979:131). Extending Khan's point, I think of psychoanalysis as the perfect therapy for a culture of alienation, for in it you pay a stranger to recover yourself. Paradoxically, psychotherapy that is bought and sold under conditions of alienation generates a "dis-ease" in both the person who pays the stranger and the stranger who is paid, and that needs treatment too. In a way, then, my goal is to explicate how alienation filters into transference and countertransference and how clinical process, by exploiting it, transcends it in a momentary, Utopian, and reparative fashion.

Commerce and psychoanalysis

What is money? So deeply embedded in our culture, daily life and history, money tends to elude definition's reach. Since one's own culture is often invisible until it is compared with a different one, let me look at money cross-culturally. The lengthy anthropological debate about money concludes that money objects are not present in all cultures (Dimen-Schein 1977:197–199). Instead, money emerges under particular political, economic, and/or ecological conditions. After much cross-cultural comparison, anthropologists offer a universal definition that, spelled out, helps us see, as if anew, money's meaning in psychoanalytic context: money is any material object that performs one or more of the following five functions – a medium of exchange, a standard of value, a unit of account, a store of value, and a standard of deferred payments. While there may be different objects serving each different function in any one society, the first function tends to be controlling; whatever is the medium of exchange likely serves the other functions too. Finally, money itself may be a commodity, as it is in capitalism, where you buy it with what we call interest; that is, with more of the same (LeClair and Schneider 1968:468).

According to this less than exciting definition, then, there's nothing mystical about money; it is, among other things, a matter of commerce. As Freud saw, however, this plain fact notoriously renders clinicians uneasy. After all these years, psychotherapists still "want to nurture their image as beneficent purveyors of good rather than as individuals who are at least partially involved in commerce" (Tulipan 1986:79) and who suffer its alienating effects as much as their customers. Even the notion of fee for service goes gently by the rough implications of trade, civilly suggesting the fair-and-squareness of being paid for the work you do so that you, like your patients, may use what you earn by your labor to buy what you need to live. But commerce? No. That we find tawdry and petty, the very opposite of the trust and professionalism on which psychoanalysis depends (Herron and Welt 1992:4).

Still, commerce is a cornerstone of the psychoanalytic edifice. It is not the only cornerstone, but it is a primary one. We sell our services to make our living. Oh, yes, sometimes analysts see patients for free. Some even argue that it may be necessary not to charge certain kinds of patients in order to treat them at all (Jacobs 1986). But even to say "for free" suggests the norm, that analysts engage in trade (see also Horner (1991:177)). Without money, there's no psychoanalysis at all. But with it comes an unavoidable anxiety. Indeed, I would be quite surprised were anyone able to think through this topic without an unsettled moment or two. Consider, for instance, that instant when you learn that your four-time-a-week analytic patient has been fired and will have to discontinue treatment. That first dip on the Cyclone at Coney Island has nothing on it. Recall the excited satisfaction when you take on a new patient at full fee for a long-term analysis. What about the envy when a colleague's practice has doubled while yours has only maintained, or even dropped an hour or two? Or the guilty triumph to find you have more hours, income, or both than a friend in great need.

Are these suggestions extreme? Perhaps there are clinicians to whom the loss (or gain) of, let us say, $600 a week or about $25,000 a year has no emotional resonance. If so, then the extremity of these examples may have something to do with the history recounted earlier: analysts who came of age before and just after the middle class began its recent descent in the 1960s are likely to have been initially less worried than those whose practices began in the 1980s and after. The original work experience of the last generation may well have created a basic sense of ease, financial optimism, and professional security that survives regardless of the economy's vicissitudes.

Nevertheless, psychoanalytic anxiety in relation to money has always sufficed to create the tacit prohibition on asking people how many hours they carry or what fees they charge unless you know them very well. Of course, it's never in the best of taste for professionals to inquire about each other's income, and laws about price-fixing dampen such discussion when it starts (as happened recently on one institute's listserv). The traditional ideology of the professional–managerial class is that they work for love, not money or power. Still, I do not suppose it would surprise anyone to find that in order to protect themselves from their anxiety about money and the alienation contextualizing it, psychoanalysts depict their pecuniary practices in ways that are, at best, confusing.

Consider, for example, an informal and anonymous survey about fees taken at an early 1980s retreat sponsored by the New York University Postdoctoral Program in Psychotherapy and Psychoanalysis, to which all the women replied they had a sliding scale, while each man declared one bold fee. Yet, we all know male analysts, both senior and junior, who "reduce" their fees, to use that rather cool and complacent euphemism for bargaining. The alleged tendency of women to charge lower fees (Herron and Welt (1992:174); see Liss-Levenson (1990)) may sometimes be a fact, and at other times, an artifact of a gendered asymmetry in self-presentation: although men may charge the same fees as women, or fluctuate their fees, public acknowledgment may conflict with masculinity, while self-sacrifice accords more with cultural and intrapsychic expectations of femininity. To let the men off the hook, I also have a female colleague who, in order to conquer her own anxiety about her recently increased expenses (as well as, perhaps, to make me anxious), rather loftily announced that she was now "taking" patients at higher fees. (And I always think, "How nice of her!")

The contradiction between money and love

The point is critical: the way analysts talk, behave, and feel in relation to money is replete with an uneasiness that is the surface manifestation of a deep, psychocultural contradiction that cannot be thought, willed, or wished away. Embedded in the marrow of our work and souls, it will not disappear until the very bones of our society change. All we can do in our work is to find a temporary and Utopian resolution to it. Money and love, the twin engines that make the known world go round, do not go together at all. Worse. They negate one another, and their contradiction funds alienation. While money may be a matter of commerce, it is, like any material object, social practice, or cultural symbol, simultaneously a matter of primitive passion.

Freud knew this. He called money the "Devil's gold," an image he found in European folklore. The Devil gives his lovers a parting gift of gold that, upon his going, turns to excrement (Freud 1908:174). Freud's psychosexual interpretation of this extravagant and primal metaphor addressed what it means to consort with what he called "the repressed instinctual life." He noted how the image contrasts the most precious and the most worthless of substances, money and feces, and considered how this contrast sublimates anal eroticism (cf. Ferenczi 1914). This interpretation brightly illuminates some analysts' anxiety about base cash dirtying up the scene of noble motives and high-minded encounters.

What awaits elaboration, however, is the relation between the gift and the act; what needs unraveling is the relation between the Devil and his lovers so that we may, in turn, decipher the relation between money and love, as well as the relation between those who exchange the two. Freud and the European folktales had something very subtle in mind, and if you have ever been loved and left by the Devil, you will know what I mean. When the Devil has left you, you know not only that you have been fooled, but that, in your longing, you have fooled yourself. You now see that you knew all along that what you thought was pure gold was false. You have searched to be better than you are, in fact, to be the best you can be. The Devil's betrayal crumbles your dreams, destroys the ideal self into which you have breathed life by imagining it in the other's form. In the end, you become less, not more, than you hoped to be.

Degradation, then, is the Devil's gold. A gift, not a payment, it is given after passion is spent. But, instead of honoring an encounter as glorious as love, this gift degrades it. Gold given to mark love becomes worse than nothing, degraded desire and lost illusions. That capacity to make everything less than it is and so to make us doubt what it was we had in mind when we worked so hard to get it – that capacity, says Freud, is the Devil's gold. Money is a pact with the Devil, as Marx, expounding on Goethe, says:

> That which is for me through the medium of money – that for which I can pay (i.e. which money can buy) – that am I, the possessor of the money. The extent of the power of money is the extent of my power . . . Thus, what I am and am capable of is by no means determined by my individuality. I am ugly, but I can buy for myself the most beautiful of women. Therefore I am not ugly, for the effect of ugliness – its deterrent power – is nullified by money. I, as an individual, am lame, but money furnishes me with twenty-four feet. Therefore I am not lame . . . Money is the supreme good, therefore its possessor is good.
>
> (Marx 1964:167)

If, as Marx goes on to tell us, money can "transform all [your] incapacities into their contrary," why would you not sell your soul to get it? If money can get you whatever you need, then it "is the bond binding [you] to human life" (1964:167). Marx asks, "Can it not dissolve and bind all ties? Is it not therefore the universal agent of separation? It is the true agent of separation as well as the true binding agent . . . of society" (p. 167). The agent of alienation, it absorbs all creative power into itself, robs people of their own potential; just as money transforms imperfections into powers, so it "transforms the real essential powers of [human beings] and nature into what are merely abstract conceits" (pp. 168–169).

In a way, money occupies the place in modern society that kinship has in premodern culture; it is the cultural nerve center, the institution that organizes economic life, structures social relations, underlies political power, and informs symbol, ritual, and systems of meaning. Kinship, however, unlike money, can't be taken away from you; as the aphorism has it, "Home is, when you go there, they gotta take you in." In contrast, "money . . . is the alienated ability of [hu]mankind" (p. 167). That's why it's the Devil's gold.

In our culture, money has the same unconscious effect no matter in what trade it is used. By reducing everything to a common denominator, it robs everything and every person of individuality and thereby debases what it touches. That is one reason we like to separate it from love and distinguish the profane, public sphere of work, trade, and politics from the sacred, private space of intimacy, love, and relationship. Perhaps that is also one reason that, in the families with which we are familiar and in which men have conventionally been the breadwinners, men, more than women, have tended to consider the money they bring home as their nurturing gift; decontextualizing money, they can thereby deny the alienation that otherwise robs them of their integrity (Rapp 1978). As feminism has taught us, these domains mix in a way that makes the personal political, so that men, too, feel about money and love the way a blue-collar worker felt about having to put in overtime to send his son to college: shamed to find himself hating his kid, he said, "Things were touching that shouldn't touch" (Sennett and Cobb 1972:200).

According to anthropologists, there are two kinds of money. "Special-purpose" money is usable in exchange only for particular objects or services. The most famous ethnographic example is used in the New Guinea Kula Ring (Malinowski 1922). Through ritualized bargaining ceremonies, chiefs of different villages or islands would exchange with regular trading partners shell bracelets and necklaces. With any given partner, a chief would give necklaces and receive bracelets, or vice versa; necklaces would travel clockwise from island to island, bracelets counterclockwise. The aim of this exchange was to acquire prestige, of which each shell ornament carried a different amount created by, and registered in, the history of the exchanges it had undergone. In other words, whatever is transacted with special-purpose money tends to retain its individuality; indeed, it is embedded in the relationship governing the transaction.

In contrast, "general-purpose" money can, as in capitalism, buy anything that can be bought. A "universal equivalent, everything becomes translatable into it," which empowers it to symbolically homogenize everything (Dimen-Schein 1977:197). For example, in Manhattan (as of this writing), $2.50 can buy, and thus *means*, both a one-trip Metro card (itself a sort of special-purpose money) and, let us say, a frozen yogurt. General-purpose money measures everything by the same standard, which nullifies the individual meaning of any object or transaction:

> As money is not exchanged for any one specific quality, for any one specific thing or for any particular human essential power but for the entire objective world . . . from the standpoint of its possessor it therefore serves to exchange every property for every other, even contradictory, property and object; it is the fraternization of impossibilities. It makes contradictions embrace.
>
> (Marx 1964:169)

In capitalism, money is a universal medium of exchange. Although everything is not in fact for sale, in principle it is. Since the same standard, whether the dollar, ruble, or yen, quantifies everything, it erases all differences between things, levels all qualities, eliminates all particularity. Money reduces everything to its abstract capacity to be exchanged.

The paradox between love and hate

We come to what happens when that most general of things, money, pays for that most personal of experiences, the psychoanalytic journey. The psychoanalytic relation, like love, is highly particular. So particular is it that, at its most intense, in the heat of an analytic encounter, no generality seems to apply at all. For example, one has to work very hard to think about what is happening, to develop a set of ideas suited to clarify the complex relation that is transpiring. In fact, this doubled tension, the struggle to engage and the struggle to conceptualize, is one mark of the curative power of psychoanalysis, making it quite distinct from ordinary intercourse.

This particularity, however, is regularly undercut by the money that permits it. As analysts, we all know how rapidly our narcissism or, as Freud would have called it, our self-preservative instinct leads us to equate the loss of an hour with a bill we'll have to find some other way to pay; how disjunctive this thought is to the personal relation that we are also about to lose; and how dysphoric the hunch that our patients perceive these feelings (Aron and Hirsch 1992; Whitson 1989). As patients, who of us has not wondered just which of our analysts' bills our own treatment services? Or thought that we are replaceable by some other patient with enough money to pay the fare for their own personal journey? What's so personal and particular then? In fact, it's so painfully bizarre to go from the feelings of special love, meant only for one's analyst or one's patient, to the money that allows those emotions to flower but could also be used to buy many other things or could disappear in a flash, that one represses the connection and asks, as did a colleague, when I told her about this paper: why are we talking about money? That monthly bill rasps against the poignant longings for love that bloom in the psychoanalytic contact. It threatens to destroy them, turn them to shit. Like the man said, things touch that shouldn't.

When love turns to hate, it seems wise to move from Freud to Klein. In the psychoanalytic contact, as in the psyche, as, indeed, in our culture, the contradiction between money and love threatens to transform love into its seeming opposite; hate in turn threatens to annihilate relatedness altogether; and analysts, not unlike infants, feel the paralysis of terror. Money incites hate, if only because there is never enough of it to go around. But this twist of social fate resembles the vicissitudes of dependency that Riviere sees as the understructure of society, relatedness, and love. She stresses

> the degree of dependence of the human organism on its surroundings. In a stable political and economic system there is a great deal of apparent liberty and opportunity to fulfill our own needs, and we do not as a rule feel our dependence on the organization in which we live – unless, for instance, there is an earthquake or a strike! Then we may realize with reluctance and often with deep resentment that we are dependent on the forces of nature or on other people to a terrifying extent.
>
> (Klein and Riviere 1964:5)

Although this emergency recognition of dependence may typify only our own culture and even only certain groups within it, what Klein and Riviere go on to say is probably universal. Not only does dependence become awful when external events deprive us of what we need; such terror also inheres in love. The "possibility of privation" tends "to rouse resistance and aggressive emotions," a murderousness that forebodes doom (p. 7). What such loss feels like to the infant is what it unconsciously feels like to the adult: Your world "is out of control; a strike and an earthquake have happened . . . and this is because" you love and desire. Your "love may bring pain and devastation" to you and to those you love, but you "cannot control or eradicate" either your desire or your hate (p. 9). Hate is a condition of love, as love is a condition of life. You must love in order to live, but loving also means hating.

This, then, is the paradox of my title, the paradox of love and hate to which Klein, and later Winnicott and Guntrip, introduced us. I do not hold, with Klein and Riviere, that these primal passions of love and hate are constitutional. Nor do I hold with Guntrip (1969:24) that only one of them, love, is what we begin with. I prefer what I call the big bang theory, in which love and hate are co-born. Their mutual birthing is what makes their relation paradoxical, for paradox denotes the indissoluble tension between contraries that themselves never change, are transhistorical, atemporal, universal. The paradox of love and hate comes into being through the primal relationship; these passions take their shape and meaning from their passage through the emotional and structural net of that intimacy in which they likewise participate. Love and hate, emerging together, become mutually meaningful in the context of failure, when babies and mothering persons disappoint each other, when, as the earlier Klein seemed to argue, babies, in hating the primary caretaker, also first sense their love, and when, as Winnicott (1947) taught us, parents, to their often denying dismay, feel for their babies what they long ago learned to disavow, the dreaded hate that portends the death of their newborn and miraculous and reparative love.

The landlady of time

That we must absorb – indeed, relish – this paradox so as to do our best work, we have learned from Winnicott (1947) and from Searles (1965), as well as from Khan, who says: "One could argue that what is unique about the clinical situation is that the analyst survives both the loving and the hating of the patient as a person, and the patient as a person at the resolution of the relationship survives it, too, and is the richer for it" (1970:111). That paradox is an acquired taste we've all learned from our clinical work. One year I moved my office to a new, upscaled location. Although my furnishings were substantially the same, the setting itself was and is far more elegant and professional than the old one. Most of my patients, including Ms Rose, as I will call her, were pleased. They read their new environment as a sign of surging hope for their therapeutic progress and, not coincidentally, a sign of my ability to survive their aggression.

About six weeks after this move, Ms Rose, whose low fee was nevertheless a struggle for her to pay, took the opportunity to push on with her analytic work. She missed an appointment, one she had rescheduled because of an upcoming conference. At the next session, she sat up on the couch and looked me in the eyes. With icy fury, she challenged me: "Suppose someone has an accident?" Would I charge them? Ms Rose, who had been in treatment with me for just over five years, then explained that her alarm clock had failed to work. Rageful that she would have to pay anyway, she had declined to call; I said that I tried to telephone her but never reached her. Her diatribe intensified. Must she, she wanted to know, be responsible for everything? Could we not share the responsibility? Somewhere in here, I said that I charged her based on my time commitment. "Of course," she said, "I understand this is a business; you have to guarantee yourself an income. But what about my interests?" The schedule was for my convenience, not hers. It's often inconvenient for her. Oh, she knew the answers: she had to conform to my schedule because I wanted her to face the reality principle. I would not change it, so she had two choices, to pay or not to pay. Anyway, why should she rely on my judgment that she needed more than one session a week? Then, like an archer at last loosing her bow, she let fly her final question: "What are you, the Landlady of Time?"

Ms Rose is a poet as well as a graduate student in political studies, and if her rage made my heart beat in anger, her metaphor hit me right in the solar plexus. I felt all the emotions of the rainbow – guilt, recognition, anxiety, excitement, hate. After all, Freud said that analysts lease their time. And one of the dilemmas with which I am trying to deal here is what happens when money turns our work into a commodity just like any other. Indeed, it did not escape my notice that Ms Rose had granted me a perfect illustration of my present argument, which I had already begun to think about. Her knowledge of my inner life was, in certain respects, as unerring as her poetic aim.

At this, for us, unprecedented point of mutual hate, we continued. I said that while she appeared to be asking about my policies, she in fact often seemed to assume my reply. She agreed. She also concurred with my view that she was treating this clash like a pitched battle and added that her anger meant not that she would not continue to analyze this situation with me but that she was no longer letting her relationships go unquestioned. She then observed that it was odd to feel the same way about our relationship, since, of all the people she had been questioning, I was the one who had been kindest to her. I asked, by way of interpretation, where else should she bring her anger? Where hate but where she loves? She nodded in agreement. I added, correctly but in a fit of bad timing that spewed straight from my anger, that it was about time she was doing this, to which she coldly replied that she knew I would say that. She then began to list my unfairnesses in regard to money, some of which I acknowledged, others of which I contested. At session's end, I wished her a good trip. Her scornful smile said, "Who needs your good wishes?" Two weeks later, when she returned, she gave me a cartoon, in which a therapist is saying to a naked turtle, "I see you're coming out of your shell."

Every clinical moment is overdetermined, and many elements had fused to make Ms Rose's rage combust. I use this vignette to illustrate my contention that in the psychoanalytic contact, the contradiction between money and love can be resolved only if we transform it into the paradox between love and hate. The Devil's gold turns love to shit only when you cannot live out the hate with the one you love. What Ms Rose and I did was to live the contradiction together, risking the hate that seemed to be killing us, tolerating imminent annihilation until she found a way to survive it, until the paradox of love and hate presented itself to her in what Ghent (1992:9) characterized as the "somewhat altered consciousness that prevails in a spontaneous moment of creativity."

While the disparity in our financial, social, and ethnic status (I am white, Jewish, and a full-fledged member of the professional–managerial class, to which Ms Rose, fair-skinned, Afro-American, and from a lower-middle-class family, aspires) had always been apparent and sometimes attended to, the envy, greed, fear, and hate stimulated by these economic and cultural differences had become far more accessible in my new surroundings. Until now, Ms Rose had denied the contradictory dimension of our strange intimacy and could feel only fragments of her love and hate. My new office, which flagged not only my standing and authority but her own aspirations for the best for herself, now permitted her to move the contradiction between money and love into the center of the relationship, where it produced the hate that it always does. There were precursors. For example, shortly after I opened the new office, we began to see how she skirted shame. One day, she noticed a most offensive but, in this context, strangely appropriate odor emanating from the lovely garden onto which my casement windows open. Sniffing carefully, she said, "Why, it smells like cats!" Then she giggled. I asked her about the giggle. She tentatively answered, "Well I just thought, you smell like a cat."

Once the river of hate began to rage, once she finally woke up, opened her eyes, and, in shock, saw me for who I am, that is, the Landlady of Time, not only the money-hate but all the others, all hate itself, could fill the space between us. Her rage was the sound of her shell cracking, heralding the emergence of the self we had previously called the waif in the cave. Naked, that waif emerged, angry yet/and still loving. Her discovery of the paradox, that it was strange to doubt me, created this Utopian moment in which there began to grow another kind of love, the kind of bond you have with someone only when you have shed blood together.

After that, Ms Rose let me in on her thought that perhaps analysis is not always the most important thing in her life. She owned more of the analytic work and, in return for permitting me to write about this encounter between us in a way that disguises her identity, read the originally published version of this paper for me. In the end, she was no longer my tenant in the cave of psychoanalysis; she had made us into an interracial and otherwise nontraditional family: in her last dream, she wondered what I saw in the little black girl I had adopted when there were so many white ones around. Hate having been accepted along with differences and inequities between us, she could begin imagining her own, still untenanted loveliness.

Conclusion: from contradiction to paradox and back

Money, along with its coordinates, space and time, belongs conventionally to what has been labeled the analytic "frame." I would like, in concluding, to argue that the frame, which Langs (1973) calls "ground rules," ought to be treated as part of the picture too (see also Horner (1991), Herron and Welt (1992:11)). While analysts and patients often find the ground rules irritating, not only their outlining of, but their presence inside the consulting room in fact potentiates the Utopian moment that makes treatment work. They enter the symbolic play the frame permits: "When there is a frame it surely serves to indicate that what's inside the frame has to be interpreted in a different way from what's outside it . . . Thus the frame marks off an area within which what is perceived has to be taken symbolically, while what is outside the frame is taken literally" (Milner 1957:158). Because money is both a constituent of the frame and in the picture, it can be played with as symbol as well as literally exchanged. Thus, in bourgeois culture, as I have argued, a money relation appears to negate love, producing the hate that signs their contradiction.[1] But the psychoanalytic situation is a case where money permits love; where, for a moment, the culture can be upended, where you can love even where you would most expect to hate, where you would not get to love unless money were exchanged, where money in fact guarantees the possibility of love, and where, therefore, the contradiction between money and love and the hate it generates become safe.

We know this paradox from Freud, even though he did not appear to know what he knew. His own case histories reveal that the money relation and, hence, alienation entered his bourgeois patients' lives through their families. Gallop (1982) points out that "the family never was, in any of Freud's texts, completely closed off from questions of economic class. And the most insistent locus of that intrusion into the family circle . . . is the maid/governess/nurse" (Gallop 1982:144). Always from a lower class, this worker symbolizes, in unconscious and text alike, the very "financial distinction" that also comes to characterize the relation of Freud and all analysts to their patients. Gallop reminds us, in this context, of the two weeks' notice Dora gave Freud with the same courtesy she would have used upon firing a servant. Gallop argues that for psychoanalysis to provide the radical encounter of self with self it promises and to contend, I would add, with alienation, "Freud must assume his identification with the governess" (p. 146), because, rather "than having the power of life and death like the mother has over the infant, the analyst is financially dependent on the patient" (p. 143).

To put it more concretely, unless money may leave the frame and enter the picture, psychoanalysis must renege on its promise. The very economic transaction that distinguishes the psychoanalytic relationship from ordinary intimacies renders the transference sensible; money mediates one-person and two-person psychologies, their ambiguous, paradoxical, and contingent interface made possible and manifest by money's unavoidable but necessary and definitive arbitrariness; by what, in a way, Freud would have called the reality principle (Ms Rose, it turns out, was right). "The fact that the analyst is paid . . . proves that the analyst is . . . a stand-in" (Gallop 1982:143). Payment, in other words, grounds the possibility of genuinely new experience in the analysis, as well as that of remembering, repeating, and working through the past: the old happens with a newcomer who would never, without money, have been known and whose job it is to interpret both the old and the new. Reciprocally, the money relation also unveils the countertransference, in the service of whose understanding analysts must be willing to confront, internally and, when indicated, interpretively, both the discomforts and the pleasures of money's powerful place in psychoanalysis.

At the heart of psychoanalysis, this most private of encounters, lies society, just as at the heart of public life lies the alienation psychoanalysis tries to cure. Psychoanalysis is not revolution, and it doesn't make the contradiction between money and love go away. But for a brief, Utopian moment, it permits transcendence. The contradiction between money and love, a relation between contraries that can be transformed, finds a temporary, reparative resolution in the paradox between love and hate, a relation between contraries that never changes. The possibility of transformation distinguishes contradiction from paradox: contradiction bears resolution; paradox does not. Or, rather, as Ghent (1992) has said, the only resolution of paradox is paradox itself, here to inhabit, without rushing to relieve, the tension between love and hate, a tension that also preserves the memory of the contradiction between money and love it resolves.

The lesson of contradiction is perhaps easier to remember than that of paradox, which is, in turn, one of the easiest to forget. That money negates love, this we know preconsciously and needs, I think, only to be surfaced to stay in consciousness. But paradox is different; it is relearned each time it is lived. This is perhaps what Freud (1923) was trying to capture when he said that "love is with unexpected regularity accompanied by hate (ambivalence)" (p. 43). That love and hate go together, this is an analytic commonplace. But that, in the hot moment of loving or hating, we never remember that they do, this, perhaps, is wisdom.

Note

1 That the dichotomy between money and love may also define love as we know it is a consideration that is important but not possible to take up here.

References

Abraham, K. (1921) Contributions to the theory of the anal character. *Selected Papers of Karl Abraham, M.D.* (D. Bryan and A. Strachey, trans.). New York: Basic Books, 1953, pp. 370–392.

Amar, A. (1956) A psychoanalytic study of money. In E. Borneman (ed.), M. Shaw (trans.), *The Psychoanalysis of Money*. New York: Urizen Books, 1976, pp. 277–291.

Aron, L. (1991) The patient's experience of the analyst's subjectivity. *Psychoanalytic Dialogues*, 1:29–51.

Aron, L. and Hirsch, I. (1992) Money matters in psychoanalysis: a relational approach. In N. Skolnick and S. Warshaw (eds), *Relational Perspectives in Psychoanalysis*. Hillsdale, NJ: The Analytic Press, pp. 239–256.

Bion, W. R. (1980) *Key to Memoir of the Future*. Strath Tay, UK: Clunie Press.

Chodoff, P. (1986) The effect of third-party payment on the practice of psychotherapy. In D. W. Krueger (ed.), *The Last Taboo: Money as Symbol and Reality in Psychotherapy and Psychoanalysis*. New York: Brunner/Mazel, pp. 111–120.

Chodoff, P. (1991) Effects of the new economic climate on psychotherapeutic practice. In S. Klebanow and E. L. Lowenkopf (eds), *Money and Mind*. New York: Plenum Press, pp. 253–264.

Denby, D. (2004) *American Sucker*. Boston: Little, Brown.

Dimen-Schein, M. (1977) *The Anthropological Imagination*. New York: McGraw-Hill.

Drellich, M. (1991) Money and countertransference. In S. Klebanow and E. L. Lowenkopf (eds), *Money and Mind*. New York: Plenum Press, pp. 155–162.

Ehrenreich, B. (1989) *Fear of Falling*. New York: Pantheon.

Ehrenreich, B. and Ehrenreich, J. (1979) The professional–managerial class. In P. Walker (ed.), *Between Labor and Capital*. Boston: South End Press, pp. 5–48.

Eigen, M. (1986) *The Psychotic Core*. Northvale, NJ: Aronson.

Ferenczi, S. (1914) The ontogenesis of the interest in money. In E. Borneman (ed.), M. Shaw (trans.), *The Psychoanalysis of Money*. New York: Urizen Books, 1976, pp. 81–90.

Freud, S. (1895) Psychotherapy of hysteria. *Standard Edition*, 2, pp. 253–305. London: Hogarth Press, 1955.

Freud, S. (1905) Three essays on the theory of sexuality. *Standard Edition*, 7, pp. 125–245. London: Hogarth Press, 1953.

Freud, S. (1908) Character and anal erotism. *Standard Edition*, 9, pp. 167–175. London: Hogarth Press, 1953.

Freud, S. (1913) On beginning the treatment. *Standard Edition*, 12, pp. 123–144. London: Hogarth Press, 1958.

Freud, S. (1918) From the history of an infantile neurosis. *Standard Edition*, 17, pp. 3–174. London: Hogarth Press, 1955.

Freud, S. (1923) The ego and the id. *Standard Edition*, 19, pp. 3–68. London: Hogarth Press, 1961.

Freud, S. (1985) *The Complete Letters of Sigmund Freud to Wilhelm Fliess 1887–1904*, J. M. Masson (trans. and ed.). Cambridge and London: The Belknap Press of Harvard University Press.

Gallop, J. (1982) *The Daughter's Seduction*. Ithaca, NY: Cornell University Press.

Gay, P. (1988) *Freud*. New York: Norton.

Ghent, E. (1989) Credo: The dialectics of one-person and two-person psychologies. *Contemporary Psychoanalysis*, 25:200–237.

Ghent, E. (1992) Paradox and process. *Psychoanalytic Dialogues*, 2:135–159.

Greenberg, J. (1986) Theoretical models and the analyst's neutrality. *Contemporary Psychoanalysis*, 22:87–106.

Guntrip, H. (1969) *Schizoid Phenomena, Object-Relations and the Self*. New York: International Universities Press.

Havens, L. (1989) *A Safe Place*. Cambridge, MA: Harvard University Press.

Herron, W. G. and Welt, S. R. (1992) *Money Matters*. New York: Guilford Press.

Horner, A. J. (1991) Money issues and analytic neutrality. In S. Klebanow and E. L. Lowenkopf (eds), *Money and Mind*. New York: Plenum Press, pp. 175–182.

Jacobs, D. H. (1986) On negotiating fees with psychotherapy and psychoanalytic patients. In D. W. Krueger (ed.), *The Last Taboo: Money as Symbol and Reality in Psychotherapy and Psychoanalysis*. New York: Brunner/Mazel, pp. 121–131.

Khan, M. M. R. (1970) Montaigne, Rousseau and Freud. *The Privacy of the Self*. New York: International Universities Press, 1974, pp. 99–111.

Khan, M. M. R. (1972) On Freud's provision of the therapeutic frame. *The Privacy of the Self*. New York: International Universities Press, 1974, pp. 129–135.

Khan, M. M. R. (1979) *Alienation in Perversions*. New York: International Universities Press.

Klebanow, S. and Lowenkopf, E. L. (eds) (1991) *Money and Mind*. New York: Plenum Press.

Klein, M. and Riviere, J. (1964) *Love, Hate and Reparation*. New York: Norton.

Krueger, D. W. (ed.) (1986) *The Last Taboo: Money as Symbol and Reality in Psychotherapy and Psychoanalysis*. New York: Brunner/Mazel.

Langs, R. (1973) *The Technique of Psychoanalytic Psychotherapy*. Northvale, NJ: Aronson.

LeClair, E. E., Jr and Schneider, H. K. (1968) Some further theoretical issues. In E. E. LeClair, Jr and H. K. Schneider (eds), *Economic Anthropology*. New York: Holt, Rinehart & Winston, pp. 453–474.

Liss-Levenson, N. (1990) Money matters and the woman analyst: in a different voice. *Psychoanalytic Psychology*, 7 (supplement):119–130.

Malinowski, B. (1922) *Argonauts of the Western Pacific*. New York: Dutton, 1961.

Marx, K. (1964) *The Economic and Philosophical Manuscripts of 1844* (D. Struik, ed.; M. Milligan, trans.). New York: International Publishers.

Mészáros, J. (1975) *Marx's Theory of Alienation*, 4th edn. London: Merlin Press.

Milner, M. (1957) *On Not Being Able to Paint*. New York: International Universities Press.

Newman, K. S. (1988) *Falling from Grace*. New York: Free Press.

Ollman, B. (1976), *Alienation*, 2nd edn. New York: Cambridge University Press.

Rapp, R. (1978) Family and class in contemporary America: notes toward an understanding of ideology. *Science & Society*, 42:278–300.

Rendon, M. (1991) Money and the left in psychoanalysis. In S. Klebanow and E. L. Lowenkopf (eds), *Money and Mind*. New York: Plenum Press, pp. 135–148.

Searles, H. (1965) *Collected Papers on Schizophrenia and Related Subjects*. New York: International Universities Press.

Sennett, R. and Cobb, J. (1972) *The Hidden Injuries of Class*. New York: Vintage.

Shainess, N. (1991) Countertransference problems with money. In S. Klebanow and E. L. Lowenkopf (eds), *Money and Mind*. New York: Plenum Press, pp. 163–175.

Stern, D. (1997) *Unformulated Experience: From Dissociation to Imagination in Psychoanalysis*. Hillsdale, NJ: The Analytic Press.

Tulipan, A. B. (1986) Fee policy as an extension of the therapist's style and orientation. In D. W. Krueger (ed.), *The Last Taboo: Money as Symbol and Reality in Psychotherapy and Psychoanalysis*. New York: Brunner/Mazel, pp. 79–87.

Warner, S. L. (1991) Sigmund Freud and money. In S. Klebanow and E. L. Lowenkopf (eds), *Money and Mind*. New York: Plenum Press, pp. 121–134.

Whitson, G. (1989) *Money matters in psychoanalysis: the analyst's coparticipation in the matter of money*. Unpublished manuscript.

Winnicott, D. W. (1947) Hate in the countertransference. *Through Paediatrics to Psychoanalysis*. New York: Basic Books, 1975, pp. 194–203.
Zaphiropoulos, M. L. (1991) Fee and empathy: logic and logistics in psychoanalysis. In S. Klebanow and E. L. Lowenkopf (eds), *Money and Mind.* New York: Plenum Press, pp. 235–244.

Chapter 3

That place gives me the heebie jeebies

Lynne Layton

I needed a garden hose and took a friend shopping with me to a store called Ocean State Job Lot. As we left the store, my upper-middle-class friend looked utterly disgusted and said, "That place gives me the heebie jeebies." I tried to find out what she meant, what emotion "heebie jeebies" describes for her, but as I asked and it became clear that the emotion had to do with a disdain not only for the lower-class goods in the store but for the lower-class shoppers, shame set in and she refused to keep talking. The incident brought to mind Pierre Bourdieu's (1984) work on class, taste, and distinction, and it suggested to me that emotions such as "the heebie jeebies" play an important role in sustaining the tastes that keep class hierarchies in place. I personally had felt completely comfortable in the store, which undoubtedly has to do with my own class origins. I hail from what Bourdieu would identify as the rising petite bourgeoisie, marked by a mild asceticism combined with the search for a good bargain that, in my case, is articulated with the Jewish immigrant experience. I have crossed over, via education, into what he would call the new petite bourgeoisie. As I discussed the connections between shopping and emotions with my friend, I recalled my own feelings of discomfort and shame in upper-class stores such as Neiman Marcus. Having found some hints in Bourdieu that emotions secure the tastes that differentiate one class fraction from another, I wanted to explore further the unexplored psychoanalytic dimension of his work. After a discussion of the clues Bourdieu provides, I turn to a very informal survey I made of my friends' and colleagues' emotional experiences when shopping in high-end vs low-end stores. While this method does not have the advantage of providing a random sample from which one might generalize, it did, because I know the people and the complexities of their class identifications, enable me to read between the lines of self-report. The results point to some of the issues that sustain class conflict, particularly connections between emotions and the unconscious, conflictual internalizations of class relations that sustain well-defended identities.

In his book *Distinction* (1984), Bourdieu largely discusses the tastes of the different class fractions as they appear to the conscious mind of his survey subjects. His empirical methods rely on self-report, and he defines each class fraction by its relative volume and mixture of social, educational, and economic capital as well as its members' personal historical trajectory (i.e., from one class fraction to another). The focus is on how each fraction distinguishes itself from the others and how all but the lowest fractions struggle to distance themselves from the necessity that marks the lives of those at the bottom. Although Bourdieu's work is not psychoanalytic, and in some respects might be seen as rather anti-psychoanalytic (see Chapter 6, where he critiques the profession), he nonetheless opens his investigation with the following sentence: "Sociology is rarely more akin to social psychoanalysis than when it confronts an object like taste, one of the most vital stakes in the struggles fought in the field of the dominant class and the field of cultural production" (1984:11). What might he mean by a "social psychoanalysis"? *Distinction*'s significance for psychoanalysis lies in the fact that the core sociological concepts Bourdieu identifies operate largely on an unconscious level. For example, his notion of habitus – the schemes and dispositions that class fractions draw upon to make ethical and taste judgments that distinguish them from other fractions – is something that performatively takes shape from repeated relational and other early tactile and visual experiences that remain unconscious:

> The schemes of the habitus, the primary forms of classification, owe their specific efficacy to the fact that they function below the level of consciousness and language, beyond the reach of introspective scrutiny or control by the will. Orienting practices practically, they embed what some would mistakenly call *values* in the most automatic gestures or the apparently most insignificant techniques of the body – ways of walking or blowing one's nose, ways of eating or talking – and engage the most fundamental principles of construction and evaluation of the social world, those which most directly express the division of labour (between the classes, the age groups and the sexes) or the division of the work of domination, in divisions between bodies and between relations to the body which borrow more features than one, as if to give them the appearances of naturalness, from the sexual division of labour and the division of sexual labour.
>
> (Bourdieu 1984:466)

This version of the unconscious might be thought of as something akin to Stern's (1997) concept of "unformulated experience," which describes a not necessarily conflictual realm of what forms one's horizon of meaning-making possibilities. But other passages, such as the following, suggest that the habitus is grounded in a dynamic unconscious and that tastes derive from relational conflicts highly charged with emotion. Bourdieu writes:

> If a group's whole life-style can be read off from the style it adopts in furnishing or clothing, this is not only because these properties are the objectification of the economic and cultural necessity which determined their selection, but also because the social relations objectified in familiar objects, in their luxury or poverty, their "distinction" or "vulgarity", their "beauty" or "ugliness", impress themselves through bodily experiences which may be as profoundly unconscious as the quiet caress of beige carpets or the thin clamminess of tattered, garish linoleum, the harsh smell of bleach or perfumes as imperceptible as a negative scent. Every interior expresses, in its own language, the present and even the past state of its occupants, bespeaking the elegant self-assurance of inherited wealth, the flashy arrogance of the nouveaux riches, the discreet shabbiness of the poor and the gilded shabbiness of "poor relations" striving to live beyond their means; one thinks of the child in D. H. Lawrence's story "The Rocking-Horse Winner" who hears throughout the house and even in his bedroom, full of expensive toys, an incessant whispering: "There must be more money." Experiences of this sort would be the material of a social psychoanalysis which set out to grasp the logic whereby the social relations objectified in things and also, of course in people are insensibly internalized, taking their place in a lasting relation to the world and to others, which manifests itself, for example, in thresholds of tolerance of the natural and social world, of noise, overcrowding, physical or verbal violence – and of which the mode of appropriation of cultural goods is one dimension.
>
> (Bourdieu 1984:77)

As Bourdieu's citation of the D. H. Lawrence story suggests, the child's relational world is the ground of a *conflictual* internalization of class antagonisms, an internalization that causes neurotic misery. To capture this dynamic aspect, I have elsewhere spoken of a normative unconscious (Layton 2002), that part of the unconscious that is produced by social hierarchies of various kinds and that, in turn, works to reproduce and secure a hierarchical *status quo*. If one casts Bourdieu's description of distinction into the terminology of a dynamic unconscious, one could say that class identities are formed via a defensive splitting off of parts of self too closely associated with anything felt to characterize other, especially lower- but also upper-class fractions. One distances oneself from the lower class's closeness to necessity, but that very splitting creates a haunting anxiety about necessity that is ever-present and must be vigilantly guarded against (see Butler (1995) on melancholy gender). In different ways, we distance ourselves as well from those who have what we can never hope to have.

The anxiety born of distinguishing oneself from both those below and those above is precisely what Bourdieu discovers to be the motor of social reproduction, but the emotions are not his primary focus and in fact get a bit lost in the welter of empirical data. Bourdieu does occasionally speak about emotions, particularly the anxiety, disdain and resentment people in one class fraction may feel when they find themselves in the institutions, sites, or among objects that are considered the legitimate domain of another class fraction. Any particular habitus, in other words, is shot through with the emotions that hold its series of dispositions and strategies in place, that mark them as morally good, nay superior to other sets of dispositions. The habitus, he writes, "is a virtue made of necessity" (1984:372), and the most common words, such as "practical," "sober," "odd," "clean" are used to defend or condemn a given habitus, used in ways that mark one fraction off from another (1984:193–194). An example lies in the way the new petite bourgeoisie distinguishes itself from the rising petite bourgeoisie by rejecting its ethic of asceticism for one of pleasure. Each fraction describes the other's choices in negative terms, e.g., what the ascetic, rising p.b. calls ethical in terms of body discipline, necessary purchases, etc., the new p.b. pathologizes in terms such as masochistic and self-denying.

So even though Bourdieu does not explore emotions, it is clear that emotions are central to his investigation of what reproduces the social *status quo*, perhaps even more central than taste: indeed, it is precisely the kind of shame or anxiety I feel in the upper-class Neiman Marcus store that keeps the likes of me OUT of Neiman Marcus, no matter how much I may like their goods. On the rare occasions that I go there, I try to make myself small and inconspicuous, anxious that at any moment I will be too loud, take up too much space, or make some other social gaffe that will give me away as not belonging. More comfortable in my own element, my unconscious anxiety is denied by the conscious thought that what I like is the best, but the anxiety that makes me stick close to my own stores simultaneously legitimizes the upper class's right to have more, to have better, and to dominate. I may make fun of what will appear to me to be their extravagance, or, more likely, morally disdain it, both strategies of the less powerful, but I will deploy my own set of values and lifestyle choices, my habitus, to justify turning my back on their domain, all the while possibly envying if not their goods, then certainly their place at the top of the hierarchy. As one respondent to my survey admitted:

> Sometimes when I am in a store like SAKS [an upper-class store: note that she prints it in large letters] and can't afford things, I feel better by telling myself that the clothes, etc. are really not worth even close to what they are asking and I feel that I am empowered by NOT buying them (whether I'd like to or not). It's my personal form of protest.

What is conscious is the shame or anxiety she and I experience in the store; what is structuring the unconscious is the taboo on having a proprietary relation to culture and knowledge. As Bourdieu writes: "Objective limits become a sense of limits, a practical anticipation of objective limits acquired by experience of objective limits, a 'sense of one's place' which leads one to exclude oneself from the goods, persons, places and so forth from which one is excluded" (1984:471).

To get more of a sense of how emotions sustain class identifications and differentiations, what gets split off and how what is split off haunts, I undertook an informal survey of friends and colleagues, most of whom are also part of the new petite bourgeoisie, a class fraction of cultural intermediaries that tends to repudiate the other fractions of the petite bourgeoisie as well as the dominant class fractions. This fraction, Bourdieu writes, in fact often sees itself as allied with the dominated classes and the dispossessed, understands itself as marginal, *déclassé*. I suspected, then, that there might be some conflict between the liberal or left values held by this class fraction and reactions, such as the "heebie jeebies," to the habitus of their lower-class allies. To begin to explore the emotions structuring the habitus of the new petite bourgeoisie, I sent around an email that said the following:

> I'm working on a research question that I need my friends to help out with. I'm writing about shopping and emotion and social class. I'm finding that some people can't bear to be in stores like the Christmas Tree Shop [a store that buys odd lots of varying quality goods and sells at a discount] – as one person put it, these stores give me the heebie jeebies. I want to know what the heebie jeebies means, what emotion does it describe and what does it have to do with class relations. I myself experience shame when I'm in places like Neiman Marcus, like I'm going to make some terrible social *faux pas* and I'll be discovered not to belong. These are examples of what I'm interested in – what emotions sustain antagonisms between classes, or, put another way, what emotions sustain class identity. In what shopping situations does one get anxious, shame-filled, repelled, and why? What do those emotions have to do with class? Do you have any anecdotes you'd be willing to share? Thanks in advance.

The responses to this question produced a few broad themes that I analyze below: responses that show how taste is underwritten by the fear of falling back into the class from which one has come and/or falling for the first time into the state of necessity of which the poor are constant reminders; responses that show that those whose origin is upper class have attained and maintain that position by disdaining whatever is associated with the lower classes; responses that reflect something that Bourdieu mentions but does not consider in any detail in *Distinction*, the way that gender and other aspects of identity intersect with class to mediate the emotions behind taste;

and, finally, responses that reflect a kind of pity or sadness for the lower classes and the quality of goods with which they are "forced" to make do.

One set of responses came from the wives of men whose social trajectory took them from white working class to highly paid professional. The wives reported that their husbands NEVER go into stores like Ocean State Job Lot, which also seems to be true of those born into the upper middle class. But there are interesting emotional differences behind the similar behavior of these two groups. In the store, both groups might feel the heebie jeebies, but it seems that the emotional reactions of those who rose from lower class origins center on the fact that it all feels painfully familiar, while those from upper class origins find such stores simply alien. For both groups, entering the stores might reactivate all that they have split off to attain what they have, and both groups' emotional responses suggest a fear of contagion by contact with the lower classes. But whereas the heebie jeebies among those born into the upper class seems to be something akin to revulsion, for the group whose class status has risen these stores also evoke shame, even humiliation. Responses suggest that low-end stores recall painful experiences of having less than other kids, the wrong kind of clothes, of seeing family members working there at low pay all their lives. One respondent who has moved, via education, from a lower- to a higher-class fraction said:

> When I was a kid, my mother used to shop at a place called King's, which I think was an early Wal-Mart . . . I felt humiliated that we were buying stuff there and embarrassed that my clothes came from these discount-y places (or were homemade) when my friends were all buying stuff at Ann Taylor [upper-class women's clothing] . . . I found the people at King's and Caldor's scary and the colors ugly and the smells horrible. I still do.

The humiliation felt in relation to the upper class seems to produce the heebie jeebies reaction toward the lower class.

In thinking about the reactions of both groups, made up largely of liberals, I was reminded of Patricia Williams's (1997) analysis of why the white lower classes don't trust liberals. Williams writes that while liberals may politically fight for the poor, they make it clear in many other ways that they don't want to be anywhere near the poor. They have nothing but disdain for the poor habitus, and the poor know it. Yet it is significant for a social psychoanalysis to recognize that the disdain has different emotional underpinnings for the two class fractions.

Respondents who have moved up in class – especially men – characteristically expressed a wish for "only the best" goods. They expressed it in terms of "better quality," but my guess is that in some cases this hides a fear of being "revealed" as not truly upper class if you *don't* have the best. In my clinical work, I had a client whose obsession with getting "only the best" consumer goods hid an ever-present anxiety about being judged inadequate. This client, who was born into the working poor but who became a successful entrepreneur in his twenties, once said that the only way he can know for sure that no one is putting him down (as he was put down constantly in childhood) is if he exclusively buys those things that legitimate culture considers the best. Bourdieu considers the psychic cost that these fractions, who come from poverty, pay:

> The nature against which culture is here constituted is nothing other than what is "popular", "low", "vulgar", "common". This means that anyone who wants to "succeed in life" must pay for his succession to everything which defines truly humane humans by a change of nature, a 'social promotion' experienced as an ontological promotion . . . a leap from nature to culture, from the animal to the human; but having internalized the class struggle, which is at the very heart of culture, he is condemned to shame, horror, even hatred of the old Adam, his language, his body and his tastes, and of everything he was bound to, his roots, his family, his peers, sometimes even his mother tongue, from which he is now separate by a frontier more absolute than any taboo.
> (Bourdieu 1984:251)

The emotional implication is that a kind of melancholia or dysthymia is the price of that separation from one's former self and earliest attachments (Layton 1998: Chapter 9; Eng and Han 2002).

Alternately, the attainment of the higher-class status might provide a manic defense against what has been lost. One respondent who moved, via education, from middle to upper middle class said:

> I used to hate getting a bargain . . . But that was 20 years ago when I was moving up class ranks. Now I'm pleased not to overpay and willing to go almost anywhere . . . although I still think of myself as belonging in the Nordstroms, Neiman Marcuses, Williams Sonomas and Bread and Circuses of the world [all high-end upper-class stores]. Guess it's sort of like dressing a certain way most of the time – but enjoying dressing in drag – because you're pushing the boundaries and somehow "getting away" with something.

This respondent, whose mother aspired to upper-class status, was one of the few Jews in his town, and I wonder if he also perceived that Jewishness, often associated with getting a bargain, stood in the way of rising in class status. He did not repudiate Judaism, just getting a bargain; his comment reveals the interesting difference between how one passes while moving up in rank, by disdaining association with those who need a bargain, and how one passes once having achieved the desired status: he can now take pleasure in frequenting the bargain store because he no longer feels an emotional kinship with those who have to do so.

The next set of responses suggest that gender inflects the habitus in particular ways; for example, within a class fraction such as the new petite bourgeoisie, men and women may have different emotional ways of internalizing class difference, ways that have to do in part with their relation to their bodies, to knowledge, and to their right to dominate. A 52-year-old female geriatric social worker, whose parents are Holocaust survivors who did factory work when they first came to the USA, spoke of her discomfort looking at clothes in Bloomingdale's [upper-class department store] in an upscale suburban mall:

> First of all, all the saleswomen were young and thin. It's not true of other large department stores like Filene's [a middle-class department store] . . . It made me feel different. The women that shopped there were all well manicured, and looked like they spent time on themselves. I felt schleppy in comparison. The clothes they were selling also left me feeling left out. There were only a few items in each size and they seemed to say "not for you" . . . On the other hand I had been to Chicos in the Burlington Mall [a more middle-class mall] a few weeks before. I felt more comfortable there. Perhaps because their clothes were geared toward someone like me (older and rounder). Also the saleswomen were friendly and there is a sense of camaraderie amongst the customers.

Aware of systemic age discrimination, she also wrote that she's aware that it is the unspoken policy of some stores not to hire older women.

Like myself, this respondent did not feel that she has the right body for these high-end stores. A male respondent to my email asked if I felt similarly uncomfortable in high-end restaurants and hotels. I do not, which made me think all the more that the shopping issue is about having the wrong body. My large educational capital, consonant with my Jewish identity, makes me see myself as someone with excellent and sophisticated taste that entitles me to frequent the finest restaurants and hotels with no sense of shame. Another Jewish female psychologist respondent seemed to feel similarly:

> I often have conversations with myself when I find myself having feelings of superiority about such things as taste in clothes, music, books (or should I say literature), accents, plays (or should I say theatre), etc. I tell myself that taste is subjective, but part of me persists in feelings of superiority, which feels good, sad to say, since like you, Lynne, I have feelings of inferiority in stores like Neiman Marcus, etc.

So it is not just class that keeps this class fraction out of high-end stores, but the intersection of class and gender.

Worried far less about his body, a male, gay, Jewish psychologist wrote:

> I don't often feel (aware of anyway) discomfort related to shame or class when shopping. However, on the rare occasions I have been in an extremely upscale store or boutique, I am more aware of "how I pass or read" than usual. In those situations, I can feel imperiled of feeling (or seeming) "less than" – so I might want to convey an air of "I know what I'm looking for" or "I know Armani," or maybe even "I am a person who could/does wear this clothing, or owns home furnishings like this."

He further wrote that he does not usually feel as though he doesn't belong in high-end stores; he has a sense of entitlement that enables him to go there. But what does cause him discomfort is to be perceived as a "neophyte, or a pretender." He wondered if there is a gender component to this, that men don't like to "not know," to be perceived as an "unknowledgeable consumer." I imagine that another aspect of the gender component is that, as a male, he feels a right to have what the upper class has in a way that the females of this class fraction might not. Although my sample was quite small (with an N of 20), I would say that most of the males claimed this right to have the best, and most of the females felt as though they did not belong in upper-class stores.

I conclude with the responses of a few avowedly left-wing members of my sample, who said that they feel sad in stores such as Ocean State Job Lot; one said she feels the stores are an assault on poor people:

> When I am in a store like a Christmas Tree shop, or a place with scented candles and knickknacks for instance, I get a sick feeling that I would describe as existential agony. I feel that everything in the world is worthless junk and that there is no point in striving or in trying to do anything of substance. I often feel this way at malls. I rarely go to them because of it . . . If I go to shop, I soon become "world weary" and just want to go home immediately. Some of the stores have sickening smells in them which I think is a combination of poor air circulation and evil gases coming from the products. It's got to be unhealthy, but beyond that it's just awful to smell. Yet, no one seems to notice it. I want to shout to everyone to wake up and see what a horrid environment they're in, but I of course know that would be "crazy."

Another respondent wrote:

> I find those low-end places horribly depressing. They make me angry for AND at the people shopping there. And maybe horrified at/scared of the idea of living that kind of life? I don't like the high-end Neiman Marcus stores, either. In fact, I really loathe shopping – except in bookstores and hardware stores, for books and hammers and paint. Those are okay. Classless, perhaps? . . . Even when I was a kid I minded [resented] the ugly brownish colors and sleazy fabrics and horrible mirrors in the dressing rooms and the way you often don't have private dressing rooms in stores like that. Maybe I was picking up my mother's resentment that she had to shop there, that my father didn't make enough money to live the way they'd been brought up to live? I find it all a kind of assault on poor people and yet, I suppose, don't like being WITH those people. Any more than I like being with the people at Saks or Neiman's or just about anyplace that isn't a small store . . .
>
> All of this is what makes catalogues such a great way to shop. You can do it at 11:00 at night if you want and you don't have to undress with those ugly fat ladies yelling at their kids AND you don't have to deal with snooty salespeople in expensive stores.

As with the upper-class respondents, heebie jeebies for these respondents had to do with the quality of the goods, the way they're thrown all over the place, the dirty floors, the noise, the overstimulation, the crowdedness – mixed in with some condescension toward the people who shop there. But the sadness also reflected empathy for those who HAVE to shop there.

Bourdieu suggests that this sadness, too, might be merely a guise of the way distinction operates. He argues that the dominant classes generally impose their own view of what is desirable (in terms of noise, clothing quality, cleanliness) on the working classes, not recognizing that their own taste marks nothing objective, nothing superior, but only their internalization of class struggle. He writes:

> So the search for distinction has no need to see itself for what it is, and all the intolerances – of noise, crowds, etc. – inculcated by a bourgeois upbringing are generally sufficient to provoke the changes of terrain or object which, in work as in leisure, lead towards the objects, places or activities rarest at a given moment.
>
> (Bourdieu 1984:249)

Bourdieu's theory has been accused of being overly deterministic/structuralist and pessimistic, and here is one place where I think we see evidence of that. For he suggests that there is no stance from which to make an objective judgment; there are only subjective rationalizations that legitimize one's own place in the hierarchy. Clearly, he has a point, and we can see it in the respondents' distaste for noise, for dressing in open rooms, for the "ugly, fat people." Yet, perhaps Bourdieu is not attentive enough to emotion and misses the possibilities for a class alliance that exist in this class fraction's empathy for the poor. If there are indeed gases coming out of the goods and the people who have to buy those goods can't, in any of several ways, afford to notice, it seems a good thing that some do notice that bad goods and unhealthy food are being dumped on the poor.

Bourdieu's logic suggests that the poor develop their habitus out of necessity. While at times he seems almost to glorify tastes that are closer to everyday needs and experiences, critiquing the aesthetic distance central to the taste of dominant fractions, would he want to argue that values that rationalize the constraints of necessity are emancipatory? Isn't part of the goal of social equality to make it so no one has to live dangerously close to the edge of not having basic necessities? Bourdieu's system presupposes a narcissistic subject and so holds little place for getting outside oneself and caring about what happens to those not of your class; he assumes that negative value judgments on the habitus of a lower class are rationalizations meant to maintain your class status at a safe distance from that class. My results suggest that this class fraction's emotions are complex, operating simultaneously to secure distance from necessity and to make one decry and fight actively against social injustice.

Conclusion

Psychoanalytic social theorists know that social change does not come about by suggesting that people "just say no;" they know that fantasy and the emotions that drive fantasy largely pull to keeps things as they are or alternatively to motivate change. What drives Bourdieu's work is the psychoanalytic view that the internalization of class relations, manifest in taste and people's fantasies about what tastes represent about them, is responsible for the social reproduction of things as they are. His work inspires a deeper investigation of the unconscious processes of internalization and the role emotions play in social reproduction. I suggest that to elaborate a social psychoanalysis, we must investigate the workings of a dynamic normative unconscious, that aspect of the unconscious born of having to suppress and/or split off whatever feelings, desires, and attributes that those who offer us love insist, consciously and unconsciously, are not part of a proper way of being human. "The Rocking-Horse Winner" exemplifies the way in which parental anxiety about money becomes a child's anxiety. Another example: a friend whose early life was dominated by a father who wanted him to go to medical school was repeatedly asked, whenever he did something that did not show enough scholarly promise, whenever he wasn't serious enough, "So what do you want to be, a truck driver?" It has been known since Freud that anxiety can signal danger, and Sullivan (1953) wrote about security operations that become a part of character and are designed to help us avoid whatever might put us at risk of losing love. The notion of a normative unconscious socializes that insight: once internalized class relations produce splits between what is proper to one's class identity and what is not (class here understood as mediated by gender, sexuality, race, and other identity variables), anxiety signals the danger of stepping out of place and losing love.

But most of us are not even aware of this anxiety, because we do not step out of our habitus. Bourdieu puts this in a less psychoanalytic way, omitting the fear of loss of love that generates conflict:

> The *sense* of limits implies *forgetting* the limits. One of the most important effects of the correspondence between real divisions and practical principles of division, between social structures and mental structures, is undoubtedly the fact that primary experience of the social world is that of doxa, an adherence to relations of order which, because they structure inseparably both the real world and the thought world, are accepted as self-evident.
>
> (Bourdieu 1984:471)

I am arguing that doxa is transmitted in conflictual relational experiences and thereafter held in place by emotions such as humiliation, shame, anxiety, love.

The truck driver example evokes the previously cited Patricia Williams essay, which concludes with the important insight that it is very hard indeed to undo hate learned in the context of love (Williams 1997). What would it take, she might ask, for my friend to feel that there is anything human about a truck driver? Equally important, the conceptualization of normative unconscious processes suggests that it isn't just the truck driver he will hate, but all those things about himself that the father associated with the truck driver. Indeed, the reason he disdains the truck driver is that he cannot come too near that part of himself for fear of retribution.

The emotions that underlie the internalization of class relations, as we have seen, entail a great deal of anxiety about being contaminated by poverty, of getting too close to need. Whether originally upper class or originally lower middle class, the respondents' fear of contagion, their "heebie jeebies," suggests a repudiation of need but also more than that. A mainstream psychoanalytic interpretation would argue that we are all born dependent and needy and have conflictual feelings about being so. But what I hear in my survey responses is that culture gives a particular definition to neediness: getting too close to need entails painful memories of being inadequate, put down, found to be not quite right. The cultural devaluation of dependency is central to most identity categories – class, gender, race, sexuality – and identities are all too often brought into being via humiliation about "weakness," which causes both self-hatred and hatred of others. Struck by Bourdieu's description of the way that moving up in class almost demands repudiation of who you were, relegation of who you were to the non-human, I suggested that the psychic cost of class mobility might be chronic low-grade depression or manic denial of need. Perhaps there is a connection, then, between our recent economic boom times and the increasing use of anti-depressants among the middle and upper middle class, especially among children of those classes. When I think about why there is so little left-wing activism in the USA and so much use of anti-depressants, I can't help but wonder if it is because of this possible origin of melancholia.

As I suggested above, in the new petit bourgeois class fraction, there is both empathy for and heebie jeebies towards poverty and the poor. My sense is that the doubleness of this left/liberal group's feelings about contact with the poor has to do precisely with Bourdieu's perception that dominant culture defines "human" as "not poor." Yet, most of my respondents are aware of class and of systemic discrimination, and this in a culture in which most class fractions are not. It is important to try to account for this awareness. One possible answer lies in Stuart Hall's (1980, 1982) discussion of oppositional readings and of active agents creating new ideological discourses by dis-articulating and re-articulating existent discourses. The way that gender, Jewish immigrant status, educational capital, class trajectory and historical moment might come together in a particular individual, for example, could account for a reading of consumerism oppositional to that of most Americans. One left-wing female respondent, an immigrant who came to America as a child, wrote that her family was "not steeped in consumerism as a means of selfhood or sense of emotional security. In fact, my parents thought Americans foolish in their spending habits."

It seems important to think about the fact that even those in my sample who were aware of systemic discrimination did not seem aware of what might underlie their fear of contagion by the poor, be it a fear of humiliation or the separation from an earlier self of which Bourdieu speaks. Recall that the friend I spoke of in my opening anecdote stopped talking as soon as she realized that her heebie jeebies was not only about the goods but about the people. I conclude by suggesting we look at the shame about need and dependency that is part of this class fraction's identity, for it may be the very thing that blocks a closer political alliance between the left-liberal new petite bourgeoisie and lower-class fractions.

References

Bourdieu, P. (1984) *Distinction. A Social Critique of the Judgement of Taste* (R. Nice, trans.). Cambridge, MA: Harvard University Press.

Butler, J. (1995) Melancholy gender – refused identification. *Psychoanalytic Dialogues*, 5:165–180.

Eng, D. and Han, S. (2002) A dialogue on racial melancholia. In S. Fairfield, L. Layton, and C. Stack (eds), *Bringing the Plague. Toward a Postmodern Psychoanalysis*. New York: Other Press, pp. 233–267.

Hall, S. (1980) Encoding/decoding. In S. Hall, D. Hobson, A. Lowe, and P. Willis, *Culture, Media, Language. Working Papers in Cultural Studies*. London: Hutchinson, pp. 128–138.

Hall, S. (1982) The rediscovery of ideology: return of the repressed in media studies. In M. Gurevitch, T. Bennett, J. Curran, and J. Woollacott (eds), *Culture, Society and the Media*. New York: Methuen, pp. 56–90.

Layton, L. (1998) *Who's That Girl? Who's That Boy? Clinical Practice Meets Postmodern Gender Theory*. Hillsdale, NJ: The Analytic Press, 2004.

Layton, L. (2002) Cultural hierarchies, splitting, and the heterosexist unconscious. In S. Fairfield, L. Layton, and C. Stack (eds), *Bringing the Plague. Toward a Postmodern Psychoanalysis*. New York: Other Press, pp. 195–223.

Stern, D. B. (1997) *Unformulated Experience. From Dissociation to Imagination in Psychoanalysis*. Hillsdale, NJ: The Analytic Press.

Sullivan, H. S. (1953) *The Interpersonal Theory of Psychiatry*. New York: Norton.

Williams, P. (1997) The ethnic scarring of American whiteness. In W. Lubiano (ed.), *The House That Race Built*. New York: Pantheon, pp. 253–263.

Chapter 4

The manic society

Rachael Peltz

> Society has relinquished its caretaking function, demolished its institutions for supporting emotional development, and shifted its priorities from the mental and emotional to the material. In the increasing violence around us, we may be seeing the casualties of this cavalier approach.
>
> (Fonagy 1999:23)

> I and others have been accused of being partisan – not just personally, which is our right to be, but involving psychoanalysis and speaking as analysts. I do not agree with this viewpoint. I think psychoanalytic neutrality must not be confused with being neutered . . . and there can be no neutrality, say, as between Hitler and his victims. One can only strive for the understanding of factors that produce certain situations, and we are entitled, and indeed ethically bound, to make known our views about the dangers we foresee . . .
>
> We have also been accused of idealism. This I do not entirely refute, but I do not consider that it is "unanalytic." One has to distinguish between idealization and having ideals. Idealization is a distortion of realities and a dangerous stance, since it is invariably accompanied by splitting and projection – idealizing oneself and one's ideas or groups at the expense of paranoid attitudes toward others. Having ideals is very different: it is not pathological to hope for a better future, for instance, for peace, and to strive for it, whilst recognizing how hard it is to attain, and that the opposition to it comes not only from others but also has its roots in ourselves.
>
> (Segal 1995:204)

The other day my eight-year-old daughter and I were visiting our local library. Her class was studying Africa and we were looking for books on African crafts to help us get ideas for her project. The woman at the information desk was only too happy to help us. She quickly logged on to her computer and located several books in different libraries which would be transferred to our branch by the next day. I thought, "This is terrific. You go to the library to get help for your child. You receive assistance from an enthusiastic employee, eager to find what you're looking for and proud of the service she is delivering. And it's all free." On our way home I was marveling to my daughter how libraries are wonderful places, and was abruptly jolted by a horrible thought. What if libraries were privatized and suddenly run for profit? What if libraries went the way of air transport, health care, schools, energy?

I have similar thoughts about museums. In 1998 I visited the Freud exhibit at the Library of Congress in Washington, DC. As it was only my second visit to DC, I had never visited the Library of Congress before and was awed by the majesty of the Jefferson building's gloriously painted walls and palatial ceilings open to viewing from the staircase that led to the different exhibits. I was curious and so inquired about the construction of this museum. I discovered it was originally conceived of in 1800, based on the belief of Thomas Jefferson that the power of knowledge could shape a free and democratic society. The Jefferson building was completed in 1897 and the others followed. From their conception these muse-inducing structures were meant to be available to the population at large, again in accordance with the belief that knowledge and democracy go hand in hand. Thus there is always a place for them in the federal budget and, unlike other tourist attractions in the USA, they are open to the public free of charge, availing them to all segments of the population most days of the week. As I enjoyed the freedom to wander through these grand museums I was struck by the sensibility they engendered – an awesome yet calming excitement that reminded me of the first time I visited the Museum of Science and Industry in Chicago at the age of eight. In retrospect, beyond my interest and excitement about what was in the museum, I think I felt very reassured that people, elders to my mind, had to have thought to build the museum and maintain it so that I could visit. I think I felt secure in that setting because it was a sign that I was being looked after and provided with such places, "evocative objects" in Bollas's (1987) words, to feed my imagination. They offered generational continuity and a contained symbolic space in which I was free to learn and let my mind wander.

The Freud exhibit, housed within the Jefferson Building, highlighted Freud's life and key ideas and the influence of these ideas in the century to come. Among them, contained in the title of the exhibit itself, "Sigmund Freud: Conflict and Culture," was Freud's conviction that culture represented the expression of desires in conflict with one another and with society. The job of society was the regulation and control of human instincts, which inevitably pit the needs of the individual and society against one another. Furthermore, Freud (1931) thought that the consequences of the unresolved conflicts between the needs of the individual and society led to society's vulnerability to "radical disruptions" in which "primal conflicts" could erupt in unthinkable violence, a fact we know he painfully registered upon fleeing Nazi Germany in the nick of time.

In 1931 Freud added a final sentence to *Civilization and Its Discontents*, originally written in 1929, in which he rhetorically inquired, "Who can foresee with what success and with what result the forces of eros will prevail over his equally immortal adversary" (1931:45). Since Freud's time analysts have sought to understand and respond to the human capacity for destructiveness. From Fenichel's roundtable discussions (Jacoby 1975), through members of the Frankfurt school (Jay 1972), to Marie Langer and her associates (Langer 1989), there have been ongoing attempts to subject social phenomena to psychoanalytic scrutiny. At times this involved revising analytic theory and suggesting alternative visions to Freud's account of the inevitable and explosive polarization between the individual and society.

Although some may refute the applicability of developmental theories of the individual to society, I agree with Winnicott's notion that "The study of the emotional development of society must be closely related to the study of the individual" (1986:241). In this chapter, I join those who believe psychoanalysis offers a great deal to understanding the social world and the direction of social and political change. That understanding can be achieved not by sustaining a neutral stance toward social issues, but by using our ideas about psychic development to inform and articulate our social policies.

I want to examine a manic characteristic of contemporary society, which originates in the operation of our current unfettered market economy. I will focus on the particular role of manic defenses and the ways they are manifested, particularly among professional and upper-middle-class sectors of this society, as a means of coping with the loss of a socially "just" vision of the future, based on "good enough" social provision and containment. I will argue that the goals of a free market (unregulated) economy are in direct conflict with the goals of a democratic society committed to providing social safety nets for its members. I will further discuss how the idealization (and ideologies) of consumption in the absence of a consistent ideal of provision aid and abet the use of manic defenses and the idealization of "pregenital states" (Chasseguet-Smirgel 1985). In this atmosphere manic defenses proliferate to ward off the sense of loss and abandonment by communal (governmental and institutional) structures of authority, and the multiple threats to social well-being, most evident in the marginalized poor sectors of society.

I will draw on the ideas of Winnicott and Bion, who were especially bold in their respective ideas about the environmental provisions necessary to humanly thrive. I will emphasize the role of social provision (Winnicott *et al.* 1984) and containment (Bion 1962a), which when present allow for what Winnicott (1986:246) described as the healthy development of an "innate democratic factor" ("internalization of authority that arises out of self discovery"). This will be followed by a discussion of the parallels between parental and societal failures of provision and containment, and the prevalence of primitive, with an emphasis on "manic" "social defense systems" (Jacques, in Hinshelwood 1991).

Manic defenses are designed to distort, deny, and denigrate the awareness that we are not the omnipotent source of life, but instead dependent on our caretakers. In the Kleinian tradition, manic defenses come into play when the pain of the awareness that we are not omnipotent becomes too much to bear. Then the combined efforts to deny and disparage our helplessness and dependence, and control and idealize (through splitting) the objects of our dependence (these internal objects return in their persecutory role), fuel what we think of as the manic cycle of response (Hinshelwood 1991:344). These defenses are regulated by the degree to which we can tolerate the pain associated with loss (of omnipotence, of the object, and of the object's love and caretaking). To the degree that we can tolerate loss in all its variations, we remain engaged with the multi-dimensionalities of psychic reality (Klein 1935; Ogden 1994). To the degree that we cannot tolerate loss and instead invoke the cycle of manic defenses, the experience of psychic reality in all its complexity collapses.

We are familiar with the widespread reliance on manic defenses in instances of war and catastrophe (Lifton 1969). I believe we are less attuned to the more subtle pressures of everyday life on our abilities to cope with the multiple losses that we have incurred. Here I am referring to the loss of safety nets, the erosion of public life, and the multiple threats that assault us as we confront the insecurities of work life, health maintenance, educational opportunities, available natural resources and the quality of those resources, finding shelter, opportunities for our children, and so on. Though this chapter is entitled "The manic society," it is as much about the need for clearly stated ideals that guide a society in its established priorities as it is about the manic distortion of ideals into idealization. Idealization, a mental state that knows no limits, and the manic attempts to ward off internal interferences to this limitless state, will be discussed in the context of what Robert Reich (2001) described as the "new economy," or what Richard Sennett (1998) called the "new flexible capitalism." Reich writes:

> The benefits of the new economy turn on innovation and the increased ease with which buyers can switch – to better, faster, and cheaper products from anywhere around the world, to higher-returning investments, and to the joint amenities that constitute the modern community. These same features of the new economy are also contributing to financial insecurity, more frenzied work, widening gaps in income and wealth, an ever efficient sorting mechanism, and the consequent erosion of personal, family, and community life.
>
> (Reich 2001:22)

I will discuss how the decision to allow the "new economy" to remain unmonitored, with market needs primarily dictating the direction of social policies (profit versus people), reflects the lack of commitment to a set of social values and priorities (ideals) aimed at guaranteeing the members of this society their "inalienable" democratic rights. This means guaranteeing the members of society provision of basic human needs, even when doing so doesn't directly benefit the market.

Failure of containment in today's society

Belief in the environment and the social provision – what psychoanalysis can tell us

"Real development can only come out of, and is the process of finding, belief in the environment," says Adam Phillips (1988:64), paraphrasing Winnicott. Though Winnicott is not known for his political work, his life's work was devoted to promoting the importance of environmental provision in the development of healthy and creative people. These are not often words we come upon in psychoanalytic circles. In the past such words connoted an uncomfortable divergence from the doctrines of conflict-ridden drive theories that bound psychoanalytic thinking. More recently, postmodernist indictments of essentialism have had a similar restricting effect. Feminists and postmodern theorists have offered a powerful and important critique of conservative definitions of family life, social values, and discriminatory social policies. One consequence of this critique, however, is that our fear of imposing cultural and class biases has made us unduly reticent about formulating what people need from society in order to thrive. Both Winnicott and Bion, psychoanalytic renegades, believed some things are essential. Both, in their own ways, described the essential role of the environment, primarily the maternal (parental) environment. Both believed that unless certain things were provided – continuous attentive care, and resilient and responsive containment of anxieties – children would suffer and their suffering would explode as adults by generating, in Winnicott's words, "the compulsion to attain power or the need to be controlled" (Winnicott, in Phillips 1988:70).

I am interested in reviving these essentials in this discussion. Rustin (1991), in his book, *The Good Society and the Inner World*, underscores the importance for a progressive social movement of understanding concepts present in British object relations theories. He argues that studying the complex developmental road to symbolization mapped out by these theorists can help us navigate our way through misguided political rhetoric and faulty logic to see our way clear to building or changing the social structures necessary for good-enough environment. Rustin argues, and I agree, that psychoanalytic theories can offer direction to a society by clarifying the conditions in which people optimally thrive. These are not value-neutral theories. They imply a social responsibility of society to provide the conditions for optimal psychic development, just as we hold parents responsible for providing these conditions for their children. I believe psychoanalysis can be used to state one's values clearly, set forth ideals for health, and utilize these ideals in the service of legislating social policies.

What emerged in Britain as a result of trying to accommodate the evacuated children of the Second World War years was the revision of psychoanalytic theories about childhood, attachment, and dependency. Interrupting the continuity of the relationship between children and their parents brought home to Bowlby and Winnicott, among others, the significance of what Winnicott called the "environmental provision." Without a "belief in the environment," a child's development (into all that s/he could otherwise become) is arrested. Pathological symptoms then develop in the process of adapting to environmental failures.

This growing awareness underscored the premise that we are inherently social beings, inextricably related to each other through culture and society, and that in order to thrive physically, emotionally and mentally we depend on our relationships and social institutions to nurture, protect, and contain us. We can no more separate the individual from society in our conceptualizations than we can sever the Winnicottian infant from its caretaker. In other words, though the infant *qua* individual has a clear and separate constitutional integrity, the social unit that is formed between infant and caretaker – likewise, the individual and society – is forever interwoven in a mutually, though asymmetrically constitutive relationship. Social institutions have the potential to shelter and contain us. Unlike Freud's scheme in which culture required the renunciation of instinct, for Winnicott (1986) culture and social institutions held the promise of supporting the development of individuals – helping parents provide "ordinary good homes" in which the creative passions that emerge out of the integration of instinct and relatedness flourish. We know culture and society can also exacerbate our most primitive fears, anxieties, and destructive potentials, unleashing attacks on life and the living that Kleinian thinkers have described only too well. But, according to Winnicott's revision, these anxieties and "anti-social tendencies" are released in response to the breakdown of the "social provision," as opposed to the innate, constitutionally destructive factors.

Authority and the containing function of institutions

In theory the familial and societal provision of shelter and containment of primitive anxieties enables both a reparative appreciation of our potential to deplete and destroy the natural and social resources we depend on and the creative urge to expand these resources. The legislation of social policies to govern and protect the social institutions and natural resources we depend on then becomes the provision of social containers for future generations.

Idealistic as this may sound, especially in these times of profound cynicism with regard to anything remotely related to government, it is precisely the commitment to the value of social provision and containment that is missing. "Big government" (governmental institutions that could monitor the needs of people over profit by overseeing the provision of societal safety nets) is the term used by the "right" to incite visions of communism, useless bureaucracy, and fiscal irresponsibility, catapulting the political "center" into a defensive retreat from such accusations. An alternative vision and redefinition is thereby lost. This loss reflects a significant breakdown in what we would call the "democratic" process. But before elaborating, a discussion of what is meant by "containment" is in order.

The concept of containment is very important to understanding the conditions under which people optimally develop their emotional, mental, and creative capacities. Bion's (1962b) model of the container–contained describes how the infant's raw sensory, somatic experiences and concomitant primitive anxieties are transformed by caretakers into mental, learning, and creative experiences if the caretakers are receptive to the infant's projections and able to process them thoughtfully. This capacity to contain teaches the burgeoning baby that its anxieties are tolerable and that good things can come of having those anxieties contained. "The containment of anxiety by an external object capable of understanding is a beginning of mental stability," says Segal (1975:134–135). Beyond introducing the infant to the world of representation and symbolization, that is, to the world of meaning, this initial communication between caretaker and infant, to my mind, introduces the infant to the world of inspiration. Inspiration is born out of gentle yet firm parental containment (Peltz 1998). When anxiety is thus transformed, not only does a person realize that s/he can survive ("go on being"), but something exhilarating is taken in – an exciting feeling of agency based on the survival of the infant–parent unit that says, in essence, "we can do it!" Furthermore, an ideal is formed about how goodness can prevail in the face of badness. As Bion (1959) notes, mental links are made between the containing object and the contained affective experience.

The capacity to contain infantile anxieties is a necessary requisite of parental authority. We could call this "Oedipal" (Britton 1989) or "moral" (Benjamin 2001) authority in that it implies an internal triadic relationship, in which an internally functioning third assists the parent in charge in the process of containment. This symbolic mental function offers parents internal guidance so that the authority that is wielded is neither heavy-handed nor wobbly. This interpretation of authority is markedly different from the classic paternalistic model. Rather than the paternalistic model that, in the words of Jessica Benjamin (1988), privileges the father's role by virtue of positioning the father as the liberator of the child from the clutches of maternal dependency and infantile helplessness, I am describing a form of parental authority in which no particular sex or family constellation is privileged, nor is an actual third person required. To return to the ideals upon which the Library of Congress was founded, parental containment creates the possibility of mental space in the child. That space, facilitated by the inspiration derived from the freeing of the child of intolerable anxieties, can then be filled by thoughts, interests, and a striving for knowledge which, to reiterate Jefferson's hope, will expand the possibilities of freedom and democracy. However, Winnicott cautioned us that "the price of freedom is eternal vigilance" (1986:257). He seemed to recognize the need to watch over the societal symbols of authority that are meant to protect the resources and socially providing institutions we depend on against a malevolent transformation of authority.

I am arguing that we are missing reliable and just symbols of communal/governing authority. As government has increasingly eroded into backroom deals made between wealthy lobbyists and elected and appointed officials, with fewer and fewer counterbalancing organizations to effectively voice the needs of ordinary people, the voices representing profit and corporate greed are most of what we hear. Most other voices have been marginalized and some are not heard at all. Deregulation and the "folly-flight of manic capital," in the words of Greider (1998), a progressive economist writing for *The Nation*, leave us with a profound sense that no one is minding the store. Instead they've emptied the registers and gone on holiday, leaving unregulated markets, lost safety nets, and a lot of hungry and frightened people behind. There is the obvious hunger of the staggering up to three million homeless in the USA. Then we have the other 33 million plus living below poverty level. Then there is the hunger for meaning that eats away at the rest of us with money to spare. In a *New York Times* review of Beck, a 28-year-old rock musician, titled "Post-modernist gives up on irony," Beck says:

> I've been guilty of irony and cynicism, those things that are symptomatic of our times. You can't really blame anybody in the way irony and cynicism are pounded into everybody's head in every t.v. commercial, as if we're all insiders on the big joke here. But there's got to be more than just the joke.
>
> (Pareles 1998)

The reviewer notes that nearly all of Beck's songs "read as impressions of a time when the only certainty is a free-floating sense of loss."

In the absence of what we might call inspiring governmental (communal) authority, or the system of governance that can't be bought off and instead legislates according to the emotional needs of its citizenry, we are caught in a cycle of manic defensiveness, warding off the loss of meaning and fears of being abandoned that accompany this absence. In keeping with the analogy to parental containment, without the provision of social containers (institutions of consistent social provision that are democratically maintained), the members of a society are traumatized – much like the child who has been abandoned either physically or psychically. The erosion and corruption of communal (embodied in governmental institutions) authority whose responsibility it is to maintain a system of "just" social provisions translates into the death of inspiration as the potential outgrowth of being held and contained. In the place of idealism, curiosity, and the love of knowledge come resignation, psychic deadness, cynicism, or an overreliance on hypomanic denial, flights into action, and omnipotence. We suffer from all of these.

The socially sanctioned solution for the loss of an inspiring communal authority, itself a symptom of the complex relationship between late capitalism and our system of democracy, is to fill the void with stuff – to buy things. And so, in the language of Showalter (1997), one of the "hysterias" of our time is addiction. In this case the addiction to buying things is an attempt to fill the void left by the lack of social symbols of a just and inspiring system of democratic governance. Without those containing symbols, anxieties of being stranded and abandoned intensify (which has indeed happened to large numbers of poor and marginalized sectors of society). These anxieties can be temporarily warded off through the compulsive pursuit of things. Having things puffs one up in the short run, connoting images – that flood us at every juncture – of limitless strength, power, and omnipotence. Buying things then becomes a concrete way of warding off the anxieties and depression associated with a profound loss of provision and containment.

The embodiment of manic defenses

Celia tells me, "I'm always in pursuit. It's always been with me. I can't think of a time I wasn't striving for more. I can't enjoy what I have. Why can't I? Why do I have to do more? Why can't I enjoy my house? I feel it has to be bigger. How did I get this way?"

The following composite case is intended to illustrate the commonplace workings of the manic defense among middle-class professionals in contemporary society. Like Celia, Rhoda is in her forties and is often tormented by the fear that she is not living her life. Instead she feels scattered and overwhelmed by the conflicting pulls of her multiple commitments and responsibilities. Married and a mother of two small children, she works two-thirds time as a lawyer and is involved in various legal and political organizations. She is also devoted to her extended family and friends, puts a fair amount of energy into her home, and knows she needs to exercise to feel well. She often laments, "How do people live?" She is haunted by the thought that she will have wasted her life by spreading herself so thinly, depriving herself and the people she loves most of a more meaningful life together. Furthermore, she feels that her involvements have been reduced to tokens, that nothing will ever come of her efforts. Yet she is unable to limit or focus herself. In fact, she increasingly finds it difficult to do one thing at a time. Instead she finds herself calculating how much she can possibly squeeze into any given block of time. At one point she called me from her car phone wondering if she couldn't have our session in her car while she drove, as she was running late.

Despite her wish for a simpler, more reflective life, she can't stop herself. When she tries she becomes depressed, feeling that she's failed in her efforts. None of her accomplishments measures up. She complains that, though she loves her home, she can't relax in it because of the many things that need to be done and the standards she imposes on herself. She loves her children but often can't relax with them either. She speaks to me often of her fear that she is missing her children's childhood. She is forever conflicted about what she should be doing, driven by multiple compelling internal pressures – to be a good mother, to be a good wife, to be a good lawyer, to be a good friend, to be a good person. She is haunted by images of the earth mother she isn't, one who spends many hours with her children generating creative projects. Instead, though she looks forward to the time she has carved out for her kids, she often feels disappointed and impatient, like their "quality time" is being squandered. She carries a heavy burden of expectation that leaves her very little room to enjoy simply "being" with them. She is similarly crowded by images of a successful lawyer whose scope extends well beyond the boundaries of her law practice into research, teaching, publishing, making public presentations.

Rhoda also feels her relationship with her husband has suffered. Though she expresses a deep love and respect for him and though he is quite successful, she resents him. She often feels critical and impatient of him yet longs for a sense of intimacy that characterized the beginning of their relationship. She feels he takes the brunt of her pressured life. In addition, she expresses anxieties about restricting her knowledge to the narrow sphere of law and losing track of what's going on in the world of culture, world events, and politics. Sound familiar?

What's wrong with this picture? Solomon Resnik describes the psychopathology of mental space. One of his patients began a session with "I have nothing to say. I work very hard and I have no time for thinking" (1995:25). Resnik muses about his patient, "This is a characteristic of our culture – keeping ourselves very busy in our everyday life. This is how we fill up space; a space that at times we cannot put up with. In my view this may culminate in a phobia of existence, of our inner world, of our unconscious" (1995:25). Rhoda has taken manic flight from the space she cannot put up with. As a child she inherited the profound and unmetabolized losses of her parents, but no person or communal connection has helped her come close to the mourning that awaits her. Instead she feels anxious and driven. Slowing down reminds her of her failings, her limitations. But we might ask, how is it that a self with limitations is a failed self? In addition to the internal psychic clinging to omnipotence, we are currently "embedded" (Stern 1991) in a world of idealization, a world of limitless potential, in which coming to terms with one's limitations and losses could easily signify failure.

In their discussion of the "mind-object," a concept derived from Winnicott's (1949) ideas about how the mind is cathected as an object that omnipotently attempts to replace the caretaking environment, Corrigan and Gordon discuss how human aliveness can be transformed into manic and precocious ego functions (1995:12). They also describe how brutally their patients criticize themselves, with severe and sadistic internal objects predominating and shaping their superego formations. The heavy burden of parental projections and expectations "fostered the premature and rigid structuring of unalterable ego ideals. Having prematurely internalized parental standards, they expect too much from themselves, are often quite unrealistic, at times, omnipotent in their self-demands" (1995:13). They add, "we must remember that precocity is a disorder of adaptation much valued in our culture" (1995:16).

Precocity is often an adaptation to trauma. Children prematurely take over their parents' caretaking functions and then hold this capacity in an unrealistic light, feeling contempt for their needful states. In a culture in which dependency is scorned, where people in need of assistance are considered freeloaders, is it any wonder that parents, insecure about their own ability to protect and provide for their children's futures, would promote precocity in their children?

Manic work

Let us shift for the moment to the bigger societal picture. Over the past 20 years there has been a growing encroachment of work time into family or private time. Not only are more family members required to work in order to maintain the same and sometimes a lesser standard of living than in previous years (Currie *et al.* 1991), but the parameters of work life have themselves changed. In *The Corrosion of Character: The Personal Consequences of Work in the New Capitalism*, Richard Sennett (1998) describes a series of shifting work-related demands that are consequences of the "Anglo-American" model. This model, operative in the USA and Great Britain, in contrast with the "Rhine" model (in the Netherlands, Germany, and France)

> gives free-market capitalism greater scope. While the Rhine model emphasizes certain obligations of economic institutions to the polity, the Anglo-American model stresses the state bureaucracy's subordination to the economy, and thus is willing to loosen the safety net

> provided by the government. The Rhine regimes tend to put the brakes on change when their less powerful citizens suffer, while the Anglo-American regime is more inclined to pursue changes in the work organization and practices even though the weak might pay a price. These regimes have different defects. The Anglo-American regime has had low unemployment but increasing wage inequality. The brute facts of current wealth inequality are indeed staggering. The economist Simon Head has calculated that for the bottom 80 percent of the American working population, average weekly wages fell 18 percent from 1973 to 1995, while the pay of the corporate elite rose 19 percent before taxes and 66 percent after tax accountants had worked their magic.
>
> (Sennett 1998:53)

Sennett describes not only the disappearance of communal safety nets for people without work but the insistence on flexibility, meaning no limits on what can be work time, with no job security. The people he interviewed blamed themselves for being laid off because they had not anticipated soon enough that the companies for which they were working were being downsized. They believed they should have been scheming ahead of time for new positions. Doing their work was not enough.

A couple I see in psychotherapy were fighting with each other, in part as a consequence of rarely making time to relax together. I expressed my concern that their relationship was suffering and asked them why they found it so difficult to make their time together a priority. The man remarked, "We're so busy, yet we have these pictures of what's supposed to happen. Somehow you're lacking if you don't have it all. It's crazy! You have the expectation of what you're supposed to feel and do, yet you can't possibly fulfill all of the expectations . . . When you're in the pressure cooker that's the norm. You don't realize it's dysfunctional. The whole work thing is a bugaboo. I don't know what to do about it. The culture of work in this society is so coercive. We live in a democracy yet work is coercive and isolating. It's supposed to be one of many roles, but that's propaganda. Work is always number one. Work is your family now, that's the religion, the efficiency model, based on how work is done. You always have to be efficient. If you don't everyone will surpass you." The woman in the couple added, "For me it's overwhelming sometimes. It's a feeling of trying to keep your head above water." I noted, "You both sound like you feel driven by expectations I don't think you're even aware of. Maybe you hold it against each other when you feel overwhelmed and exhausted, like no one is protecting you or your relationship. Maybe each of you is waiting for the other one to slow things down." The woman responded, "You saying this many times gives us more permission. Maybe we think we shouldn't have to [find time to be together]." I say, "In your fantasies it's supposed to just happen. Your relationship shouldn't need anything to flourish." The man responded, "It should just be wonderful, romantic love. It ends up being one of those things you just don't get to." She added, "Then as the gap widens, we don't deal with it." I commented, "There's something about this work mode that neither of you can help each other disengage from. You become task masters at life and then it stops feeling like living." The man lamented, "Society doesn't do anything to help. It's part of our culture." If we follow the chain of signifiers, beginning with Celia and Rhoda, we find torment, frantic pace, haunting images of failure, conflicting internal pressures, impatience, no space for reflection, precocious development, parental demand, changing parameters of work life, lost safety nets, staggering inequality, impossible expectations.

Weaving this chain together might suggest that parents, anxious about their own futures and the futures of their children, aware of the inequalities that give rise to a growing sector of the poor, inflict this anxiety onto their children in subtle and not so subtle ways. Knowing it is quite possible to be forgotten in this society, perhaps we anxiously drive ourselves and our children in an attempt to fortify ourselves with the images of success we are fed, which ultimately return to haunt us. But, as Resnick maintains, manic flight is a form of self amnesia. We become fearful of open spaces. Open spaces remind us of empty spaces, lost spaces, forgotten spaces. We suffer from agoraphobia of the soul, crowding our lives with pursuits, accomplishments, commodities, symbols of achievement that don't scratch the surface beneath which lies the fear of emptiness and failure for ourselves, for our relationships, and for our children.

We run from our internal worlds and any space that might exist in which our losses – in this instance, our loss of societal provision – could be felt. We want to protect our children against these anxieties by giving them every opportunity. But wouldn't we do better by them if we created the space to think seriously about what is wrong with this crowded, anxious picture?

Conclusion

British authors Kraemer and Roberts (1996) advocate a "politics of attachment." They argue that the political domain would benefit from incorporating some of the tenets of attachment theory in the hopes of building a more "secure society." They close their introduction with the following question: "How then can we ignore what we know about the ways in which we humans grow, develop, and relate with others: an ordinary yet fundamental part of life?" (1996:18).

In conclusion I would like to report a patient's dream that I felt brought home one of the central themes of this chapter. In the dream the patient and several other people were driving along the railroad tracks. Again in the dream, the patient thought, "This is cool because I can avoid being in traffic while also being safe." It was understood that the larger locomotives would slow down for the cars.

The analyst had the immediate association, in part as a result of writing this chapter, that, in the dream, "public" tracks were available to this analysand to use, in contrast to having to make a go of it on his own, which meant tackling the congestion and competition of traffic. "Traffic" seemed to epitomize the worst aspects of modern life: being on your own, trying to get ahead, and feeling frenzied and thwarted by the mass of other cars. The people in those cars then become reduced to their most primitive mental states of rage, greed, and envy. In contrast, public "tracks" elicited images of a calm system of transport, in which everyone could get to their destination with time to spare.

This analysand happened to be considering the idea of terminating his analysis for the first time. In our discussion of the dream we understood together that, indeed, the patient felt that foundational "tracks" had been laid down for him by his analysis. Furthermore, he felt that these "tracks" could be shared by the "big locomotive" analyst and himself. He felt he could consider navigating his own path without worrying, as he had in the past, that if he ventured off on his own he'd either be mowed down or abandoned to the chaotic frenzy of traffic by the "larger locomotives," i.e., internal parental objects. He expressed gratitude toward his analyst for helping him believe he need not get on her "train," in exchange for protection, and instead could pursue his own ideas, while knowing she would remain alive as a supportive figure on whom he could rely to provide a safety net for him as he tested the road ahead. He also noted that he enjoyed the feeling of being part of "humanity," which he felt was evident in the dream, given that the tracks were available for anyone who wanted to use them. (Soon after this dream, the patient, a man in his forties, voted for the first time.) This represented a marked shift from previous times when he believed he could only gain access to opportunities (and the love of authority figures) by setting himself apart from others through seductive, less honest pathways to success.

This moment in an analysis illustrates once again how, given the support of and relationship to a facilitating, containing person (environment) that lends itself to be used, it is possible to generate a uniquely creative path through life. Of course, navigating one's way is fraught with struggle, both in analysis and outside. And the urge greedily and manically to "have it all" can pose any number of obstacles, as it did for this patient. However, I believe that it is the job of society – people casting their votes – to insist that communal–governmental institutions similarly provide its citizens with a set of public "tracks." These tracks or social provisions are meant to inspire creative usage by the members of society in the course of discovering their own pathways through life.

It doesn't take a psychoanalytic education to recognize that the potential for human destructiveness intensifies in situations of parental neglect, abandonment, or trauma. The same logic applies to the relationship between society as reflected in social institutions of provision and the members of a society. Knowing what we know as psychoanalysts underscores the importance of reminding people that this is true, and that if we don't do something about it we are headed for more trouble than we are already in.

References

Benjamin, J. (1988) *The Bonds of Love: Psychoanalysis, Feminism, and the Problem of Domination*. New York: Pantheon.

Benjamin, J. (2001) *Two way streets: recognition and intersubjective economy*. Paper presented at Division 39, APA Spring Meetings, Santa Fe, NM, April 2001.

Bion, W. R. (1959) Attacks on linking. *International Journal of Psychoanalysis*, 40. Reprinted in *Second Thoughts*. Northvale, NJ: Jason Aronson, 1967.

Bion, W. R. (1962a) A theory of thinking. *International Journal of Psychoanalysis*, 43. Reprinted in *Second Thoughts*. Northvale, NJ: Jason Aronson, 1967.

Bion, W. R. (1962b) *Learning from Experience*. London: Karnac Books, 1984.

Bollas, C. (1987) *The Shadow of the Object: Psychoanalysis of the Unthought Known*. New York: Columbia University Press

Britton, R. (1989) The missing link: parental sexuality in the Oedipus complex. In J. Steiner (ed.), *The Oedipus Complex Today*. London: Karnac.

Brownstein, R. (2001) The government, once scorned, becomes savior. *Los Angeles Times*, 19 September.

Chasseguet-Smirgel, J. (1985) *The Ego Ideal: A Psychoanalytic Essay on the Malady of the Ideal* (trans. Paul Barrows). New York: W. W. Norton.

Corrigan, E. and Gordon, P. E. (1995) *The Mind Object: Precocity and the Pathology of Self-sufficiency*. Northvale, NJ: Aronson.

Currie, E., Dunn, R., and Fogarty, D. (1991) The fading dream: economic crisis and the new inequality. In E. Currie and J. Skolnick (eds), *Crisis in American Institutions*. New York: Harper Collins, pp. 104–112.

Fonagy, P. (1999) Male perpetrators of violence against women: an attachment theory perspective. *Journal of Applied Psychoanalytic Studies*, 1:7–27.

Freud, S. (1931) Civilization and its discontents. *Standard Edition*, 21, pp. 59–145. London: Hogarth Press, 1961.

Greider, W. (1998) The global crisis deepens: now what? *The Nation*, 267(12):11–16.

Hinshelwood, R. D. (1991) *A Dictionary of Kleinian Thought*. London: Free Association Books.

Jacoby, R. (1975) *Social Amnesia: A Critique of Contemporary Psychology from Adler to Laing*. Boston: Beacon Press.

Jay, M. (1972) *The Dialectical Imagination*. Boston: Little, Brown and Company.

Klein, M. (1935) A contribution to the psychogenesis of self-depressive states. *International Journal of Psychoanalysis*, 16:145–174.

Kraemer, S. and Roberts, J. (1996) Introduction. In S. Kraemer and J. Roberts (eds), *The Politics of Attachment: Towards a Secure Society*. London: Free Association Books, pp. 1–20.

Langer, M. (1989) *From Vienna to Managua: Journey of a Psychoanalyst*. London: Free Association Books.

Lifton, R. (1969) *Death in Life: Survivors of Hiroshima*. New York: Vintage.

Ogden, T. (1994) *Subjects of Analysis*. Northvale, NJ: Jason Aronson.

Pareles, J. (1998) A pop post-modernist gives up on irony. *New York Times*, 8 November, 36.

Peltz, R. (1998) *The primal envelope and the origins of loving authority*. Paper presented at Division 39, APA Spring Meetings, Boston, MA, April 1998.

Phillips, A. (1988) *Winnicott*. Cambridge, MA: Harvard University Press.

Reich, R. (2001) The new economy as a decent society. *The American Prospect*, 12 February, 20.

Resnick, S. (1995) *Mental Space*. London: Karnac.

Rustin, M. (1991) *The Good Society and the Inner World: Psychoanalysis, Politics, and Culture*. London: Verso.

Segal H. (1975) A psycho-analytic approach to the treatment of schizophrenia. In M. Lader (ed.), *Studies of Schizophrenia*. Ashford, UK: Headley Bros, pp. 87–144.

Segal, H. (1995) From Hiroshima to the Gulf War and after: a psychoanalytic perspective. In A. Elliott and S. Frosh (eds), *Psychoanalysis in Contexts*. New York: Routledge, pp. 191–204.

Sennett, R. (1998) *The Corrosion of Character: The Personal Consequences of Work in the New Capitalism*. New York: Norton.

Showalter, E. (1997) *Histories, Hysterical Epidemics and Modern Media*. New York: Columbia University Press.

Soros, G. (2000) *Open Society: Reforming Global Capitalism*. New York: Public Affairs.

Stern, D. B. (1991) A philosophy for the embedded analyst. *Contemporary Psychoanalysis*, 27:51–80.

Winnicott, C., Shepard, R., and Davis, M. (1984) *D. W. Winnicott: Deprivation and Delinquency*. London: Tavistock.

Winnicott, D. W. (1949) Mind and its relation to psyche-soma. *British Journal of Medical Psychology*, 27; reprinted in *Through Pediatrics to Psychoanalysis*. London: Hogarth, 1975.

Winnicott, D. W. (1986) *Home Is Where We Start From: Essays by a Psychoanalyst*. New York: Norton.

Winnicott, D. W. (1988) *Human Nature*. New York: Schocken Books.

Chapter 5

Despair and hope in a culture of denial

Nancy Caro Hollander and Susan Gutwill

This chapter is about the relationship between psychic and social reality – specifically, the experience of despair and hope in relation to the present culture of violence and denial. It was conceptualized in September 2002, a specific historical moment in which we were interested in examining the relationship between, on the one hand, the traumatogenic social environment produced by the terrorist attacks of September 11th, exaggerated by the aggressive political/military responses adopted by the Bush administration, and, on the other hand, a population whose psychic defenses, while serving to protect them from feelings of helplessness, anxiety, and despair, prevented an effective oppositional discourse and movement that could represent real hope. As we begin to write in March 2003, we have been encouraged by the emergence of a national and international peace movement that represents a challenge to the escalating cycles of violence in the world. In response to this development, we shifted the focus of our analysis to consider the potential for hope within the new circumstances; that is, within the tension between the increasing authoritarian trends in our society and the growth of a critical alternative vision being expressed in city councils, schools, churches, unions, and professional organizations, as well as in the streets. Our intention is to provide understanding of the specific subjectivity of this extraordinary time, within both the culture at large and the ways the culture has been experienced by our patients and ourselves.

We begin with a brief sketch of the initial traumatogenic environment, a picture that we will develop more thoroughly in the course of the chapter. North Americans were terrified by 9/11. The response of the government further alarmed an already shocked population. There were the alerts: "more terrorist attacks on the way . . . anthrax, chemical or biological weapons, dirty nuclear bombs." Then came the color code of danger – green, yellow, orange, red. The alerts bombarded us with confusing and ineffectual instructions: "don't worry, but be careful;" "be patriotic and shop to support your country;" "wave your flag and seal yourselves into your individual homes with duct tape." Meanwhile, the White House hired an advertising agency to convince the population that only war would make the USA safe (Rampton and Stauber 2003:38–39). Moreover, war would bring freedom and democracy, first to Afghanistan and then to Iraq.

In the initial months following 9/11, the government mobilized manic defenses among a frightened population that could then experience community in an uncritically shared enthusiasm for its aggressive retaliatory policies. Displaying "united we stand" slogans implicitly held the false promise that we would be safe if we rallied blindly behind government authority, war-making, and chauvinistic "pride." Simultaneously, President Bush told us to "go shopping," i.e. US citizens were encouraged to buy things, thereby associating feeling good and safe through consumerism and the private relationship with commodities rather than through engagement with others in communities of shared critical thinking and informed civic participation.

Because a large proportion of the population received most of its information from corporate network television and newspapers, they knew little of the occasional dissenting perspectives that raised critical questions, such as why it was that the World Trade Center and the Pentagon were terrorist targets, why during previous decades the USA had funded and supported the Taliban and Saddam Hussein, how US sanctions against Iraq had already destroyed Hussein's military power long before the invasion, why so many Islamist fundamentalists hated the USA for its policies in the Middle East, Africa and Latin America. Neither mainstream media nor the government facilitated a sustained national exploration of the complex factors that produced September 11 or considerations of alternative responses capable of containing rather than exacerbating international violence. Instead we witnessed the political exploitation of widespread anxiety.

We believe this phenomenon can be illuminated by insights derived from psychoanalysts and social theorists who study the intersubjective context for the development of self and one's attachment to others. From the beginning of life, we are interdependent social beings, developing first in the context of our attachment to family and later through our group membership in the larger social order. At the earliest stage of life, the culture is introjected through the conscious and unconscious communications of caregivers, inevitably based on their insertion in the socioeconomic order. As we develop, we continue to internalize the political culture directly through its institutions and symbolic discourse.

Certain psychoanalytic concepts can be elaborated to help explain the emergence and dynamics of political subjectivity. For example, Winnicott (1971) proposed the concept of the potential space to describe the optimal conditions that would provide for the growth of a subject able to sustain a sense of feeling "real" while recognizing the other and the demands of external reality. When neither inner nor outer experience dominates, a transitional or symbolic space – a third – develops. Such a space permits creative negotiation of the inevitable tensions in life between our needs for dependency and individuation, "authentic" voice and compliance with the social group, healthful narcissism and the recognition of the needs of others. The failure of the potential space exacerbates what Melanie Klein (1952) called paranoid/schizoid states of mind, in which primitive defenses such as splitting, projection, idealization, and projective identification protect the subject against intolerable paranoid experience that threatens annihilation from external as well as from internal sources. Ogden (1990) offered an integration of aspects of Winnicott and Klein in his description of the pathologies of the potential space. He showed how these pathologies are characterized by the psychotic experience of an individual who has little capacity to negotiate with external reality or of an individual utterly taken over by authoritarian domination of external reality. While Winnicott, Klein, and Ogden are commenting on the vicissitudes of parent/child relationships within the family, we think that their ideas may be extended to explain the relationship between the subject and the social order.

An important aspect of interpersonal experience is realized through the medium and psychological use of social symbols. Winnicott and the object relations theorists who followed him have led the way in understanding the range of experience that is negotiated through social symbols. Winnicott emphasized symbolization as a constructive, expansive intrapsychic capacity as well as a relational process in which one authentically negotiates a balance between internal wishes and needs and external reality's expectations and demands. He recognized that individuals extend their object-seeking to their symbolic environment to feel connected and integrated. Winnicott observed that the mother could fail the baby, her own narcissistic needs impinging on the child's development. We extend his notion to the social order and argue that power structures through symbolic media impinge upon people's capacities to function as critically minded citizens in a democracy. In other words, just as individuals extend their object-seeking to the social order, the social order is what we call subject-seeking (Gutwill 1994). The prevailing cultural symbols maintain attachment to values and principles that ultimately support the *status quo* of inequitable economic and social relations. Lacan (Frosh 1987) captured this view of social symbols, especially from his perspective in terms of the function of language, as the demanding "Other." He saw a social order that inevitably takes one out of oneself, alienates, requires. Lacan is especially important to our understanding of the conflictual relationship individuals have to the social order and its dominant ideology and discourse.

In the post-9/11 political environment, the government's discourse imposes a symbolic world that, as Lacan would see it, is decentering in that it ruptures the capacity of citizens to use their minds. "Seeking peace" is the symbolic language used for waging war. Bombing civilians is referred to as "liberating" them. "Collateral damage" and "soft targets" are reported rather than the number of mothers, fathers, and children being killed by US bombs. The president uses language to obfuscate and to lie: George W. Bush claims we have tried every means at our disposal to use UN diplomacy when it is later revealed that he has wiretapped the members of the Security Council, bribed countries to support the US invasion and threatened those who have opposed it. "Orange alert, danger, be careful, don't worry, be patriotic, go shopping" – this is the insidious backdrop to US war-making. The repeated reminders of a potential imminent terrorist attack carried out with weapons of mass destruction wind up terrorizing us without the actual attack itself. We increasingly see police and military in our cities. Some of us know – and then "forget" – while others of us were never exposed to the information that our ports, public buildings, nuclear power plants, waste sites and weaponry storage centers, our chemical and biological research facilities are still not safe because of lack of oversight and protective strategies. We know – and then "forget" – or we are not aware that the budgets necessary for such protection have not been supported by the Bush administration even as it warns of imminent terrorist attacks. Instead, we are told that the government will protect us through making war on other countries and expanding exponentially the definition of a terrorist to anyone who opposes the policies of the current regime.

As trauma theory tells us, when people are frightened, as we are, by the real threat of terrorism as well as the government's exploitative use of it, the denial of vulnerability alternates with overwhelming feelings of impotence (Davies and Frawley 1994; Herman 1992). Fantasies of being rescued by a strong leader/parent combine with wishes for revenge. The inability to tolerate ambiguity produces a bifurcated view of the world as good and bad, with the tendency to identify with an all-powerful goodness while all that is bad is projected on to a demonized other who becomes the target for aggressive attacks. This split constitutes a manic defense that protects against the anxiety of helplessness. These psychological tendencies make us vulnerable to the government promotions forced upon us through the mass media, which become "an offer we can't refuse." They are so powerful because they constitute the relationship between the deep structures of the psyche and the ideological underpinnings of the culture.

In the context of the post-September 11 environment, the ongoing traumatic assault that citizens have been exposed to in the USA also illustrates Lacan's notion of the alienation of the self by the Other – the social order – and Michel Foucault's understanding (1979, 1980; Jaggar and Bordo 1990) of the disciplining of the individual citizen in the interest of the power structure. We suggest as well that Italian political philosopher Antonio Gramsci's notion (1999) of hegemonic ideology is useful for understanding the class relations of domination and subordination that are simultaneously inherent to the economic and political system and denied in the dominant discourse, i.e. the "official story," in the USA.

Gramsci was particularly interested in exploring how capitalism, with its inherent inequities, can sustain itself without serious threat from subordinate social classes. He posited that in advanced capitalist societies the ruling elites are able to sustain their domination through hegemonic ideology rather than physical coercion. Ideological hegemony for Gramsci included the whole range of values, attitudes, beliefs, cultural norms, legal precepts and so on that infuse civil society via the state, legal system, workplace, schools, churches, bureaucracies, cultural activities, the media, and the family. Widely accepted prevailing views always include justifications of the elites' power, wealth and status, thereby securing citizens' acceptance of this arrangement as "natural," part of an eternal social order and therefore unchangeable. Hegemony lends a secure and enduring quality to power that the coercive institutions of the military and the police cannot, giving it a kind of psychological validity. As Carl Boggs argues, "it mystifies power relations, public issues and historical events; it encourages fatalism and passivity toward political action; it justifies various types of system-serving deprivation and sacrifice" (1984:161). Although hegemony is dynamic and characterized by an always-shifting complex of relations, once it is institutionalized and stable, when confronting a crisis the ruling elites are able to mobilize the ideological "resources" and manipulate popular consciousness. At the same time, as Gramsci himself pointed out, hegemony within constitutional democracy is not totalistic. Indeed, there are moments of disruption, when oppositional ideas come to the fore, resulting in shifts within the existing power relations and degrees of reorganization of relative wealth and influence. Examples that come to mind are the impact of the militant trade union and civil rights movements in the USA. Often oppositional ideas are reconfigured and absorbed by the dominant ideology, easily visible in the ways the advertising industry appropriates the radical language of revolutionary movements in order to sell commodities. We have only to recall well-known ads, such as "You've come a long way, baby" that sells cigarettes to women and "the Dodge revolution" that sells fast cars to men, to see how the language of the radical movements that reflected people's aspirations to alter exploitative relationships is put to the crass purpose of increasing corporate profits (Kilbourne 1999).

We can see Gramsci's idea of the consensual basis of power via hegemony if we look at the deterioration in the quality of life during the past several decades, the systemic causes of which have remained hidden from view. The symptoms have included an increase in the working poor and of homeless populations, the erosion of family and community, the corrupt relationship between government and corporate wealth, continuing racial and gender discrimination, urban plight, a drug-addicted youth, and a violence-addicted media reflecting and motivating an escalating real-world violence, to name but a few. Furthermore, below the surface of the stock-market-driven "roaring nineties" but peeking through the recession-impacted first few years of the twenty-first century, a pervasive anti-democratic trend has characterized the USA. The dramatic pattern of concentration of wealth – and thus power and influence – increasing during the Reagan period has continued apace: today, the wealthiest 1% of all households control about 38% of national wealth, while the bottom 80% of households hold only 17%. In addition to increasing inequality, middle income families with children have added 20 hours of paid work per year to make ends meet, even while acquiring more indebtedness. The median male wage in 2000 was still below its 1979 level, although productivity increased during that time by 44.5%. Today there is less mobility out of poverty and fewer families are financially prepared for retirement (Economic Policy Institute 2002–2003).

These deeply worrisome developments on the domestic front have been accompanied by a foreign policy for the past several decades that has enriched corporate profits through exploitative trade relations, often buttressed by military expansionism and support for repressive regimes abroad. US global reach has exacerbated domestic inequities as corporations put American workers in competition with low-waged foreign workers and used technology to downsize their workforces internationally. US policies have fostered anti-Americanism throughout the world that, except for a brief period following September 11, has dramatically accelerated in recent years as the result of the Bush administration's unilateral and pre-emptive aggressive policies.

Those in power maintain their privilege to the extent that the rest of us deny or disavow the causes of our own disempowerment. To prevent collective psychic and social alienation, i.e. detachment from hegemony, it is incumbent upon the elites to hide the real nature and purposes of their political agenda. We have only to imagine the feelings of betrayal if citizens knew that the policies of the Bush administration had, in fact, been in place long before the traumatic events of 9/11. For example, behind the rhetoric of the Bush administration's justifications for making war on Iraq, uncritically reproduced by the media, lies a well-developed plan of a small group of right-wing think-tank intellectuals and policy makers who, since the early 1990s, a full decade before 9/11, were designing the strategy to protect US corporate global interests and to ensure that the USA would remain the world's only superpower. In 1997, this group founded The Project for the New American Century (PNAC 1997), which includes, among others, Vice President Dick Cheney, Secretary of Defense Donald Rumsfeld, Deputy Secretary of Defense Paul Wolfowitz, Elliot Abrams, member of Bush's National Security Council, and Bruce Jackson, Chairman of PNAC and former vice president of weapons manufacturer Lockheed-Martin.

PNAC members are in strategic positions to see their ideological and economic interests implemented, because they now control the White House, the Pentagon and the Defense Department, and thus the armed forces and intelligence communities. The control over the government and media secured by this small group of men is reinforced by a Republican-dominated Congress that is more than willing to approve legislation, including the repressive Patriot Act, that helps implement their goals, even when it means the suppression of US democracy. The PNAC seeks to establish a "Pax Americana" across the globe by transforming the USA into a planetary empire by force of arms. Its project requires a massive increase in defense spending, which the Bush administration has just secured from Congress. In its plan, the war in Iraq has a threefold function: (1) to acquire control over Iraqi oil so as to fund the entire enterprise; (2) to stand as a warning to every leader in the Middle East not to oppose the USA; (3) to establish in Iraq a military staging area for a PNAC-inspired plan to extend the "axis of evil" to include Syria, Lebanon, Libya, Saudi Arabia, Egypt and the Palestinian Authority. PNAC members also advocate control over Middle East oil for purposes of controlling when, if and how to supply it to competing economies, such as those of Europe and China (Pitt 2003). Corporations, such as Halliburton and Bechtel, with close ties to Bush, Cheney and other members of the PNAC, are being awarded – without competitive bidding – billion-dollar government contracts for military expenditures in general, for building and supplying permanent US military bases in Iraq and neighboring countries and for activities related to oil, natural gas and construction in the Middle East and Asia. These and other American corporations buy the rights to "reconstruct" Iraq and Afghanistan, a process through which they then own and sell to the Iraqis water, health care and education, among other basic necessities, which prevents national development and promotes economic dependency and poverty. In reality, US global reach will be implemented at a staggering cost to the working people of the USA and to the recipients of US "aid."

The systemic and class-based causes of domestic inequities and dangerous foreign policies, as well as the connections between them, are masked through the manipulation of hegemonic symbols of "freedom," "democracy," "equality" and "liberty" in an attempt to organize citizens' beliefs that the USA is the most advanced civilization with respect to social equity, in terms both of economic opportunity and political representation. These convictions can exist alongside the paradox that US citizens live in a world increasingly characterized by impediments to their realization. The unconscious maneuvers, such as denial, disavowal, projection and splitting, that we use to sustain our attachment to these internalized symbols while our experience contradicts them are facilitated by the mass media, which either obfuscates relationships of power – especially of class – or produces a cynical acceptance of the inevitability of inequality and injustice. The media's role in dampening critical consciousness is expectable both because of its customary function of perpetuating hegemonic ideology and in this period because of its economic integration with the ruling elites. Since the 1980s, and rising alarmingly in the past several years, mega-corporations have used the state to institute policies of media deregulation. This corporate take-over of all aspects of the media industry has resulted in a staggering concentration of ownership and thus ideological power. In 1983, for example, 50 corporations controlled the vast majority of all news media in the USA. In 1992, fewer than two dozen corporations owned and operated 90% of the mass media, that is, almost all the country's newspapers, magazines, TV and radio stations, books, records, movies, videos, wire services and photo agencies. Today, that number has fallen to five major corporate monoliths, including the Walt Disney Company and AOL Time Warner, and their holdings now extend to the ownership and operation of the expanding internet market (Bagdikian 2004; Media Reform Information Center 2004).

This concentration of media ownership by the most powerful corporations has profoundly affected the news and information branches, which have become the representative of the state. According to journalists Norman Solomon and Reese Erlich (Solomon and Erlich 2003), the intimate relationship between the press and the government means that instead of providing critical reportage that opens the potential space by inviting citizens to engage in informed, reflective exploration of the causes of complex social, political and economic problems, the media forecloses this possibility through policies of editorial constraint and journalistic self-censorship. In 2001, Fairness and Accuracy in Reporting (FAIR) confirmed that one-quarter of television-viewing homes, representing two-thirds of the US public that claims to follow current events regularly, watched primarily ABC *World News Tonight*, CBS *Evening News* and NBC *Nightly News*. Another FAIR study, "Who's on the news?" found that 92% of all US sources interviewed were white, 85% were male and, where party affiliation was identifiable, 75% were Republican. It is not surprising, then, that media critics argue that the more Americans watch televised news, the less informed they are. As popular hip-hop performers Disposable Heroes of Hiphoprisy (1992) sing it, "television, the drug of the nation, breeding ignorance and feeding radiation . . ."

Understandably, the current US-led invasion of Iraq is depicted within narrow political parameters, a fact reinforced by the new policy of embedding journalists with US fighting forces, whose reportage uncritically reproduces the administration's self-serving war narrative. By conflating our soldiers and our government, these media monoliths erase the true story of the former's wounds, dead bodies and traumatized souls. This pro-government propagandistic function of the media encourages citizens' identification with the troops and thus their support for their government's unilateral preemptive strike against another country. Typically, the complex motives and goals of the war, as well as the major players who have orchestrated it, are largely invisible in the media. A collapsed potential space impoverishes our capacity for empathy for the victims of war. Because government propaganda equates Hussein first with 9/11, then with terrorism, then with Hitler, then with Iraq, and then with the Iraqi people, war and occupation are experienced as justifiable. The real deaths, suffering and destruction due to "shock and awe" vanish from our consciousness.

The traumatic impact of September 11 prompted many citizens to deal with their feelings of vulnerability, loss and fear through an identification with the aggressive retaliatory response by the US government. The wishful reliance on promises by a powerful authority to keep us safe from further terrorist attacks has permitted many citizens to embrace the simplistic division of the world into good (us) and evil (them) and to accept military aggression against anyone the government defines as a threat. The government has thus not provided the reflective space for the development of the intersubjective capacity to negotiate conflict aimed at reconciliation and reparation. Instead, it has manipulated the psychological defenses of a population's rage, loss and fear to support its covert economic and political aims.

However, US citizens must negotiate the challenges of living in a culture whose familiar discourse about democracy and freedom is countermanded by a new reality, whether we are aware of it or not. The basic principles of our political culture and economic security are under attack. The Patriot Act has undermined our right to free speech, a free press, transparency of government, freedom to assemble and to dissent, and freedom from arbitrary detention and torture. The social services upon which we have relied, including health, education, and welfare, have disintegrated as our tax dollars have been redirected to support the corporate welfare for Halliburton and other major players in the military–industrial complex. We face anxiety as our attachment to the dominant ideology of the social order is increasingly contradicted by our lived experience. Increasing numbers of citizens are hard-pressed to offer support to a government that assaults the very democracy it purports to export through war. In Gramsci's terms, we are experiencing a crisis of consensual power in the USA.

Alongside the government's aggressive, nationalistic and militaristic discourse and policies, a culture of resistance has emerged. This culture represents an oppositional ideology, a fundamental critique of war and of the hidden power relations that sponsor it. This antiwar movement is itself the beneficiary of the mobilization of millions of people over the past decade by the global justice movement. From Seattle to Genoa, from Bhopal to Pôrto Alegre, that movement has confronted the US and other governments in the First World, powerful transnational corporations and international financial institutions on behalf of labor, human rights, and environmental struggles for equity and social justice. These issues reappear in the contemporary antiwar movement, offering an alternative explanation of the current crisis in our country and in the world. With the accelerated growth of this oppositional movement a new public culture is being born. While the oppositional forces, representing millions of activists around the world, do not have the military, the media, and the wealth of the largest corporations on their side, they are carving out a new set of possibilities for popular participation in the political process.

Much like the therapeutic third of Winnicott or Ogden (1994), the rapidly growing oppositional movement opens public space for mentalization, reflection and symbolization about US domestic and global policies. It is revitalizing in ways similar to the therapeutic experience in that people can break through denial to see what they see, connect to others in ways that help them develop their thinking, validate their feelings and make critical observations about the complex world in which we live. These are people who, as bell hooks says (1992), stand apart and therefore see apart from the stupefying vision perpetrated by the hegemonic mass media – citizens who seek alternative information in books and on the internet or independent radio networks, who meet with neighbors in candlelight vigils, who join with thousands of others in song at demonstrations, or who invent humorous ways to confront hegemony: we have simply to think about the small group of women friends who spontaneously dressed as bunnies and went to Wal-Mart and Kmart to protest the sale of Easter baskets from which the bunny had been removed and replaced by a GI Joe holding a gun and a bomb.

This oppositional movement can open up a space for citizens to question the dominant ideological forms and the class relations they represent. However, while this opportunity represents new possibilities, it can also be experienced as potential new psychological threats. When our belief in and attachment to our political authorities are undermined, we may face a profound psychological as well as political challenge. Just as in the therapeutic experience, in the political domain as well, disengaging from attachments to bad objects, individuating from relationships that hold us back, and acknowledging painful realities can lead to feelings of despair and dread. Only by mourning our losses, facing the uncertainties and feeling our vulnerability will we be free enough to make the new attachments that help us reach beyond despair to a new kind of hope.

References

Bagdikian, B. (2004) *The New Media Monopoly*. Boston: Beacon Press. Website: http://www.benbagdikian.com

Boggs, C. (1984) *The Two Revolutions: Gramsci and the Dilemmas of Western Marxism*. Cambridge, MA: Southend Press.

Davies, J. M. and Frawley, M. G. (1994) *Treating the Adult Survivor of Childhood Sexual Abuse*. New York: Basic Books.

Diamond, I. and Quinby, L. (eds) (1988) *Feminism and Foucault: Reflections on Resistance*. Boston: Northeastern University Press.
The Disposable Heroes of Hiphoprisy (1992) Television, the drug of the nation [music track]. On *Hypocrisy is the Greatest Luxury*. Island Records.
Economic Policy Institute (2002–2003) The state of working America 2002–03. Website: http://www.epinet.org/content.cfm/books_swa.2002_swa2002intro
Fairness and Accuracy in Reporting (2001) Website: http://www.fair.org
Foucault, M. (1979) *Discipline and Punish*. New York: Vintage Books.
Foucault, M. (1980) *Power/Knowledge: Selected Interviews and Other Writings, 1972–1977*. Brighton, UK: Harvester Press.
Frosh, S. (1987) *The Politics of Psychoanalysis: An Introduction to Freudian and Post-Freudian Theory*. New York: New York University Press.
Gramsci, A. (1999) *Selections from the Prison Notebooks*. New York: International Publishers.
Gutwill, S. (1994) Women's eating problems: social context and the internalization of culture. In C. Bloom, A. Gitter, S. Gutwill, L. Kogel, and L. Zaphiropoulos (eds), *Eating Problems: A Feminist Psychoanalytic Treatment Model*. New York: Basic Books.
Herman, J. L. (1992) *Trauma and Recovery*. New York: Basic Books.
hooks, b. (1992) The oppositional gaze. *Black Looks: Race and Representation*. Boston: South End Press.
Jaggar, A. and Bordo, S. (eds) (1990) *Gender/Body/Knowledge: Feminist Reconstruction of Being and Knowing*. New Brunswick, NJ: Rutgers University Press.
Kilbourne, J. (1999) *Deadly Persuasion*. New York: The Free Press.
Klein, M. (1952) *Envy and Gratitude and Other Works, 1946–1963*. New York: Delacorte.
Media Reform Information Center (2004) Website: http://corporations.org/media
Ogden, T. H. (1990) *The Matrix of the Mind*. Northvale, NJ: Jason Aronson.
Ogden, T. H. (1994) *Subjects of Analysis*. Northvale, NJ: Jason Aronson.
Pitt, W. R. (2003) Blood money. Website: http://www.truthout.org/cgi-bin/artman/exec/view.cgi/1/53/printer
Project for the New American Century (1997) Website: http://www.newamericancentury.org
Rampton, S. and Stauber, J. (2003) *Weapons of Mass Deception*. New York: Penguin.
Solomon, N. and Erlich, R. (2003) *Target Iraq: What the News Media Didn't Tell You*. New York: Context Books.
Winnicott, D. W. (1971) *Playing and Reality*. Harmondsworth, UK: Penguin.

Chapter 6

Class and splitting in the clinical setting

The ideological dance in the transference and countertransference

Susan Gutwill and Nancy Caro Hollander

On the night that Bush was to announce his decision to declare formal war on Iraq, a women's psychotherapy group asked whether they should end early to go home and listen to the President's address. They began to waver about whether or not this was even a subject to discuss in therapy. Two of the women each said, "I am a pacifist but Saddam is so bad and dangerous." One of the two went on to insist that we had to stop a Hitler: "We can't just let Saddam dictate to the world and hurt people." Three others opposed the war. They wanted to know how the therapist felt.

A politically liberal 35-year-old single female patient, seven months pregnant, has had difficulty securing affordable health care through her work. In one session she describes feeling exhausted, overwrought and anxious in general, and, to point out how difficult life has become, describes bitterly having had to go grocery shopping after a particularly difficult day at work. She has gone to a local supermarket, part of a chain that is the target of a much publicized strike by workers – many of whom are women – over wages and demands for health care coverage. The strike has been a major news story for weeks and received much public support, but she says nothing about crossing the picket line.

These vignettes represent cases we will return to later, and they raise questions about how we analysts deal with our relationship to the social and political world. Important studies on the unconscious experience of gender and race have influenced our psychoanalytic appreciation of how significant these aspects of our membership in the social order are in helping to determine our intrapsychic and intersubjective life. But in the USA especially, the domain of politics, class, and each subject's relationship to the larger sociosymbolic order is almost taboo. With the exception of the tradition established by Harry Stack Sullivan and the cultural school, it has been the least analyzed category of power in American psychoanalysis. In this paper we want to explore our patients' and our own resistance to and yearning for political/emotional literacy, paying special attention to our relationship to the world beyond the private domains of family and work and to how the larger social sphere impacts on our psychological experience. We in the United States live in a socio-economic system wherein a tiny minority of people representing a political and economic class has inordinate power and influence over how we live, think, and feel. Contemporary psychoanalytic treatment in this country too often leaves our relationship to this social reality largely unexplored and therefore unconscious.

We believe that we are living at a historical juncture that not only offers the opportunity, but demands that we take up the question of the relationship that we and our patients have to a system dominated by class dynamics. We want to reflect on how psychoanalysis can provide individuals and groups with the possibility of exploring how their psychological conflicts and states of mind are affected not only within the private realm, but also with respect to their insertion in the larger social order. For many scholars of social theory and psychoanalysis, it is futile to speak of psychic and external reality as if they were two separate registers. From the beginning of life, they argue, subjectivity is fashioned out of the intimate interplay between the imaginary dimensions of the unconscious, which is characterized by representations, drives, and affects, and the sociosymbolic order, composed of asymmetrical relations of power and force. Freud emphasized that our earliest experiences are rooted in dependence on parental authority and dominance and that the formation of the superego constitutes such a powerful identification with authority because it is saturated with the vicissitudes of sexuality and aggression. In other words, subjectivity is constituted from the beginning of psychic life in an identification with and a resistance to authority so deep-seated that it is destined to be repeated throughout life, not only within the family, but in one's relationship to the larger social group – the sociosymbolic order (Elliott 1999).

We want to argue that the relationship of the subject to the social and political world and one's role as citizen is so central to identity that it ought to be a legitimate part of the psychoanalytic enterprise. As British group psychoanalyst, Earl Hopper, puts it, "An analyst who is unaware of the effect of social facts and forces . . . will not be able to provide a space for patients to imagine how their identities have been formed at particular historical and political junctures, and how this continues to affect them throughout their lives." Moreover, Hopper goes on to argue that such an analyst "cannot be sensitive to the unconscious recreation of [these social facts and forces] within the therapeutic situation" (Hopper 1996:7). We argue that Hopper's view is made extraordinarily meaningful by the conditions that pertain in the USA today. And, along with many of our colleagues, we believe that understanding the impact of our increasingly traumatogenic social environment on individual and group psychological life and the ways that it may be reproduced unconsciously within the patient/therapist relationship will make for a more thorough and elaborated psychoanalytically informed treatment.

Let us begin by describing what life is like in America today. Since George W. Bush was elected president in 2000, the neoconservative movement and its agenda for America have been able to take advantage of the traumatic after-effects of 9/11 in order to consolidate their 30-year organizing effort. The project for US global hegemony has been implemented through the following policies:

- an overt war effort in two countries, Afghanistan and Iraq, and a covert war in Haiti, Venezuela and Colombia
- the establishment of a number of new military bases in the Middle East and Asia
- guaranteed multi-billion dollar government contracts for US energy companies, such as Halliburton and Bechtel, and various defense contractors
- tax cuts for corporations so that the average person is paying for the corporate profits made from these government contracts
- social service funding slashed, including education, health care, medicare, environmental protection, law enforcement programs, and veteran benefits
- Homeland Security budget cuts, leaving Americans more vulnerable than ever to potential terrorist attacks with weapons of mass destruction
- unemployment and underemployment of growing numbers of people vulnerable to the downscaling of unemployment programs and a government that provides no protection for American jobs
- the Patriot Act and other legislation that legalizes the government's repression of dissent, which threatens to compromise our democratic rights and civil liberties.

These policies represent a massive redistribution of wealth and power from the majority of us to a small government and corporate elite, and have had deleterious effects on citizens of this country. It is often impossible for people to understand what is responsible for the deterioration in the quality of life for their families and their communities, in part due to a complicit mass media that is owned by a few mega-corporations in whose interest it is to control information and limit diversity of perspectives on major current issues.

The media and its mystifying function are but one instance of the general role of ideology in cementing the relationship between individuals and the social order. Ideology provides the lens through which citizens negotiate the contradictions between public discourse and real lived experience. What is ideology and how does it function? As psychoanalysts, we know that interpersonal experience is realized through the medium and psychological use of social symbols. Winnicott thought of symbolization as a constructive, expansive intrapsychic capacity as well as a relational process in which one authentically negotiates a balance between internal wishes and needs and external reality's expectations and demands. Winnicott did not conceptualize this process, as have other psychoanalytic theorists such as Lacan, in light of how the dominant cultural symbols represent the social order and the forces of privilege and power. Lacan's view of the Symbolic Order is that it inevitably takes one out of oneself, alienates, requires. Political philosopher Antonio Gramsci argued that the dominant social symbols of the culture – the whole range of values, attitudes, beliefs, cultural norms, legal precepts and so on that infuse civil society – together constitute the dominant ideology, which he called "hegemony" (Boggs 1984). Transmitted through the major institutions, including the family, they generate a belief in a particular system. French Marxist Louis Althusser's study of ideological apparatuses, including the family and the educational system, emphasized how from birth onwards each individual internalizes ideology, the fundamental principles and values of which become a significant aspect of unconscious life. While Althusser understood that the *raison d'être* of ideology is to facilitate the maintenance of the hidden relations of power, he also believed that ideology has an important psychological function. From his Lacanian perspective, the subject engages in an imaginary search for unity and coherence to escape the fractured and decentered nature of human experience. The subject's true state of diffuseness or decenterment is able to be transcended through the encounter with a consolingly coherent image of oneself reflected in the mirror of the dominant ideological discourse. The individual locates himself/herself through ideology, which is a thought-practice located in concrete behaviors of everyday life. Since hegemonic values are taken as natural, our conscious awareness about them is pre-empted and we are habituated to them (Althusser 1994). In Lacanian philosopher Slavoj Žižek's words, from birth on we are being "hailed" by the social order so that we unconsciously assume our appropriate position within it. Žižek puts the matter simply, "we do not know it, but we are doing it" (Myers 2003:63). Earl Hopper agrees that ideology functions to hide the unequal power structure and access to resources, and he argues that it is difficult for the subject in any sociosymbolic order to perceive the truth hidden by ideology because to see the truth and feel one's impotence in the face of it would constitute a narcissistic injury (Hopper 1996).

We might say that in the wake of the terrorist attacks on 9/11, ideology came to our rescue. Bush's aggressive policies were justified by a discourse that split the world into good and evil – US democracy pitted against totalitarian evil throughout the globe. Most citizens could uncritically identify with the ideological assumptions underlying Bush's crusade because of the history of US expansionism, ideologically rationalized in various incarnations of Manifest Destiny for well over a century. In Žižek's words, we did not know it, but we were doing it – that is, citizens were unconsciously identifying with the hegemonic ideological justifications of the policies instituted by the powerful who rule the USA. By rationalizing government policies aimed at ensuring US hegemony in the world, covering over the psychological experience of individual and group decentering and discontinuity, and protecting us against the narcissistic injury of impotence and helplessness in America provoked by 9/11, ideology worked.

Elsewhere we have discussed contemporary subjectivity from the standpoint of trauma theory, which sensitizes us to the dilemma of the disjuncture between the nature of one's personal experience and the official story offered by those in a position of authority (see Chapter 5, this volume). Since 9/11, military expansionism as a response to the terrorist attacks has been experienced by many people as a solution to feelings of insecurity and impotence on the one hand and rage and aggression on the other. While today many important questions are being raised about the nature of the present US administration and its policies, they are limited to specific symptoms, such as the illegal and immoral behavior of corporate "special interests," rather than directed to the inequities inherent in the system of late capitalism and globalization. As we understand it, whether we are inserted into the sociosymbolic order as members of the working and middle classes or members of that segment of the wealthy class who own and control capital and the means of production, we are all unavoidably engaged in the competitive struggle for jobs or profits, and are always in danger of being vanquished by others. The neo-conservative solution for this dilemma at the level of the wealthiest in the USA is the philosophical underpinning of the current administration's policies. It is articulated in the Project for the New American Century, which calls for US domination of the world and its resources, and at home for the elimination of the social infrastructure (Project for the New American Century 1997). This "modest proposal" inevitably provokes antagonism toward the USA and its citizens, most of whom know nothing about their leadership's long-range vision.

We believe that today the public sphere is characterized by what Thomas Ogden has noted with reference to personal relationships within the family and the self, a pathology of the potential space. There is no negotiation between self and other; the symbol and the symbolized have been collapsed. For example, in the initial stages of the US occupation of Iraq, if we/America were not all good and they/Iraq were not all bad, then we were bad as well as good; if they/Iraqis hated Saddam's dictatorship, then they would want a US military occupation, an assumption maintained in the USA despite all evidence to the contrary. The inability to achieve a depressive position acceptance of ambiguity and ambivalence results in the paradox that if we are all good we are endlessly threatened by the all bad other who will attack us. Robert Jay Lifton speaks of this dilemma in contemporary America in a slightly different way when he analyzes the pathology of the "superpower syndrome," which contains a basic contradiction stemming from the need to seek to eliminate the experience of vulnerability. This need puts the superpower on what Lifton, emphasizing vulnerability, describes as a psychological treadmill. He writes that "The idea of vulnerability is intolerable, the fact of it irrefutable. One solution is to maintain an illusion of invulnerability. But the superpower then runs the danger of taking increasingly draconian actions to sustain that illusion. For to do otherwise would be to surrender the cherished status of superpower" (Lifton 2003:129). In this pathological transitional space, primitive defenses among a frightened, angry and aggressive population come into play, overdetermined by public discourse as well as individual unconscious states. In today's traumatogenic environment, paranoid-schizoid mechanisms can prevail at the most terrifying moments; for example, in response to ongoing color-coded alerts and news that focuses on nuclear proliferation or global warming, each of which conveys a threat to our very survival as a species. The more frightened and angry we are, the more difficult it becomes to separate and individuate from the authority of government and its discourse, especially when they appear to promise safety in a dangerous world. The capacity to reflect, to allow oneself to think critically and to take an independent position with respect to what in society is responsible for endangering our safety and wellbeing can itself feel threatening. We analysts know how difficult separation is under the best of circumstances. Grieving losses, feeling vulnerabilities, and facing uncertainty and one's own aggression are painful when disengaging from attachments to bad objects because of the terror of retaliation. We argue that these dynamics operate in the relationship between the individual and the sociosymbolic order. And we believe that psychoanalysts have a role to play in creating a transitional space that permits the possibility of this process to unfold. In order for it to take place, however, we are obliged to pay close attention and take seriously the ways that concerns and anxieties about the social/political world emerge in patient material, either as they are articulated or even by their absence. We need to consider how the transference/countertransference dance either enables or inhibits the mutual capacity of analyst and patient to elaborate this important dimension of life.

We turn now to an elaboration of case examples that we hope will illustrate some of the assertions we have been making. We will attempt to demonstrate some ways to think about why the analyst is or is not willing to take up social and political questions as they present themselves in treatment and to interpret the consequences of doing so or of failing to do so.

We will begin with an example of the problems generated when the analyst does not take up a political issue by returning to the patient mentioned at the beginning of the chapter. If you recall, Mary is a pregnant woman in her mid-thirties who described going grocery shopping and said nothing about having crossed a workers' militant picket line to do so. Since Mary has periodically referred with a sense of helpless indignation to the injustices of the world as well as to her experiences of being exploited in the workplace, I was shocked that she crossed the line and perplexed that she said nothing. I hesitated to say anything because of my doubts about the appropriateness of focusing on something "political," in this case external to her personal life and her own emotional preoccupations. At that moment, she was complaining about feeling exhausted and disappointed by the limited support she felt from friends and family when her working-class husband left her while she was pregnant. I could have made yet again a transference interpretation in response to her repeated laments that unlike her fantasies of my successful life in love and work, she had failed in her attempts to sustain a relationship with a man in order to have a baby. Or I could have once again focused on her resistance to experience herself as independent and capable, even though her decision to now be a single mother had been the most important autonomous act she had engaged in as an adult. But I found myself distracted: I felt angry because these militant strikers included many poor women and mothers fighting for basic rights for themselves and their kids, while the patient had grown up the child of a wealthy family. Now, as a "declassed" adult she still maintained her privileged sense of entitlement, which was constantly disappointed and frustrated. The grocery workers had been out for months at great personal sacrifice and had received a good deal of support from the public – except from this patient! I felt guilty that I had become preoccupied with what was for her apparently not the salient aspect of her experience. I also believed I had to be quiet lest my anger damage her. Moreover, I suspected that my need to take up a conflicted political issue about which she seemed unconscious would collude with her consistent proclivity to attack herself for failing to live up to her own very harsh superego demands that she consistently experienced as emanating from others, including me. So the moment was lost, and neither of us referred to the event in subsequent sessions.

I suggest that my inhibition in that single moment illustrates some of the problems that result when we analysts are unwilling to take up social reality within the treatment. In this session's aftermath, for example, how can we know about its effects in the transference and the degree to which she feels compelled to absent herself from the relationship for fear of being attacked by me in retaliation for her wrongdoing? How can we know whether my reaction was not the effect of projective identification, in which she found a way to let me experience her own self-denunciation as well as the vulnerability she consistently insists she feels when having to deal with conflict? How can we know how my countertransference reaction might be covertly expressed but dissociated from its origins in my own history as well as in the relationship with this particular patient?

I believe that my decision not to say anything constituted an enactment in response to anxiety stimulated by transgressive wishes and their inhibition. I was agitated, but wanted to be "good" and obey the psychoanalytic rule: don't politicize my patient, don't coerce her, don't talk about politics. Mary had crossed a picket line, and I had not dared to cross the psychoanalytic line. However, if I had made an interpretation calling attention to the political issue that for her remained out of consciousness, many issues that had emerged previously in the treatment could have been explored anew in a different context. And, especially if we had found ourselves politically on different sides of the "line," my patient might have had an invaluable opportunity to experience being able to hold onto difference within the context of mutual caring and regard. Further, such an exchange within our transference–countertransference dance might have potentiated her ability, at least in fantasy if not in action, to combat one instance of her chronic feelings of isolation through an identification with a group of people acting in concert to fight for the very things my patient had passively longed for: a livable wage and quality health care.

As it turned out, months later, after Mary had her baby, we found our way back to this incident. In the context of our exchanges about the meanings of a dream she presented, I was able to refer back to the session described above. Together we came to see that crossing the picket line had had various meanings for Mary and represented the convergence of unresolved oedipal as well as class issues. In light of the focus of this chapter, I briefly comment only on the latter. We discovered that Mary's actions had represented an actively class-based disidentification with the striking women. Mary envied the privileged lifestyles and gratified dependency needs of her upper-middle-class friends who were married to wealthy or high-income-generating husbands. She resented her own declassed situation based on her economic autonomy, which translated into an earning capacity permitting at best a lower-middle-class lifestyle always threatened by financial insecurity and potential disaster. Her economic situation exacerbated her chronic inability to feel pride in herself and her independence; rather, she felt inadequate, helpless and humiliated by it. Her insensitivity to the striking women workers represented a dissociative process that enabled her in fantasy to assert her difference rather than her similarity to their class-based plight. Her psychological growth in response to the birth of her baby enabled her to reflect on these unconscious dynamics. Through her experience of motherhood, as she transitioned from initial feelings of insecurity and anxiety with her newborn to a sense of her capacity and increasing empowerment as a mother, Mary began to feel more optimistic about her abilities and to make concrete efforts to improve her work situation and income-generating possibilities. From this vantage point, she was able to understand the meanings of having crossed the picket line and not addressed it in the analysis, and we were able to interpret its significance in the transference and countertransference. In the process of revisiting this issue, Mary came to identify with the striking women, not only as the unfortunate victims of poverty and marginalization, but as protagonists of their own lives who were assertively fighting against the social forces – their corporate bosses – responsible for their low wages and lack of medical care.

Another clinical example demonstrates a positive outcome when the analyst takes up the content of the political material directly. Peter is a 34-year-old engineer, previously diagnosed with a mood disorder. Although his medication was helping his mood swings, he reported feeling anxious and agitated much of the time. It was clear from Peter's preoccupation with politics that he was critical of both major political parties and held a left perspective. But his cynicism about the possibility of citizens being able to make an impact on those in power left him marginalized from any kind of activism. The morning after the invasion of Iraq, Peter came to session in a manic state. He was convinced he was "crazy," as he put it, and the proof was that he had taken it upon himself in a helpless fury to write letters to the President and Secretary of Defense, outlining the injustices of the immoral and illegal invasion of another country and protesting this use of his tax dollars. As I listened to him, I was thinking about his history and how Peter had always felt alone in his family. His biggest complaint had been that, as the youngest of five siblings, he had never been taken seriously by anyone in his family, including his chronically unavailable father and enveloping and intrusive mother. He believed his parents had simply run out of emotional supplies after rearing so many children before he came along. I knew I felt respectful of his action and wished for him to have the experience of being treated with respect and taken seriously.

The following conveys my interventions and not Peter's part of our exchange: I made a decision, in Andrew Samuels' language, not to regard political material exclusively on the level of symbolism, intrapsychic process or transference (Samuels 1993:Chapter 10). I suggested that the problem did not lie in his having written the letters to our political leaders, but in his interpretation of the significance of it. He was certain that writing the letters and trying to communicate what he thought and felt proved that he was crazy, and this was because of his experience over a lifetime of not feeling that he warranted the serious attention and respect of others. That conviction prevented him from appreciating that he was being a responsible citizen in a democracy by writing to government officials who are supposed to represent the will of the people. Then I took up the issue of his isolation, which was also a chronic problem from childhood, in part a defensive maneuver to ward off his intrusive mother and badgering older siblings. I suggested that it was precisely his isolation that kept him from realizing how many other people were also writing letters to Bush and a host of elected officials to register their opposition to the war. In this sense, it was his isolation that made him feel crazy. Finally, and this is where I felt anxious about sticking out my political neck: I went on to say that if he were not so isolated and anxious about having passionate feelings about politics, given his knowledge and experience, he would know surely more about the organizations, like Moveon.org, that are mobilizing tens of thousands of people who feel the same outrage he does about the current government's policies. At the end of the session, Peter said he no longer felt crazy, but relieved and calm.

In the months that followed, the analysis became more intense, his connection to me stronger. I think my decision to take seriously his political feelings and perspective opened up a potential space in which he could appreciate an authentic aspect of himself reflected positively in the transference/countertransference dance. He has been able to use his experience with me to begin to separate and individuate from the destructive aspects of his relationship with his family members and to find friends with whom he shares similar values. During this same period, Peter has found ways to express his social concerns in a context that he feels he can emotionally manage and through which he has a positive sense of making a social contribution in such a way that his strong feelings and political perspectives can, indeed, be heard.

Let me remind you about my therapy group meeting on the night Bush was to formally tell the nation he would declare war on Iraq, based on the ostensible danger of Saddam Hussein's weapons of mass destruction and the need to sustain a war on terrorism made necessary since the attack of 9/11. I was furious about this when my group began that evening. A woman whom I call Jane suggested it was our responsibility to be informed by and about the president's speech. But some ambivalence was expressed: was it appropriate, worthwhile, and safe to talk about this subject within the therapy setting? The group members assumed I would be against the war because they knew that I think about the impact of the larger society on emotional life and that, since 9/11, I have been involved in an organization called Psychotherapists for Social Responsibility. Three of the women opposed going to war against Iraq. Two of them were strongly opposed, but wanted to be better able to explain their positions. The most intensely charged sentiments, however, were expressed by two other women, both of whom said, "I am a pacifist, but Saddam is so bad and dangerous."

Jane said she was passionately antiwar, but that "Saddam is so bad and he endangers Israel." Sofia, also defining herself as a pacifist, felt strongly suspicious of George W. Bush, but as a Latina who had escaped a fascist takeover of her native country claimed that any strong opinion, any black or white position, could be dangerous. Her reasoned middle was that Saddam was like Hitler and had to be stopped. I listened to their conversation and felt myself becoming furious. I was thinking that there was no knowledge of history in the discussion, no reference to the sanctions, to the US arming and propping up of Saddam, to a systemic class analysis of who wanted this war and why. Our war was good because Saddam was bad: it was a character analysis. And I was thinking, "these are good people, and are they the ones I have to depend on to help protect democracy and decency in my world?" I knew they were aware of the dehumanization of people by US government/corporate reach. Where was that knowledge? In my attempt to hold my empathy for the group, I found myself thinking about what Danny Schecter (2003), the media critic, has called the electronic colonization of our minds, by which he means that people cannot help but respond with terror when the media endlessly repeats images of destruction, like the towers coming down, while simultaneously making invisible the suffering of the people of Iraq. We cannot help but feel the annihilation fantasy that I believe we all shared in that group. Some thought Saddam was the threat. I felt that the aggressive policies of our country would eventually be just as threatening. We had to hold our terror. I struggled with myself trying to listen to them, as well as to my own angry and frightened inner experience.

Why was I so quiet, they insisted? I asked what their fantasies were regarding what I thought and felt. Jane and Sofia correctly imagined that I was furious at them, that I felt I was better than them, that I was a radical, worked for peace and looked down on them. Others thought that I might have information that could actually help them in their opposition to the war. They all knew my position, but wanted to hear me articulate it. My silence infuriated and scared them. They wanted me to talk and quit hiding and "playing therapist." So, I decided that I would tell them my views and why I held them. I told them the following: that based on the reports of the weapons inspectors and on the battering of Iraq's infrastructure after a decade of sanctions, I did not believe that Saddam had weapons of mass destruction that would be dangerous to us; that I agreed that Saddam was a horrible dictator, but if that was the case, that the USA should take responsibility for having armed and financially and diplomatically supported him; that I believed that the media, as tightly merged as it was with the government and military, could not be relied on to provide us with real information, but was instead terrifying the population to uncritically support the administration's plans; and that, finally, I believed that more violence would make us less, rather than more, secure.

Now what? To my surprise, there was palpable relief among them. All but one woman felt they had learned something, and that I really knew about this issue. Everything I had said seemed clear, plausible and well founded, which led to an expression of gratitude that I could be a source of information, and that furthermore, information was available, albeit not on the major networks. The relief in the group came first, and then later in that session and in subsequent sessions we dealt with transference–countertransference reactions to my knowledge, to my being in opposition to the *status quo*, to my being different from or the same as them. Each exploration has been very useful. But before any good work of that sort could be done, I think we had to live through this enactment, with a capital "E," as Anthony Bass puts it (2003). I believe that the sociosymbolic bifurcation of good and evil in our larger culture was enacted in my therapy group. They feared that I would annihilate them, destroy their self-esteem and therapeutic relationship with me and each other. I believed they would annihilate me/the Iraqis with their willingness to be bystanders to the Bush administration's destructiveness. I feared my own rage would kill them, that I would be thrown out of good professional standing for being intrusive and out of control. I felt "isolated" professionally and culturally, even though the majority of group members were against the war and so were (and still are) millions of people throughout the world! Certainly my own history came into play here, but in the context of this discussion I want to emphasize the aspect of my response that was conditioned by the social order.

In an article entitled "The social unconscious in clinical work" (1996:19), Earl Hopper argues that when a society is experiencing a shared threat of annihilation, there are, to use Bion's notion, "basic assumption group" responses (Bion 1959). One of these is what Hopper calls a bipolar incohesion, a form of merged collective splitting, including scapegoating. As group members spoke, the way I held my opposition to the war partially amounted to an enactment, in which I felt that they were the doers and I was the done to (Benjamin 1998). On the other hand, they feared me as the doer and they the done to. As they and I spoke, I was struggling between omnipotence and helplessness, two positions I tried to hold within me – slippery as they were. In one I was aware of how destructive I felt, and I wanted to use what I believed to be my expertise to whip them into shape. But I knew I could not do that and struggled to overcome my impulses. It was not a simple process. In retrospect, I believe I was simultaneously enacting our shared trauma and creating a potential space. Feeling, thinking, and doing are difficult to hold and juggle at once (Aron and Benjamin 1999). As the discussion progressed, the destructiveness was contained and we all became safe with our differences and with hearing each other. Working through this enactment increased the capacity of the group-as-a-whole, the individual members, and the therapist to explore constraints on development imposed by the social world, both past and present. We were all supported within the group to observe the resonances, or what Hopper calls equivalences, among historical, social, familial, and intrapsychic contributions to defensive inhibitions and painful re-enactments. This process has continued in the following months, as has the rest of our rich and robust group life.

The most dramatic outcome and continuation of the work that began on the eve of the war in Iraq is exemplified by a group meeting held about two years later. Sarit began this meeting by sharing her anxiety about her upcoming visit to Poland with her mother and brother, where they would visit her mother's childhood home as well as Auschwitz and the other concentration camps in which her mother had been interned. She and I had identified in several individual sessions that in her present life, Sarit alternately felt helpless and victimized by, and then aggressively enraged with, her partner. She was shocked by the unreasonably desperate quality of feeling narcissistically "wiped out" in the face of her partner's idiosyncrasies and felt simultaneously ashamed and justified for "freaking out" on her. Together we had understood that both of these stances were traumatic re-enactments of Sarit's painful childhood experiences with her traumatized mother. As Sarit spoke in the group I felt a stilted silence fall over the room. Sofia, the Argentine *émigrée*, began to say something about her experience but cut herself off because, as she said, "it couldn't compare with the Holocaust." Sarit and I encouraged her to speak.

Thereupon Sofia burst into tears and seemed terrified as she shared, for the first time, her experience of living through the Dirty War in Argentina. She told about having seen the military junta dropping bodies into the river from helicopters. The politically repressive environment felt too frightening to say anything. Moreover, she told us that her own husband was in the right-wing police, a secret she was not supposed to have known. She said: "I was afraid to know, but I could have been Mrs Eichmann." Not knowing what to do with her feelings and the omnipresent threats, Sofia explained that she had felt most safe at work on a top floor of a huge building where she was employed by an American corporation. She had felt that both the right and the left were dangerous. Although she had wanted to be a teacher, she could not because teachers were considered leftists. Finally, her father had been able to arrange for the family's emigration to the USA. In response to these experiences, as Sofia put it, "I had to believe that America was completely good, totally democratic." And then she told the group what she had told me after the session on the evening of Bush's address, that she had been furious with me for questioning the goodwill of American foreign policy in Iraq, a feeling that was ultimately replaced with a sense of gratitude because it had permitted her, for the first time, to share her traumatic experiences in Argentina and how she still felt she could say nothing about them within the American Argentine community.

Sarit and Jane were deeply moved, even though they said they did not know about the junta to which Sofia was referring. I had to make an important decision at that point. Should I speak about that part of US foreign policy that had secretly supported the Argentine military coup, just as in Chile, whose repressive policies had intimidated most citizens into an unknowing bystander position? If I broke the silence about such matters in our group, would I be doing wild analysis or didactic political organizing? Would I be evacuating my rage at institutional violence by taking an ideological stand at the expense of my psychotherapy group? I was frightened once again as I had been on the night of Bush's speech. This time, however, I was much less frightened because our group was ever more vigorous and honest, which gave me faith in the ability of the members to supervise me. Moreover, I knew that the information would offer another opportunity for them to contain the experience of being a bystander in the face of seeing the relationship between victims and perpetrators. After Sofia and the others had worked with the affect expressed, I shared the thought that in fact Sofia was not entirely alone because we, as members of the larger social group America-as-whole, had been bystanders to fascist repression in Argentina. As I spoke, I realized that I was not preaching nor was I evacuating my guilt or rage by inducing guilt in a sadistic way. Rather, I felt that I was widening the circle of consciousness and the possibility of achieving a kind of compassionate responsibility that as therapists we try to build in psychotherapy.

While the above case examples reflect concerns about explicit political events, it is important to remember that ideology is always present as a thought-practice of everyday life and emerges in more subtle ways as well. As therapists, we have probably all encountered clinical sessions such as the following: a patient complains about extreme weather conditions without any mention of dangerous patterns of global warming; or she feels bad because she is unable to find employment commensurate with her training or able to yield her a livable wage, but does not refer to the national underemployment and unemployment trends or the global pattern of job outsourcing or runaway factories; or she complains about her child's increasing aggression or consumerist values without noting the violence and consumerist ethic propagated ubiquitously by the media, which is owned by fewer and fewer profit-driven media conglomerates that establish the premises of taste. In these instances and countless others like them, people feel the symptoms, which are disconnected – one might say dissociated – from their systemic causes because of the convergence of ideology and psychological defenses. They thus lack an "observing ego" (Fairbairn 1986) with which to understand why they may feel powerless, self-blaming or rageful toward socially created scapegoats. When we live without critically questioning the sociosymbolic order that we take as a given, we embody what Žižek means when he asserts about ideology that "we do not know it, but we are doing it."

As we have tried to show in this paper, our patients and we are required to make repeated negotiations between psychological positions – between the paranoid-schizoid and the depressive, between the pre-oedipal and oedipal – with regard to our intrapsychic, interpersonal and larger social group relationships. In light of the intrapsychic import of dealing with what Christopher Bollas calls "the unthought known" (Bollas 1987), we have suggested that good psychoanalytic work is best and most fully understood as a commitment to helping ourselves and our patients develop the capacity to observe the attachments upon which we depend so as to expand the choices we make about them. We argue that our clinical work should involve helping our patients to be able to differentiate and separate from destructive attachments, not only within the self and with others, but in relationship to the larger social order as well. As we help to make the unconscious conscious, we open up the potential space for observation of our relationships to authority and thus help to make the movement between submission and resistance to authority a more fluid one. This challenge potentiates not only emotional health, but good citizenship as well. For the weather is changing, and the democratic rights and economic abundance that so many of us in the developed capitalist world have enjoyed, often at the expense of others, are – as the air we breathe and the earth we know – quite threatened. In light of contemporary political and social trends, we believe it is essential that we reclaim our radical tradition within psychoanalysis.

References

Althusser, L. (1994) Ideology and ideological state apparatuses (notes toward an investigation). In S. Žižek (ed.), *Mapping Ideology*. London: Routledge, pp. 100–140.

Aron, L. and Benjamin, J. (1999) *The development of intersubjectivity and the struggle to think*. Paper presented at Spring Meeting of the Division of Psychoanalysis (39), American Psychological Association, New York, April 1999.

Bass, A. (2003) "E" enactments in psychoanalysis: another medium, another message. *Psychoanalytic Dialogues*, 13(5):657–677.

Benjamin, J. (1998) *Shadow of the Other: Intersubjectivity and Gender in Psychoanalysis*. New York: Routledge.

Bion, W. (1959) *Experiences in Groups*. London: Tavistock.

Boggs, C. (1984) *The Two Revolutions: Gramsci and the Dilemmas of Western Marxism*. Cambridge, MA: South End Press.

Bollas, C. (1987) *The Shadow of the Object: Psychoanalysis of the Unthought Known*. New York: Columbia University Press.

Elliott, A. (1999) *Social Theory and Psychoanalysis in Transition: Self and Society from Freud to Kristeva*. London: Free Association Books.

Fairbairn, W. R. D. (1986) *Psychoanalytic Studies of the Personality*. London: Routledge, Kegan Paul.

Hopper, E. (1996) The social unconscious in clinical work. *Group*, 20(1):7–42. Reprinted in E. Hopper, *The Social Unconscious. Selected Papers of Earl Hopper*. London: Jessica Kingsley Publishers, 2003.

Lifton, R.J. (2003) *Superpower Syndrome: America's Apocalyptic Confrontation with the World*. New York: Thunder's Mouth Press.

Myers, T. (2003) *Žižek*. London: Routledge.

Project for the New American Century (1997) Website: http://www.newamericancentury.org/statementofprinciples.htm

Samuels, A. (1993) *The Political Psyche*. London: Routledge.

Schecter, D. (2003) *The media making a difference panel*. Paper presented at American Spirit, Values and Power Conference, CUNY Graduate Center, New York, May 2003.

Chapter 7

Attacks on linking

The unconscious pull to dissociate individuals from their social context

Lynne Layton

Cultural norms erect barriers to what can be thought, felt, and articulated in speech. Because in certain ways they share the same dominant middle-class culture, therapists and their clients often adhere, consciously and unconsciously, to some of the same cultural norms. These norms not only condition thought, feeling, and behavior, but create dynamic unconscious conflicts as well. Such unconscious conflict, in turn, can generate particular kinds of clinical enactments, ones in which therapist and patient unconsciously collude in upholding the very norms that might in fact contribute to ongoing psychic pain. For example, as I have described elsewhere (Layton 1998, 2002, 2004a, 2004b, 2005; in press), shared dominant gender norms can lead patient and therapist alike to unconsciously legitimate particular ways of splitting connection and agency, ways that make agency conflictual for women and intimacy conflictual for men. I call "normative" that aspect of unconscious process that works to uphold dominant ideologies, and I assume that the motive for doing so, even at the cost of much psychic pain, is to secure the love of intimates and the approval of one's social world. Normative unconscious processes, I argue, result from narcissistic wounding inflicted by sexist, racist, and other power hierarchies whose norms mark one group of people as inferior to other groups. Identities, I believe, are forged in part from conflict between those normative unconscious processes that are the product of narcissistic wounding, and other conscious and unconscious processes that strive to undo the wounds (Layton 2004a).

In this chapter, I want to focus on a particularly dominant norm in US culture: the unlinking of individuals from their social contexts. This unlinking derives from many historical and social sources. Its origins lie in the rise of capitalism in mid-nineteenth-century America, in response to the increasingly sharp separation of the public from the private sphere that was mandated by both urbanization and industrialization's division of labor. Patriarchal norms split and gendered the two spheres, and the disparate functions of these separate male public and female private spheres created the psychic split between agentic capacities and relational capacities that for so long has defined dominant gender positions (even though women played key roles that melded the private and the public in such historical movements as the fight to prohibit prostitution and alcohol, and for the right to divorce, own property, and work in healthy conditions). Emotional attachments were culturally valued only in the private sphere, not in the dog-eat-dog world of capitalism (Lasch 1977). Indeed, despite today's public rhetoric in favor of family values, now, as always, if a corporation or the military want to send you and your family to a different part of the country or world every few years, you go – regardless of what clinicians and others know about how significant a prognosticator for psychological difficulties frequent moves can be.

The liberal ideology that legitimates the public/private split has traditionally idealized an autonomous male whose subjectivity resides in reason and will. The ideology of the "free individual" is, particularly in the US context, closely connected with self-reliance and an extreme individualism that denies connections of all kinds. As Barthes (1957) and others have written, two of the main tropes by which bourgeois ideology operates are dehistoricization, which involves naturalizing and universalizing what is actually specific to a given historic moment and a given constellation of relations, and what Barthes calls ex-nomination, by which the class that has the most economic and symbolic power refers to itself as "man" or "human," anything but white or upper-middle-class or owners of the means of production. As Barthes writes:

> practised on a national scale, bourgeois norms are experienced as the evident laws of a natural order – the further the bourgeois class propagates its representations, the more naturalized they become.
>
> (Barthes 1957:140)

Both dehistoricization and ex-nomination are ideological forms of decontextualization, the unlinking of things that, if experience is to make sense, need to be linked. Indeed, what primarily sustains the ideology of the "free individual" is an active and continuously constructed process of decontextualization, most obvious in the media but clear as well in every one of Bush's speeches, in most discussions of corporate wrongdoing, in the medicalization of psychological problems, in discussions of what is wrong with our schools, and in most discussions of social policy. Dominant ideology works very diligently on a number of fronts to hide the systemic nature of inequalities of all kinds, to make sure that an individual's problems seem just that – individual.

As political theorist Wendy Brown (2004) claims, liberal ideology has always been deeply suspicious of groups and their public display of passions such as anger and love. Ardent attachments are deemed dangerous and must remain private and individualized. Brown cites Freud's *Group Psychology and the Analysis of the Ego* (1959; orig. 1922), which, like other important documents of liberal ideology, views groups as sites where perfectly rational individuals become regressed, primitive, and de-individuated beings. Liberal ideology then draws on such "expert evidence" to relegate group aspects of identity, such as culture and religion, to background status, to a place that is not deemed constitutive of subjectivity.

As entrepreneurial capitalism gave way to consumer capitalism, liberal individualist ideology became ever more entrenched. The autonomous individual, once figured in liberal discourse as public citizen, is now largely figured in the media and elsewhere as private consumer. The continuous subordination of sensuous human existence and morality to the "facts" of the marketplace and technical rationality severs, instrumentalizes, and commodifies connections between individuals and between individuals and their environments. All of these processes unlink individuals from each other, from themselves, and from their social and natural world.

Even to speak of the individual and the social as separate is a distortion, except insofar as that separation is the truth of this society's dominant culture, and, as such, appears to most of us as "common sense" (see Adorno 1967, 1968). As Althusser (1971) argued, all the apparatuses of capitalist culture – the family, the education system, the media, religion – function to shore up the notion of a free individual separate from social context. Free individuals, free to succeed or fail on their own, generally have no idea that their freedom is conditioned by the lack of freedom inherent in the wage-labor system (Žižek 1994). Yet, despite the mystifications of ideology and the way ideologies are enacted consciously and unconsciously, it is clear that social context is woven into one's psychic fabric in myriad ways, from the ways bodily processes are experienced and tastes developed (see, for example, Bourdieu's (1984) discussion of class, habitus, and taste; see also Chapter 3, this volume), to the ways one experiences and enacts the most taken for granted psychoanalytic staples, such as dependency and agency. The way the power structure of a culture defines what counts as dependency and what counts as agency, the way it mandates which social classes or strata will be "dependent," which "independent," plays a large role in determining the kinds of psychic conflicts inherent to that culture.

Certainly, there are subordinate cultures in the USA whose members are painfully aware of the connections between social systems and their own individual struggles. Nonwhite minorities, for example, are far less likely to buy into the unlinking norm than are whites of all classes. Nonetheless, all subcultures have to wrangle psychically with dominant ideology; it is hard to imagine that even the most impoverished black man doesn't on some level feel self-hatred for his failure to be successful. And because dominant ideology is so tied into the one system NO ONE is allowed to question – capitalism – we find that as minority subcultures rise in social status their prominent members often become the most rabid defenders of the unlinking norm: think of the Ward Connerly's and Clarence Thomas's of the world who, once achieving individual privilege, seem to want to close the privilege gate behind them.

By limiting to the family the context in which it views patients' conflicts, psychoanalytic therapy is one of the many practices that enforce the norm that unlinks the psychic from the social. Following Cushman (1995), Altman (1995) and others, I argue that, in so doing, we establish a norm for what counts as mental health that aims far lower than it might. As a consequence, we contribute to constricting the possibilities of our patients, even as we are enhancing them in many other ways. Indeed, if we believe that the individual ought to be a social individual and that his or her happiness should have something to do with connections beyond the self and beyond intimate relations, we should perhaps be troubled by the fact that, too often, our work produces only healthier and happier versions of narcissism.

Although many psychoanalytic theorists have spoken about the relation between the psychic and the social (my notion of normative unconscious processes owes a debt, for example, to Fromm's (1941, 1962) notion of social character), Samuels (1993) was perhaps the first to insist that the political development of the person is a proper and necessary topic for inquiry in the clinical setting. In the clinical vignette that I describe below, we can see that the patient's political conflicts are also psychic conflicts. What I want to add to Samuels' observations is (1) an analysis of the way that norms that separate individuals from their "political psyche" generate unconscious conflict and (2) the way this shared conflict plays out in unconscious collusions between therapist and patient.

Clinical vignette: work and love and the passion for civic life

In the spring of 2003, just after the USA went to war in Iraq, a patient reported a dream in which she wondered whether or not to tell her state senator her views on what was currently going on politically in American life. In exploring the dream with her, I found myself struggling throughout the session against the urge to close off this inquiry with an interpretation that would reduce what she was saying to the kind of psychological insight that separates the psychic from the social. Granted, we are living in difficult political times, times in which historical events such as September 11 force their way into the consulting room. But this experience revealed to me my own resistance to linking the psychic and the social, a resistance of which I was largely unaware. Fighting my urge to interpret enabled the two of us to discover that there are realms beyond those of work and love that are clinically relevant.

Before reporting the patient's two dreams from that session, I want to say something about other ways that the separation of the individual from the social affects this patient's psyche. The patient owns a small business, and like many small businesses these days, hers has not been doing well. But she never understands her failure in that context. She, after all, is part of the Smith family, and Smiths are winners, not losers. She suffers in a special way, one that doesn't seek affinity with other forms of suffering and makes it seem as though to suffer or not depends on her capacity to get it wrong or get it right. She is failing, she thinks, because she isn't organized enough, isn't getting enough done during the day. In the childhood scenes to which she associated one day as we discussed this, she was a very special person by virtue of being a Smith, but there was always a particular way to be a Smith if you wanted love, and that way included wearing your hair and your shirt collars a certain way; not reading when you're supposed to be out playing with friends; in short, figuring out what it entailed to be the right kind of person. The psychic cost of living the ideology of the free individual is precisely in living this paradox: self-reliant, what common sense calls independent, but always unsure of oneself and therefore utterly dependent on the outside for clues as to how to be (a dependency consumerism is only too happy to manipulate).

On the particular day in which the enactment I report below took place, she entered saying that she was feeling very good about certain things at work; for the first time in memory, she said, she felt that she was instituting changes that were making her small business function more the way *she* wanted it to. She also reported that as she had become more hands-on in her workplace, she felt more connected to her staff. A primary focus of treatment had been in analyzing her desire to feel connected to people and her equally strong defenses against that desire. Then she reported two dreams that she had written out in a dream journal:

> *Dream #1*: She is in the backseat of a car with someone else. John Kerry is outside the car and he's in a wheelchair. She lets him into the car and wonders if she should use the opportunity to tell him what she thinks about what's going on politically.
>
> *Dream #2*: She's with a group of people and they have to flee. She's supposed to make a fire by rubbing things together and it works. She's very surprised that it has worked and feels good about herself. But the fire is going to burn everything up and she's anxious that it will all burn before she and the others figure out what they need to take with them to start over.

I asked for her associations to the first dream and asked her what she would want to tell the senator, who had recently declared his interest in running for President. She began to talk about her political opinions, that she didn't like what was going on and that she'd been annoyed with Kerry because he wasn't sufficiently critical of the Iraq war. Her wondering about whether or not she should say something to him made me associate to what we'd recently been talking about: that it was difficult for her to make herself accountable for things. A psychic dilemma we had long looked at involved her tendency either to give everything over to another, to make that other all-powerful, or to take it all on herself and be unable to ask for help. Often she felt that she was not accountable for things such as the upkeep of her house or her business; she put herself in a child position, hoping the adults would get the job done. I said something about this dilemma, but I also thought to myself that I'd like to hear more about what she wanted to tell Kerry, and when I allowed for that she began to go more deeply into what she felt about the state of the country, evincing a level of passion and a state of conviction that I rarely had glimpsed in her.

Passionlessness, an unlived life, had been her chief complaint. As she began to get more passionate, she pulled her legs up on the couch and sat cross-legged. She looked at me and hesitantly asked: can I really talk about this? I asked her why not. She wasn't sure if it was a proper therapy topic. I assured her that it was certainly a legitimate topic. I told her that I wanted to know what she was passionate about, and I could see that she felt deeply about this. As I said that, I realized I should just let her talk without jumping in with psychological interpretations, that jumping in and interrupting her experience of passion would in fact repeat her original wounds. For, in childhood, her spontaneous passions of all kinds were often found wanting and even mocked. But also, I realized that I in fact was struggling with the same question she asked: is this a therapy topic? At that moment, I didn't think that we could have explored her question further and perhaps understood more about her doubt. At that moment, I was wondering more about my own doubt. I know her politics are left of center, as are mine, and it was perhaps knowing this that made me mistakenly feel that what she was going to say was known territory, that I was just indulging my own wish to hear her bash the Bush regime and the Iraq war. She broke into my reverie when she asked if it was alright to have her feet up on the couch like that – she said she was thinking about that on the way over: is there a couch etiquette? I wasn't sure what to make of this sudden concern, but in retrospect I wonder about the meaning of the associative sequence. Does speaking about one's political convictions in therapy carry the same kind of taboo of impurity or of being uncivilized as does putting one's feet on the furniture? Was there a connection between her child-like attitude toward political responsibility and her child-like feelings about putting her feet on mommy's couch? Was she simply doing all in her power to interrupt her *own* experience of passion?

She went on to say that she would tell Kerry that she felt that everything she grew up believing about America was being taken away from her, all the values she learned, like doing unto others. She began to cry and I asked what was upsetting her. Crying more intensely, she wailed that she felt betrayed. This is a woman who rarely is able to cry in another's presence, who, in fact, has spoken many times about her longing to be able to express feelings while with me in the room.

She then brought in the second dream, associating to what she called a Jewish theme, "maybe like there was a pogrom." Her association to the fire burning was that something very bad was happening and it would be too late by the time we realized what it was. Again, I thought about what was happening to her business, which was falling apart, and felt pulled to interject something about that; but I had the sense that while her passion about what was happening politically might have had multiple psychic sources and motivations, it would be a mistake to understand what she was saying as mere displacement. In part, I did not interpret in this other frame because I shared her feelings that what the USA stood for was being rapidly dismantled; her passionate feelings of betrayal were clearly valid in their own right. I also just wanted to see where she would go next.

Still crying, she repeated, with more intensity, that everything she felt America stood for was being betrayed and she felt helpless to do anything about it. I asked her to say more about her feelings of helplessness. She said that she supposed she could write letters but she didn't write them. I asked her why not. She answered: last night she got home and her partner wanted to watch the Red Sox game and she didn't. She wanted to sit outside and read the newspaper (the day before she had told me she stopped reading the newspaper because it was too depressing). And then she talked about her partner, who was very left-wing and very voluble about it. Apparently *she'd* been writing letters. At this point, a link between the psychic and the social became clearer – in the face of her partner's very big passion, my patient's passion drained away and she detached, letting the partner carry the political feelings and political activity. My patient didn't feel quite the same as her partner on these issues, but her feeling of helplessness seemed to come from a sense that the partner owned this realm because her passion and anger were so much bigger. I thought about Bush's 70% approval rating (in that period) and wondered if she might be allowing the other side to own civic life because the other side was louder and so deaf to dissent. Again, a part of me was thinking that, like all other roads, this political road led us back to a particular psychic conflict, the one that gets in the way of her feeling like an autonomous and passionate being. Her parents were also louder, and also deaf to dissent. My first association, the one about accountability, fit into this larger repetition scenario, for she long ago had made a conscious and unconscious pact with her parents that went something like this: "I'll do as you say but then you're in charge: I refuse to take any responsibility myself for my life." And yet, again, I felt that we were both discovering something new that day, which I stated at the end:

that her passion for a certain kind of America was not a lesser passion than the ones we had been exploring, the passion to work well and to love well. Indeed, the parental interference with her autonomy and passion had led to a kind of isolationist machoism, which coexisted with a smolderingly resentful feeling of helpless passivity. All too frequently the resentment issued in acts of passive aggression. Her character style well illustrates one typical way that American ideology's unlinking of the individual and the social is psychically enacted.

The session ended with what I consider to be an enactment worth thinking about, one I'm a bit embarrassed to admit to: I told her about some political letter-writing activities on the Internet that I was aware of. She smiled and left. I think that through the session she was consistently inviting me to be larger and louder, as when she asked me about whether it was okay to talk about this, okay to put her feet up on the couch. Each time I resisted making an interpretation, I think I was resisting that pull to be larger – although I *did* give permission rather than ask why she sought it. And then at the end, in suggesting something she might do, I went large, and I am not sure why.

The next day she told me how good the day before had felt to her. She was quite surprised and a little embarrassed that her political feelings had made her cry – she didn't think that most people take these political things so personally. She'd have to describe herself as in some way an innocent, she said, and that was embarrassing. And when I asked what about the session had made her feel so good, she told me that it was because she allowed herself to follow my questions without resistance, that there was something about my encouraging her to keep speaking about it that had put her in touch with her feelings and enabled her to go on expressing them without shame. My sense was that what enabled the passion to emerge, enabled her resistance to recede, was precisely my capacity to put a muzzle on my interpretive impulse. Here was the anti-enactment: shutting up made me less large, which enabled her to come forward.

Again, what was striking to me about this hour was how hard I had to struggle to stay out of her way and simply let her feelings develop. I do not generally find myself having irresistible urges to cut in and interpret in my sessions with her. My guess is that this urgency reflected at least two things: (1) my anxiety that because I did not explore what Samuels (1993) calls the symbolic/intrapsychic/transferential aspects of my patient's speech, I wasn't being a proper analyst – had I expressed the doubts I had at the point when the patient asked if it was a proper therapy topic, we might both have unconsciously colluded with the social norm that keeps the psychic and the social separate; and (2) the sense of urgency about jumping in may well have come from an unconscious pull (hers? mine? ours?) to re-enact this patient's repetition compulsion – to quash her spontaneous gestures by finding them not quite right, to play the larger one and make her small.

This illustrates a paradox of the American version of autonomy – we are encouraged to pull ourselves up by our bootstraps, by experts who tell us how to do it (Lasch 1979)! How many of our patients come in wanting the therapist to provide the "Ten Easy Steps to Thinking for Yourself"?

In more recent work, this patient has confronted on a deeper level her tendency to see the world and its rules as adversaries that endanger her individual autonomy. She has become aware of how she passive-aggressively breaks rules in simple ways such as not paying bills on time or trying to send a package five minutes after the post office closes. When the other refuses to "cut her slack," she self-righteously positions herself as a victim. She has also confronted the way that her sense of being an individual has been based on a refusal to be part of ANY group, again because she experiences others as intruders on her autonomy. As she has become more able to feel that she can remain a self while engaged with others, as she has had less fear that she will be taken over by others, she has tentatively begun to sustain connections to others. And, most interestingly, some months after the reported vignette, this patient, who is gay, became terrifically excited by politics and made the first political gesture of her life: she sent out an email to friends and acquaintances with a copy of an article a straight woman had written about gay marriage. The writer, who was about to be married, had a gay brother, and the article revolved around her conflicted feelings about her own right to marry and the state's attempts to limit the rights of her brother. My patient noted that in the past she might have sent the article around with an introduction such as, "Here's an article you might find interesting." But this time she wrote a preamble in which she urged people to call their representatives and senators or just to intervene when they hear homophobic conversations. She spoke in that session of feeling alive, and ended the session with the statement, "I'm pumped."

Several things strike me about both this vignette and another enactment I experienced with a patient, this one about class privilege. Most striking is that at the end of each session the patient shamefully admitted, "I'm not politically active." Hollander and Gutwill (Chapter 5, this volume), from an object relations perspective, and Althusser (1971) and Žižek (for example, 1989), from a Lacanian perspective, see psychoanalysis as uniquely suited to shed light on how and why people attach to the very social forms that oppress them. In this patient's history, and in the histories of so many of my patients, a choice was made to constrict spontaneity in the face of parents who were certain they were right. This was the only way to preserve some autonomy, even if it was a form of autonomy that doomed the patients to a sense of ineptitude and helplessness. These phenomena open up two areas for further investigation concerning the relation between the psychic and the social: (1) how that sense of helplessness is transferred from the familial to the relational and then to the political realm; and (2) what it is about the society that makes so many parents absolutely certain about how things ought to be done, that makes them frightened of the otherness of their children. This is more than just a question of generational difference; I am questioning a particular way that generational difference is lived. In this form, children are mere extensions of their parents, props the parents need to accomplish psychically and socially whatever it is they feel they have failed to accomplish (Kovel 1988). The child's response of submission, on the other hand, brings about a form of "autonomy," if we can call it that, that results in attacks on the self and a conviction that failure is individual and not systemic. The continuous enactment of this unlinking norm produces narcissistic personalities, defined both by the difficulty in regulating self-esteem that Kohut (1971, 1977) theorized, and by the difficulty in establishing relations of mutuality that Benjamin (1988) theorized. In splitting the individual from the social, bourgeois ideology brings about an impoverishment of individuality in which dependence is repudiated and difference not tolerated. This dynamic leaves so many of us vulnerable to manipulation by media, government, advertising, public relations – even as we desperately try to assert our individuality and autonomy. Rather than enable people to live happier lives as "free individuals," I feel strongly that clinical theory and practice has to figure out how to re-establish the links between the psychic and the social that dominant ideologies work tirelessly to unlink. Somehow we have to find a way to allow the passion for civic life to take its rightful place beside work and love in the clinic.

References

Adorno, T. (1967) Sociology and psychology. *New Left Review*, 46:67–80.

Adorno, T. (1968) Sociology and psychology. *New Left Review*, 47:79–91.

Althusser, L. (1971) Ideology and ideological state apparatuses (notes towards an investigation). In B. Brewster (trans.), *Lenin and Philosophy and Other Essays*. New York: Monthly Review Press, pp. 127–186.

Altman, N. (1995) *The Analyst in the Inner City*. Hillsdale, NJ: The Analytic Press.

Barthes, R. (1957) *Mythologies* (A. Lavers, trans.). New York: Hill & Wang, 1972.

Benjamin, J. (1988) *The Bonds of Love*. New York: Pantheon.

Bourdieu, P. (1984) *Distinction* (R. Nice trans.). Cambridge, MA: Harvard University Press.

Brown, W. (2004) Paper presented at Radcliffe Institute for Advanced Study conference on Cultural Citizenship: Varieties of Belonging, Cambridge, MA, 20 February, 2004.

Cushman, P. (1995) *Constructing the Self, Constructing America*. Reading, MA: Addison-Wesley.

Freud, S. (1959; orig. 1922) *Group Psychology and the Analysis of the Ego*. New York: W. W. Norton.

Fromm, E. (1941) *Escape from Freedom*. New York: Holt, Rinehart & Winston.

Fromm, E. (1962) *Beyond the Chains of Illusion. My Encounter with Marx and Freud.* New York: Simon and Schuster.
Kohut, H. (1971) *The Analysis of the Self.* New York: International Universities Press.
Kohut, H. (1977) *The Restoration of the Self.* New York: International Universities Press.
Kovel, J. (1988) *The Radical Spirit.* London: Free Association.
Lasch, C. (1977) *Haven in a Heartless World. The Family Besieged.* New York: Basic Books.
Lasch, C. (1979) *The Culture of Narcissism.* New York: W. W. Norton.
Layton, L. (1998) *Who's That Girl? Who's That Boy? Clinical Practice Meets Postmodern Gender Theory.* Hillsdale, NJ: The Analytic Press, 2004.
Layton, L. (2002) Cultural hierarchies, splitting, and the heterosexist unconscious. In S. Fairfield, L. Layton, and C. Stack (eds), *Bringing the Plague. Toward a Postmodern Psychoanalysis.* New York: Other Press, pp. 195–223.
Layton, L. (2004a) A fork in the royal road: on defining the unconscious and its stakes for social theory. *Psychoanalysis, Culture & Society*, 9(1):33–51.
Layton, L. (2004b) Relational no more: defensive autonomy in middle-class women. In J. A. Winer, J. W. Anderson, and C. C. Kieffer (eds), *The Annual of Psychoanalysis Volume XXXII. Psychoanalysis and Women.* Hillsdale, NJ: The Analytic Press, pp. 29–42.
Layton, L. (2005) Notes toward a non-conformist clinical practice. Paper presented at the Spring Meetings, Division 39, American Psychological Association, New York, 14 April, 2005.
Layton, L. (in press) Racial identities, racial enactments, and normative unconscious processes. *Psychoanalytic Quarterly.*
Samuels, A. (1993) *The Political Psyche.* New York: Routledge.
Žižek, S. (1989) *The Sublime Object of Ideology.* London: Verso.
Žižek, S. (1994) How did Marx invent the symptom? In S. Žižek (ed.), *Mapping Ideology.* London: Verso, pp. 296–331.

Chapter 8

The normative unconscious and the political contexts of change in psychotherapy

Gary Walls

I would like to elaborate Lynne Layton's concept of the normative unconscious, particularly the norm to unlink the individual from his or her social context. She calls this the unlinking norm and relates this to psychotherapy's role in the reproduction of the social values of the dominant groups in society (Chapter 7, this volume). As therapists we at times unconsciously operate to maintain prevailing social norms in the commission of our roles as defined by the social institutions to which we belong. Our training teaches us how to conduct treatments in ways that convey the social values that are embedded in psychotherapy as a culturally defined process of healing. In the case of psychoanalytic therapy, the norms that implicitly structure our activity are individualistic and quasi-medical. We usually do not reflect on the normative aspects of our work that are derived from society's ideological underpinnings: these normative assumptions are taken for granted as the very ground of our work; they are our marching orders, our commission as psychological healers in contemporary American culture.

As Layton argues, one particularly important norm in our culture is to unlink the personal from the political. This norm locates psychotherapy within the health care industry and defines emotional suffering as the result of defects or deficiencies in the psychological functioning of the individual person. In the fundamental realms of both love and work, Freud's original dimensions of emotional health and illness, the individual is viewed in terms of adaptation to a fixed and unquestioned societal, economic and political environment. Since the societal context is excluded from consideration, most contemporary American psychotherapists construe the meaning of psychological problems as if they could be understood and resolved by addressing only variables operating within individuals and in their personal relationships. This framework constitutes the unlinking of personal from societal contexts in psychotherapy, and it operates in the ways we define our therapeutic task as well as in the way patients define their own suffering.

A female patient who has aspirations to be the CEO of a large corporation provides an illustration of such an unlinking. Her personal aspiration is supported by the political idea that in America one can become anything one wants to be if one works hard enough to achieve it. However, the split-off and contradictory political reality is captured in the fact that in December 2003, not a single one of the 50 biggest corporations in the Chicago metropolitan area had a woman as CEO. Often a belief in a politically normative idea (in this case, one that forms the basis of a personal aspiration) requires a person to keep the awareness of a political reality out of consciousness. How do we as therapists address the splitting off of awareness of such political realities when we see it as contributing to our patients' depression, anxiety, low self-esteem, and other psychological symptoms?

Unconscious ideas, such as the unlinking norm, may operate as mechanisms of a culture's dominant ideology to produce and maintain political, social and economic inequalities. A relevant definition of an ideology is "a system of practices and representations that produce, maintain and reproduce social relations of domination" (Sloan 1996:101). This defines ideology as non-neutral to show that it may operate to structure society in ways that serve some individuals at the expense of others, typically while denying or obscuring the fact that it is doing so. Every culture has particular sets of ideas that may be regarded as dominant, in that they serve the dominant classes of that society, and that are also generally acknowledged as defining the mainstream of the society as opposed to marginal currents (Layton 2002). One way a dominant ideology works is to present an idealized value as representative of the society, while submerging any antisocial implications of the ideal in an unconscious element of the norm. As one aspect of the dominant ideology of American individualism, the unlinking norm presents individual freedom and responsibility as conscious idealized values, while submerging awareness of the relationships of dominance and exploitation that such an unregulated, competitive and anti-communal society requires (Walls 2004). The question then becomes: do we want to practice a psychoanalysis that is itself a form of ideology, in that it enforces a norm to maintain the unlinking of the awareness of the individual from his or her social context, an unlinking that is manifestly operating in the service of obscuring relations of domination? Or do we want to practice a psychoanalysis that is committed to a process of making the unconscious conscious, including the political unconscious, when doing so may ameliorate our patients' suffering?

Andrew Samuels (1993) advocates that we include the political as a legitimate topic of psychotherapy. But Samuels' characterization of the political falls prey to a common flaw in thinking about the political that is itself a product of the unlinking of the individual and the political: he depersonalizes the political by taking it to be an entity. The political is not a thing, an entity. A political system is, as Charlton Heston's character in the 1973 movie *Soylent Green* cries, ". . . people! It's PEEEEOPLE!!!" Samuels obscures the fact that all social arrangements, including political ones, are acts of living people that take place entirely within the medium of everyday relationships. Political acts may be legitimated under the cover of enshrined historical documents, robed dignitaries, and shared unconscious norms, but all political acts are the responsibility of human actors and take place in the present.

I am not trying to reduce political processes to the intrapsychic determinants of public figures, nor am I trying to argue that political processes can be understood in the same dynamic terms as we understand psychological processes. I am concerned with the relationship of the psyche and the social, the individual and the political, as they constitute and co-determine one another. As the outcome of these co-determinations sometimes results in individual personal suffering, we are called upon as therapists to address the question of how we can understand and address this suffering therapeutically.

Psychoanalysis works, in part, by making unconscious processes conscious and thereby open to greater freedom and choice for the individual. As long as forces of which we are pointedly not aware determine our behavior, our ability to choose our course of action is pre-empted. In the case of politically unconscious material, particularly the unconscious norm to unlink the meaningful connections between the individual and the social, we have every reason to believe that what is at stake is some form of domination or exploitation that is maintained by the disavowal that it is taking place. Further, it is clear that the patient unconsciously has some stake in colluding in the disavowal. One may reasonably surmise that patients' motivation to collude in their own oppression is almost always some version of fear, although other motivations, such as guilt, or self-sacrifice for a loved one, may also enter the picture.

The interesting thing about the psychoanalytic situation is that in the United States, for so many decades, patients and analysts have tacitly agreed to the exclusion of the political context from the therapeutic agenda (Jacoby 1983). Both parties have behaved as if the therapeutic and the political context were unlinked. Perhaps this is due to the preponderance of privileged patients in our caseloads, who may have had less to gain by contextualizing their problems in relation to the political system. Perhaps one reason that working class, poor, and minorities have sought out analysis so infrequently is that they sense that doing so will fail to address the systemic sources of their misery. But for me it has been striking that even though my patients have occasionally mentioned political topics, virtually none has ever spontaneously raised the political context as a topic relevant to the suffering that brought them to therapy.

How is it that intelligent, sophisticated adults uniformly seem to know, without being told, that their psychoanalytic session is no place to discuss their relationship to the political world? How is the unlinking norm established? Robert Coles is an analyst who has studied the political life of children (Coles 1986). Just as Freud undercut the popular assumption that children have no sexual lives, so Robert Coles undercut the idea that they have no political lives. His research counters the assumption that children's political views are empty echoes of what they have heard their parents or teachers say.

Political socialization, including the internalization of the unlinking norm, takes place not only within families ("never discuss politics, sex or religion"), but in extrafamilial contexts as well. Subliminal political messages are conveyed by the display of flags, political speeches, the visible idealization by adults of powerful public figures, the celebration of the 4th of July, military memorials, the Pledge of Allegiance, etc., all of which instill not only the content of acceptable political attitudes, but the implicit idea that this, and nothing else, is what the very idea of being an American is. Think of the sentiment induced by the image of a two-year-old sitting on a curb waving a tiny American flag as the 4th of July parade goes by. Such versions of patriotism induce unreflective loyalty to one's political system, and convey the norm that questioning the social order to which one belongs is wrong. Patriotic messages teach us that questioning the terms of anyone's place in the social system is an act of disloyalty. The unlinking norm asserts that the fate of the individual is in no way the consequence of the organization of society, and establishes our adherence to disregarding the contradictions between our own best interests and the requirements of the dominant groups, by whom and in whose interests society is primarily organized.

While children do learn political views by identification and imitation, they also can, at an early age, say six to ten years old, recognize lies, hypocrisy, and contradictions (Coles 1986). Children who are members of oppressed or disadvantaged groups become more critically aware of the realities of their political situation earlier than children of the privileged. As Coles discovered in his conversations with many children, children of the poor and oppressed minorities are more likely to have direct encounters with the coercive power of the state, such as the county sheriff or the beat cop, than more affluent children. They are also more likely to be confronted with obvious, painful discrepancies between their own lives and the public images of American society that are presented in school and the media. However, both privileged and poor children learn political skepticism by observation at an earlier age than is popularly believed.

Children also learn something else at an early age: it is not safe to express your political thoughts and feelings openly if you are going to be critical of the *status quo*. The early attainment of political awareness by children, and their almost simultaneous recognition of the dangerousness of the open expression of political dissent, has something to do, I think, with the fact that our patients rarely raise politics as a context for the problems that brought them to therapy. Granted, if they realized that their problems were related to their position in the political system, they probably also would recognize the likely helplessness of their analyst to do anything about it (for an interesting and relevant exception, see Ruth Fallenbaum's (2003) essay "The injured worker," in which she intervenes with her congressional representative on behalf of a patient, to secure her Worker's Compensation benefits). But ultimately, the efficacy of a psychoanalytic understanding of our patients' problems depends on the relevance of unconscious factors in their formation and maintenance, not on the analyst's power to solve the problem directly, politically or otherwise. By the time they become analytic patients, the unlinking norm guards against the direct emergence of these political elements into the psychoanalytic dialogue, and so we are left to interpret the derivatives of politically unconscious material against a different kind of resistance.

The development of a political unconscious is a socialization process, not unlike the development of the Freudian unconscious. Sexual drives are not primordially unconscious, but become unconscious precisely as a response to the suppression of sexuality by society. It is psychologically unsustainable to maintain sexual thoughts, images, and impulses in consciousness that, if expressed outwardly, would result in public rejection, shaming, or humiliation. In order to minimize the experience of anxiety, social suppression is internalized by the ego as sexual repression. Like all effective defensive maneuvers, the repressive function itself is unconscious. In a parallel way, politically dangerous thoughts and impulses are first suppressed, then internalized and dissociated. The fact that the political unconscious is dissociated rather than repressed is evidenced by the fact that we are not amnesiac for the material, but that it usually remains split off from our personal/relational consciousness. As Stern (1997) has argued, anxiety-provoking experiences tend to be experienced indistinctly and to a large degree remain unformulated, and so are more readily forgotten or dissociated.

Within dissociated realms of experience, we tend to alternate between different states of consciousness with access to conflicting experiences of reality. We can readily see this in the biting cynicism about government that people will at times express, alternating with feelings of intense patriotism when the situation calls for it. The mechanism of dissociation, in contrast to repression, is seen as the ego's way of managing awareness of overwhelming threats of violence, and is prevalent among victims of physical and sexual abuse, for example (Davies and Frawley 1994). Dissociation seems to be regularly employed as the psyche's defense against fears of violence of one kind or another, while repression is more often used as a defense against sexual and social shame or guilt. Not surprisingly, given the violent, traumatic nature of many political activities and feelings (war, imprisonment, economic impoverishment, police brutality, the rage of the oppressed, the hatred directed at political figures), the political unconscious is maintained by dissociation rather than the more stable and centrally organized mechanism of repression. The ego maintains dissociation in the usual ways, including avoidance of material that would invoke the feared situation, as well as the mobilization of signal anxiety to provide vigilance for danger situations, so that awareness is never approached. But like other dissociated states, split-off threats are also managed by more primitive ancillary defenses, such as denial, projection, projective identification, idealization and devaluation, and grandiosity. Chronically dissociated states become organized around quasi-independent self-systems (Davies and Frawley 1994), and may not participate in the maturational processes that accompany the interactions of the more centralized self-system with day-to-day realities. The idea that political development for most people has been split off from other psychological maturational processes may partly account for the irrational, polarized, overly intense, and often childlike and immature qualities we associate with so much of the political thinking and activities that we see or read about.

Freud provided many examples of how sexual repression worked, and he used everyday situations that we all could relate to in *The Psychopathology of Everyday Life* (1922) to convey his ideas experientially.

One everyday example of political dissociation that I think everyone can relate to is the following. I don't fly very often, but when I do, I often suffer a breakdown in my political awareness barrier. Now I regard this as an idiosyncratic symptom of mine, but nonetheless it may evoke some hint of recognition in even the healthiest of citizens. I was walking onto the plane with my six-year-old daughter, and we were making our way toward our seats in row 16. On the way, we had to walk past the three rows of seats in the first-class section: you know, the wider seats with the people about to receive their complimentary cocktails. My daughter asked me, "Are these our seats?" I found myself barely able to suppress an explanation that would have gone like this: "No, honey, our seats are farther back. These seats are the seats that only rich people are allowed to sit in. Or for people who are in charge of flying around the country to get more money for rich people." I just know she would have asked "Why?" And I imagined myself explaining "Honey, in our country, people who have more money are believed to deserve nicer things than people who have less money, even if they didn't do anything themselves to earn that money." But I experienced a sudden burst of signal anxiety, and instead I said only, "No, honey, our seats are down there a little ways," with no explanation at all. Even so, I didn't get away with that self-indulgent political fantasy scot-free. Along with the anxiety at being aware of my bout of near-impulsiveness, I began to have images of myself being asked by the flight attendants to please deplane, where I would be interrogated by Homeland Security Personnel, followed naturally by scandal, unemployment, prison, etc., etc. To this day, I don't know how much of that fantasy of political retribution is neurotic. I had another set of feelings as well, including a sense of guilt, shame and inadequacy for my cowardice in once again saying nothing about a situation of injustice, and, in effect, serving as the agent for socializing my daughter to accept without question the unjust economic inequality of first-class seating.

My point is that the unlinking norm is part of what allows us to adapt and accommodate to an unjust society with less anxiety than if we were aware of our complicity or our dissent. In the above example, the unlinking norm was no longer operating to exclude the connections between our class position and the system of airline seat assignments, and so I experienced anger, envy, anxiety, and guilt that most people usually do not in that situation.

Our norms of separating individual from societal context are nearly ubiquitous in our everyday experience and therefore, not surprisingly, also a feature of the psychoanalytic situation. The rub comes from the conjunction of two points in our work: first, as analysts we are committed to ameliorating suffering by addressing its fundamental psychological causes. Second, we espouse as our method the uncovering of unconscious determinants, especially the unconscious determinants of unbalanced or unhealthy relationships. If we agree that political domination is the source of significant amounts of our patients' suffering, and we realize that part of what reproduces that pain is the fact that it remains unconscious, then how are we to rationalize our complicity in ignoring it? Samuels is right; we must address the political dimension with our patients in psychoanalytic psychotherapy.

The reason we usually do not is the silent operation of the internalized unlinking norm. However, once we become aware of our defensive avoidance of the political implications of our patients' clinical situation, we find ourselves in a similar spot to mine on the airplane. We consciously feel the political conflict and the pressure to conform to a socially sanctioned norm. We are made to feel it is inappropriate to address the issues, and our fears of social reprisal if we do are based in at least a partially realistic assessment of the social situation.

The reason we conform to the unlinking norm is to avoid an external clash with people more powerful than ourselves. It is the mechanism of a Pax Americana, maintaining a permanent truce in the class war that allows us safely and passively to enjoy whatever is our allotment of satisfaction within a consumer society organized by relations of dominance and exploitation between different economic classes. When we make interpretations to our patients that connect their depression, or low self-esteem, or anxiety, or chronic rage to an actual set of unequal, exploitive power relationships on which they depend, it threatens to undermine the dissociation of those feelings, ideas, and impulses, and our patients may become more anxious, uncomfortable, angry, and perhaps more likely to express their dissatisfaction outwardly. This, I think, could be a good thing, but it is also easy to see why it is avoided. During the civil rights protests of the 1950s and 1960s, much was accomplished, but many were killed, or fired, or suffered ostracizing or other very real destruction to their network of social relations. Psychoanalysis that engages at the societal level will quickly reach the political, and this is not always a quiet, non-violent realm.

However, be that as it may, I have over the past several years cautiously, and usually with some trepidation, addressed the social/political context with my patients in psychoanalytic therapy, and I would like briefly to describe one of those patients. Roger is a 43-year-old attorney whom I have seen for many years for severe depression, as well as for the emotional distress and the interpersonal conflicts that attend a narcissistic personality disorder. During twice-weekly psychoanalytic therapy Roger made progress in many ways, both in his career and in his intimate relationships. In fact, he terminated therapy after about 10 years because he was no longer depressed, he was successful in his career, and he had formed a stable, loving relationship.

Four years later he returned, with a reappearance of depressive symptoms. He related this to changes in his career. He did not know why, but he had become extremely unsatisfied in his work. He hated his law firm, which was always pressing him to increase his billable hours, while giving him less than stellar reviews because he left the office at six and rarely came in on weekends. Because of this, he felt angry but also inadequate: he had never been able to generate the billing that other partners he knew were able to do. He hated his boss, who he felt was a selfish and domineering egomaniac. He also felt inadequate and resentful because his clients were very demanding, and more and more, it seemed, insisted on same-day service, with the implied or expressed threat of taking their business elsewhere. Even though he was a partner in the firm, respected in his field, and making more money than he ever had, he felt unhappy, unfulfilled, resentful, and depressed.

Roger went around in circles describing his complaints. We revisited the family dynamics that he had struggled with the last time he was in therapy. Yes, they were playing a role here again, no doubt. But that was not all there was to it. So with some trepidation I initiated a series of interpretations that connected his individual struggles with a bigger social context. I told him that in many professions in America, things were changing. When he first trained as a lawyer, a law firm was a partnership of professional lawyers. Like physicians, lawyers had professional ethics and standards of practice, which were something like the Hippocratic Oath. Although law firms were businesses, they were seen as a special kind of business that followed ethically more rigorous standards than, for example, retail stores. Law services were not something to be advertised in order to create a demand for lawyers, or thought of as commodities to be shaped to accommodate the tastes of the consumer. The fact that they were regarded as officers of the court meant that their primary allegiance was to a system of laws and to principles of justice rather than to customer satisfaction. Clients were not always right. In addition, lawyers determined to a significant degree the conditions of their work. They, not their clients, were considered competent to determine how much time a matter required, and obliged to perform up to professional standards that clients were entitled to expect, but generally not qualified to judge. If a lawyer's professional opinion displeased the clients, well, that meant the clients had to alter their plans in accord with the professional advice they received, because the lawyer was considered to be an expert.

Much had changed over the previous 10 years, and it struck me that while Roger connected these changes to his increasing dissatisfaction with his work, his eroding self-esteem, and his burgeoning depression, he did not see how these changes were the expression of broader political changes in American society. Law firms were being transformed into corporate structures that were run more like other corporations and less like traditional law firms. Partners were no longer really partners except in title; they were really employees of the corporation. They no longer had much control over the conditions of their work. Roger was pressured to respond to rush jobs on a routine basis, no matter how long he felt it would take to research a legal matter properly. He was forced to prioritize clients by how much business they represented rather than how truly urgent their problem was, or who requested service first. He was expected to act as salesman to drum up additional business from existing clients, in other words to sell law services like any other service commodity. His firm began to design advertising posters intended for the washrooms of upscale restaurants and bars. This offended Roger, who said that one of the main reasons he became a lawyer was that he didn't want to have to sell anything, which to him felt somehow debasing and shameful. And his opinion was no longer respected, as legal opinions in general no longer carried the authority with clients that they once did: if an important client who represented a substantial revenue stream wanted legal advice as to their liability in a project, it became Roger's job to devise legal cover for whatever they wanted to do, rather than to advise them against it.

I did not find it difficult to understand the sources for a significant portion of Roger's distress. I began a dialog during his sessions, making the connections I have described above. As Roger came to understand the changing structure of the practice of law in a large law firm, and its relationship to the broader political changes taking place in the USA, he did not become less dissatisfied, but he did become less depressed. His feelings of conflict with his superiors at work intensified, and he entertained fantasies of confrontation, which he by and large managed to avoid. He came to realize that if he wished to practice law according to his own values, he would have to give up the security and other benefits of a large law firm. Over the course of about two years, he first changed to a different, smaller law firm in which he would have more autonomy, but eventually realized that even this firm was being forced to adapt to the new corporate environment for the practice of law. Eventually, he left that law firm too, and he has set up an independent practice. He is currently considering a change in career altogether.

For me, this case illustrates the need to understand a patient's symptoms in a political context. Roger's symptoms were a reaction to political developments in society (the corporate takeover of law firms and the consequent commoditization of professional services) that were invalidating his identity and some of the values in which he had invested in becoming a lawyer. I don't believe he was wrong to resist changing along with the field of law. To maintain a feeling of integrity in his response to the changes in the way law was practiced in his firm, Roger needed to examine his political values and increase his awareness of the political and economic realities of the world in which lawyers now practice.

For Freud, the formation of psychological symptoms and their meanings could be fully understood in a system in which the dynamics of instinctual desires and the interactions within family relationships varied, but the cultural and political contexts were regarded as fixed and universal. This worked for him because his patients lived in a social context that varied across a narrow political and cultural range in nineteenth-century middle- and upper-class Vienna and Europe. We now realize that a therapeutic approach that assumes a fixed and universal societal context results in therapy that includes unacceptable elements of indoctrination based on dominant ideologies, much of which is conveyed unconsciously – Layton's normative unconscious. We need to develop theories of therapeutic process that include societal contexts as co-determinative of the meanings of psychological symptoms. Žižek (1989), for one, has discussed a parallel in Marx's theory, as interpreted by Lacan, to Freud's theory of symptom formation. From this perspective, psychological symptoms are created when irrational elements (internal contradictions) in the ways society is organized are rationalized ideologically (disavowed) in order to cover the conflict of interests involved. The disavowed societal conflicts create a fissure in the consciousness of its citizens that holds at bay the eruption of interpersonal disputes over the conflicts of interest. Instead, individuals internalize the conflict as a split in their own political awareness. The unlinking norm (the unconscious demand to unlink the individual and the societal) is a name for the societal force that motivates this fissure. When the relations of domination and servitude are dissociated, they re-emerge as symptoms, such as depression, anxiety disorders, alienation, anomy, narcissism. In this way of thinking, the psychoanalytic model is extended from a theory of symptoms that represent compromise formations expressing/disguising unconscious instinctual or relational conflicts, to a theory of how psychological symptoms may express/disguise unconscious societal and political conflicts. Such an extension expands the power and reach, but also the risks, of engaging in psychoanalytic therapy for both the patient and the analyst.

References

Bourdieu, P. (1984) *Distinction* (Richard Nice, trans.). Cambridge, MA: Harvard University Press.

Coles, R. (1986) *The Political Lives of Children*. New York: The Atlantic Monthly Press.

Davies, J. and Frawley, M. (1994) *Treating the Adult Survivor of Childhood Sexual Abuse*. New York: Basic Books.

Fallenbaum, R. (2003) The injured worker. *Studies in Gender and Sexuality*, 4:72–92.

Freud, S. (1922) *The Psychopathology of Everyday Life*. New York: W. W. Norton, 1960.

Fromm, E. (1962) *Beyond the Chains of Illusion. My Encounter with Marx and Freud*. New York: Simon and Schuster.

Jacoby, R. (1983) *The Repression of Psychoanalysis: Otto Fenichel and the Political Freudians*. New York: Basic Books.

Layton, L. (2002) Cultural hierarchies, splitting, and the heterosexist unconscious. In S. Fairfield, L. Layton, and C. Stack (eds), *Bringing the Plague. Toward a Postmodern Psychoanalysis*. New York: Other Press, pp. 195–223.

Samuels, A. (1993) *The Political Psyche*. New York and London: Routledge.

Seltzer, W., Thacher, R. (Producers), and Fleischer, R. (Director) (1973) *Soylent Green* [Motion picture]. USA: Metro-Goldwyn-Mayer.

Sloan, T. (1996) *Damaged Life*. New York: Routledge.

Stern, Donnel (1997) *Unformulated Experience: From Dissociation to Imagination in Psychoanalysis*. Hillsdale, NJ: The Analytic Press.

Walls, G. (2004) Toward a critical global psychoanalysis. *Psychoanalytic Dialogues*, 14:605–634.

Žižek, S. (1989) *The Sublime Object of Ideology*. London: Verso.

Chapter 9

Racism, classism, psychosis and self-image in the analysis of a woman

Gary Walls

I am going to describe a patient to you that I have been seeing in therapy for over 10 years, usually two or three times a week. This patient, whom I will call Maggie, came to me as a 34-year-old single woman, identified racially as black. She had suffered a psychotic break four years previously after a period of unemployment in an eastern city. She had returned to her childhood home in a Midwestern city and was admitted to a psychiatric hospital, where she was given the diagnosis of "schizoaffective disorder," and her condition was stabilized with medications. Following this brief inpatient treatment, Maggie was discharged, and referred to a day hospital program, where she received psychoanalytically oriented group and individual therapies for the next four years. After making much progress in this program, she was referred to me for continuing outpatient therapy.

This patient is interesting, I think, because she is outside of the usual patient parameters for treatment by outpatient psychoanalytic psychotherapy, for several reasons. Two of the most obvious are that she is socially identified and self-identified as racially black, and she presented with serious psychotic symptoms. The conventional wisdom is that psychoanalysis is not culturally appropriate for members of culturally marginalized groups, since it is the product of Western European culture. There is much merit to this criticism, not because there is something lacking in the cultural preparation of identified members of subjugated populations but because psychoanalytic theory contains embedded racist and classist elements within its structure (Dalal 2002). However, contemporary psychoanalytic approaches attempt to broaden their application by viewing all emotional disorders within the particular societal contexts of the patient. Also, many have come to regard psychoanalytic therapy as not appropriate to treat psychotic symptoms, which are regarded more and more by the mainstreams of psychiatry and psychology as biologically determined symptoms. The results of this case challenge both of these beliefs.

In this paper I will eschew the use of conventional racist and classist categories. Following Dalal and others, I regard race, ethnicity, class, and other such categories to be socially constructed for the purpose of making distinctions between the haves and must-not-haves. The continued use of such categories perpetuates the idea that the groups they seem to define actually exist as coherent, bounded entities, which they do not. Race is not the biological grouping it is purported by some to be, and instead is socially constructed in ways that render it not meaningfully distinguishable from the constructions of class, culture, and ethnicity. The use of such categories as "black" or "African-American" inevitably racializes any discourse that contains them, and tends to serve the ideological function of maintaining dominating and exploitive power relations between such groups and the dominant classes. I will, however, use the words "racism" and "classism," because these words describe activities pertaining to domination and exploitation that do exist even as the group categories on which they are putatively based do not.

I would like to discuss this case with an emphasis on certain aspects that are usually relegated to the background, if they are mentioned at all, namely the political and societal environments in which Maggie developed her sense of self. I think doing so makes a difference because when these aspects are viewed as merely background, it results in an underestimate and a misunderstanding of how integral these contexts are to the emotional disorders that we are called upon to treat. It is well known that in the United States, people assigned to racialized categories are diagnosed with mental disorders at a much higher rate than people identified with dominant groups. Even when this is not frankly attributed to racialized genetic causes, it is usually understood as a by-product of the fact that the oppressed are also more often raised in economically, educationally, and emotionally impoverished environments secondary to their lack of success and affluence within the larger society. While I do not discount these ideas, they tend to blame the victims, and I feel they do not adequately grasp the specific psychological experiences of being a dominated, devalued, exploited person, and the ways this contributes to the forms of emotional disorder from which many subjugated people suffer. The conventional wisdom reduces to a version of diathesis-stress theory, in which subjugated people suffer from the same mental disorders as the privileged do, but in greater frequency because of the greater stresses to which they are subjected. I don't think this is the case: I think that subjugated people suffer from mental illnesses that are significantly different and that are partly shaped and determined by politically specific factors.

Before I go into more detail about the particulars of Maggie's case, I would like to convey an idea of how I understand the relationship of the political context to the individual's experience of emotional disorder. If we are going to take seriously the influence of societal factors in psychological "illness" then we must go beyond regarding these factors as a superficial or secondary overlay. As Clifford Geertz has written, the biological evolution of human beings required adaptation to a cultural as well as the natural environment at least for the last one million years of biological evolution. We have thereby acquired a "social brain," within which all meaningful mental activity is structured by the internalization of cultural experiences. Geertz wrote, "A cultureless human being would probably turn out to be not an intrinsically talented, though unfulfilled ape, but a wholly mindless and consequently unworkable monstrosity" (1973:68). In this fundamental sense, culture cannot be seen as an overlay of basic mental functioning, but as a necessary constituent of the mental structure of every person, including the structures of mental disorders. Considering this, we can see how the medical model or even traditional psychoanalytic models fall short in failing to incorporate cultural and political experiences in any fundamental way in their understanding of mental disorders.

Since the topic is so large, I hope only to point in the direction of what I have in mind, and to utilize the work that Maggie and I have done to illustrate a radically different way of conceptualizing psychotic disturbances. W. E. B. Du Bois (1903) wrote about what he called the "double consciousness" and "the veil" through which all people racialized as black are required to experience themselves. As we all know, many subjugated people from Africa became part of American society originally as slaves, as property, and the legacy of violence, cruelty, and inhumanity of this form of inclusion in our culture is still manifest in the continuing necessity for this double consciousness. The formation of this double consciousness is a result of the need for protection against various forms of violence, exploitation, and victimization that began as the horror we know as slavery, but survived in various other historical forms, including Jim Crow, segregation, job discrimination, stereotyped devaluation, depersonalization, and the other more often covert and disavowed forms of racism that persist today. Double consciousness refers to the mental strategy of viewing oneself through the eyes of one's oppressor. This is one of the psychological effects of a dominant ideology on the people it oppresses: it is dangerous not to internalize the dominant ideologies' definitions of who you are, because those in power will feel threatened if you present yourself in any other way; for example, as an equal. But to maintain a sense of sanity and self-respect, one also must maintain a separate non-racialized definition of who one is, and this constitutes an effortful and dysphoric (conflictual) double consciousness, one not shared by people assigned to the dominant groups. Du Bois said the following about the psychological effects of double consciousness:

> With this come . . . peculiar problems of their inner life . . . From the double life every American Negro must live . . . must arise a painful self-consciousness, an almost morbid sense of personality and moral hesitancy which is fatal to self-confidence . . . and this must produce a

> peculiar sense of doubt and bewilderment . . . and tempt the mind to pretence or to revolt, to hypocrisy or to radicalism.
>
> (Du Bois 1903:xx–xxi)

In other words, the development of "double consciousness" can be considered a form of self-protective but also self-limiting social adaptation imposed by the violence of racism. This has striking affinities to the psychological splitting seen in survivors of sexual abuse, particularly the double consciousness they manifest in the silent day-time disavowal of the night-time realities. Such disavowal hides the crimes of their abusers and masks their own suffering in order to preserve the relationships they depend upon for emotional and physical survival.

Having set the stage, let me return to Maggie. Her mother, Flo, was born in a small town in the Midwest, one of three sisters, and she describes her grandparents as very poor. They ran a boarding house that catered to transient men as they were passing through town. The family was not only poor but, as Flo described it, disreputable, with gambling and liquor in the house. Flo became very sensitive to what others thought of her, to appearances, differences in class, and the power of money.

Flo's biological father was not her mother's husband, but a white farmer from a nearby town. Her mother's husband had collaborated in getting his wife and the farmer together, in hopes of financial gain, although no gain ever came of it. Still, the parents raised Maggie's mother as their own. Graduating from high school in the top 10% of her class, she qualified for a scholarship to the University of Illinois. However, in the 1940s, the campus at Champaign-Urbana was segregated, and Flo felt that she would not be able to afford the clothes that would allow her to be accepted on the terms she needed, and so she decided to move to Chicago and get a job. Not having attended college was a decision that Flo later came greatly to regret.

Maggie's father, Ned, was also born in a small town, an only child. Ned's father worked hard in various jobs – as a waiter and in factories. His mother worked as a "shampoo lady" in hair salons. The family moved to the big city when he was in high school. As an adult, he remained close to both parents. Maggie describes him as more like his mother, even though they didn't get along, and he felt he could never please her. When Ned's mother was older, she developed paranoid delusions. Ned's father was more supportive: he frequently helped him out in one way or another, and they sometimes lived together after Ned was an adult.

Maggie's father was rarely home when she was growing up, as he was in the Navy. She remembers his frequent comings and goings, and her "whining and complaining" to convince him to stop leaving her. Eventually, she learned to cut herself off from those feelings of longing for her father. At age 13, Maggie decided she wanted to get closer to him. However, when she tried to, he responded by making sexual advances, and she withdrew. She told her mother about the transgression, but Flo remained silent and did not address the issue. Later, Ned made sexual advances to both daughters, and while Maggie left the room when he did this, her twin sister Miriam remained. Maggie feels some envy that her sister was able to establish a closer relationship to her father, but she also knows she paid a high emotional price for that closeness. Maggie's father died several years into her treatment with me, and only a month after his own father had died at the age of 102.

During the first two years she spent in the day hospital program, Maggie was quite withdrawn, said very little in her group therapy, and was only somewhat more open in her individual therapy. However, an extraordinarily painful history emerged during her day hospital treatment that she elaborated on in her outpatient therapy, and that was clearly related to her breakdown and to her specific psychotic symptoms. Maggie was born a twin, though Miriam was not identical. In fact, unlike her sister, Maggie was born with a cleft lip that extended to involve severe disfigurement of her nose. This facial deformity became a center of focus in that it defined her as the damaged twin, and her mother added to the trauma inflicted on her self-image by telling her that she believed that the deformity was punishment for her (the mother's) sins. This left Maggie in the painful position of feeling her deformity was a source of pain for her mother, and feeling as well that she herself somehow deserved such punishment.

In an effort to correct the deformity, but in a way that also led to further emotional trauma, Maggie was subjected to multiple facial surgeries that occurred nearly every summer until she was eight years old. When she was in the waiting room of her plastic surgeon, Maggie would be surrounded by many patients with deformities much more severe than her own, but she often felt this was the world of "freaks" to which she belonged. Her mother told her at the time that the surgeon who repaired her face also performed sex change operations on transsexuals, and she remembers that this, too, disturbed her very much. At home, Maggie felt there was much emphasis on appearing "polished" on the outside, rather than being judged based on what is "inside."

As she grew older, Maggie maintained a close but conflicted relationship to her mother. She describes her mother as intrusive, controlling, and critical, involved but perhaps over-involved in her and her sister's lives. Her religious beliefs seemed superstitious, and she expressed magical ideas about God's role in everyday life, but she did not push religion on her daughters. She worked as a secretary/receptionist for a university Dean, and developed aspirations that her daughters would someday become educated professionals like the one she worked for. She pushed them to achieve academically, and they did, both attending an elite college on the east coast.

Maggie worked in a city on the east coast for several years after graduating from college, also earning a Master's degree along the way. She was happy in her work, but she worked long hours, and most of her social life revolved around her colleagues at the job. Realizing that her personal life was failing to progress, and troubled by the fact that she was frightened of men and of sex, she began seeing a therapist once a week. In retrospect, she realizes that she never really opened up enough to that therapist to receive the help she needed.

The trouble that led to her breakdown began when she was fired during a downsizing at her company. On the one hand, losing her regular social interactions at work left her socially isolated. On the other, she became emotionally involved with a man who was himself seriously depressed and who, following the death of his mother, developed religious delusions and hallucinations of the voices of angels and of Jesus. In the process of seeking and providing support in this relationship, Maggie became drawn into a world of religiously tinged delusions. As this relationship became filled with fear and disintegrated, she began to experience frightening hallucinations: when she looked into the mirror, it looked as if large scabs were forming on her face, and she saw different colors, like pieces of shredded orange, flying out of her face. A large ugly nose took up an entire corner of her apartment, and her scabs spread to cover the ceiling. Following this, she began to hear voices, soothing and comforting at first, but then turning critical and punitive. Finally, her life in ruins and alone, she confessed to her sister what she was going through, and returned to her hometown where she began her treatment.

It is important to note that this is a young woman who went away to school, did well, and did not decompensate. She also went overseas to study for her junior year and did not decompensate. She was academically successful and socially active, although she avoided dating and was frightened of sexual involvements. At the same time, her struggles were not new: her mother told her that she remembers that Maggie first heard voices when she was praying at the age of 14. There is a continuity in this woman's symptoms that frames their meaning across the entire span of her life, but which does not easily fit into conventional formulas for the development of schizophrenic illness.

The processes of splitting in Maggie's personality are apparent. On the one hand, they enabled her to partition off thoughts and feelings that might be overwhelming to her and therefore prevent her from functioning and finding success in the world. On the other, the lacunae in her awareness of her own inner life that these splits created for her also made her feel incomplete, unfulfilled, and avoidant of areas of living that she recognized were too limiting. When the splitting began to break down, what first emerged was an overwhelmingly powerful depression, and when this took control over her life, the partitions crumbled and the contents of the split-off parts of her experience came gushing out, a world of bad objects that overran her carefully and conscientiously constructed world of good objects and good selves.

One might ask what the foregoing psychoanalytic account of splitting has to do with Du Bois's notion of double consciousness. Splitting is a costly, self-distorting response to trauma, and both sexual abuse and racism are forms of trauma that are very disturbing to one's self-image. Schizophrenia is also conceptualized psychoanalytically as involving severe forms of splitting of the personality. The powerful experiences of double consciousness that Du Bois describes seem to bear some relationship to both splitting and to psychological responses to trauma, even though it is also clear that they are not completely synonymous terms.

Dalal (2002) argues that in a complex interplay of linguistic and societal development over the past four to six centuries, the color-names black and white, along with the societies they have come to define, have become racialized. Dominant groups from Europe came to associate their lighter skin with ideals of purity, goodness, and beauty, and so progressively "whitened" their self image. Blackness became associated with non-European, colonized people with darker skin, and the negative human qualities that the dominant group wished to disavow were assigned to "blackness." The purpose of the social act of creating groups defined by whiteness or blackness was to secure and legitimize the relational fields of domination that the more powerful had achieved through the violence of colonial conquest.

I believe that Maggie's processes of splitting were in the service of maintaining a self-image that allowed her to assimilate her identity to the white paternalistic relational field, while sealing off from her awareness the most intense aspects of what was described by authors David Eng and Shinhee Han (2000) as "racial melancholia." Conceptualized in this way, Du Bois's notion of "double consciousness" and Eng and Han's idea of "racial melancholia" provide alternative, more relational, and more politically contextualized bases for understanding Maggie's emotional life than the psychiatric nomenclature of "schizoaffective" allows. At the same time, psychoanalytic concepts of splitting and unconscious dissociation can deepen our understanding of the interiority of "double consciousness."

Eng and Han (2000) developed their notion of racial melancholia to help them to understand the psychological effects and meanings of the losses that subjugated people experience by the very fact that they live their lives in a society that regards them as marginalized outsiders, or "others." Part of their purpose is to relocate the site of the causes of pathology from the individual to society's racism, classism, and other systems of economic exploitation.

They begin with Freud's definition of melancholia as mourning without end. The melancholic is unable to relinquish lost objects, and unable to love new ones. Instead, the melancholic preserves the lost object by incorporating it into the ego and identifying with it. However, such a maneuver is inherently ambivalent, because of the cost to the ego of maintaining emotional loyalty to what has become an absence. As Freud described it, in identifying with a lost object, the ego itself becomes "poor and empty."

For Eng and Han, in racial melancholia what is lost is the ideal of whiteness. Our society is deeply racist in both its social devaluing and its economic exploitation of women and other subjugated people, and yet this state of affairs is routinely denied in favor of the myth of liberal individualism, equality of opportunity, etc. While these ideals are posed in abstract terms that seem to invite anyone of any color or gender to succeed, behind the abstraction is a raced and gendered model. The denied ghost behind the abstraction is a white male. If you are born non-white, or female, you will *never* be a white male, and in a racist society in which being a white male really matters, this is an irrecoverable loss.

The reasons that this becomes a matter of individual limitation and suffering, and is removed from the arena of social conflict, are twofold: (1) dominant societal ideology supports an uncompromising individualism that disavows any negative effects inherent in the structure of society, and (2) at the individual level the loss is refuted, and the refutation is disavowed, that is, split off from conscious awareness, a process that represents the internalization of what has been societally disavowed; in other words, it represents the "social unconscious." Even the marginalized often fail to fully acknowledge racism, since to do so would mean to admit aspiring to join a racist society. Since becoming a white male is not possible for many, what remains to the marginalized is, according to Homi Bhabha (cited in Eng and Han (2000)), mimicry. Mimicry involves a form of condensation, like in dreams, but also as represented in the kind of lifestyle advertising in which we are encouraged to believe that we can be happy, admired and successful if only we wear the same wristwatch as Donald Trump. We convince ourselves that if we make ourselves similar in some ways to those whom we want to be like, we can be like that person in all essential ways. Such mimicry is unconscious, because if we were conscious of what we were doing, it would fail from the beginning. But mimicry also must always in the end betray itself anyway, as long as racism remains operative. As Homi Bhabha said, "Almost the same, but not white" (cited in Eng and Han (2000:676)).

The ambivalence of racial melancholia hinges on the inability of the marginalized either to achieve or to renounce whiteness. All people, even oppressed people, internalize the race system. It is not only part of the culture, but is embedded in the language we use to think. Too much is felt to be lost, because renouncing whiteness leads to the despair of being perpetually subjugated. Even apparent success perpetuates the melancholia, albeit in its manic form. For oppressed people to succeed at whiteness (remember, in a society in which success is unconsciously raced and gendered) is to reject one's racially congruent internal good objects, with which one has had emotionally real (actual as opposed to fantasized) good experiences, and to replace them with whitened internalized good objects that are based on fantasy, and on less intimate relationships, or on internalizations of intimate others who themselves were engaged in mimicry. Meanwhile, the internalized racially congruent object becomes the bad object, and thus self-hatred is increased at the same time as a deeply felt aloneness in the world is established.

In many ways, Maggie seems to be a case in point. Her mother felt very much marginalized, and in her effort to overcome this in moving to a big city, she accepted a position in society that was within the bastions of white male privilege, but in the role of clerical aid, not professional. She aspired for more for her daughters. Her other daughter, Maggie's twin sister Miriam, went on to marry and become a secondary teacher, and so in what appears to be a reasonable compromise, given that such teaching is less defined as the domain of white male privilege and yet is still regarded as professional, she carried out her mother's aspirations. Still, Miriam has not come through unscathed, and suffers from depression and an eating disorder.

Maggie had more obstacles to overcome. Her sense of inadequacy was doubled by her facial disfigurement, which she sensed threatened her mother's self-esteem as well as her acceptance of her. She needed to stand out in some way to compensate for her mother's disappointment in her, and the way to do this was to fulfill her mother's manic intergenerational quest to succeed in a white man's world. One way she did this was by pursuing the career path of a degreed professional.

Along the way, Maggie also became interested in the literary arts, and I think that this served several unconscious purposes. For one thing, I think her notion of success was based more on fantasy than on personal experience. No one in her immediate or extended family had stepped outside the bounds of blue-collar versions of success. So I think she turned to literature and theater to answer her questions and relieve her perplexity about what kind of life she was supposed to live. This also allowed her to actualize her intellectual gifts and academic abilities, and to simultaneously constitute a version of the success she was after while exploring its meaning.

In the midst of this, her world collapsed. She was employed in the creative end of theater production when her company downsized and she went into a major depression followed by the psychotic decompensation I described earlier. That her adjustment was so fragile and shattered so irreparably is an indication of the hollowness and precariousness of the internal world that was supporting it.

When she began her therapy with me Maggie had done considerable work already in putting herself back together again. She was in graduate school in the literary arts, pursuing a doctorate and aiming to become a professor at the college level. She was still relying on substantial doses of antidepressant and neuroleptic medications, but was no longer as socially withdrawn as she had been.

What needed to happen in therapy, I think, was that Maggie had to become aware of the emotional life she split off, and she needed to comprehend the real losses she had experienced in her life so that she could mourn them. She needed to rebuild her life based on what she desired, and that, of course, involved helping her begin to know what her desires were. She had learned to avoid self-reflection, for fear of learning things about herself that she didn't want to know, but she realized that her future depended on her turning to that self-reflection now.

The transference/countertransference dynamics, as one would expect, replayed important aspects of her relationships with her parents. She felt that her fears of closeness were due to her mother's intrusiveness, and often my interest in her was experienced as intrusive. My vacations stirred up her feelings of abandonment and the painful longings she felt for her father when he was in the Navy. When she described her feelings of disturbance and revulsion about pornography, my "neutrality" made her very anxious because it seemed to condone an exploitive version of sexuality. She managed her anxiety about intimacy in the sessions by idealizing me; she denied our emotional involvement by seeing our relationship as merely professional. But she also realized that protecting herself in these ways risked impeding her progress by keeping our relationship distant and superficial.

A key part of our work was focused on her splitting off of painful affects. Often, when she would be on the verge of success, such as when she was nearly finished with her dissertation, or when a relationship changed, or ended, or became closer, Maggie would experience psychotic symptoms. What we learned together was that when she refused to feel loss, or anxiety, she would begin to have symptoms. So I told her that when she began to have symptoms, she needed to make an effort to figure out what might be upsetting her, and to try to tolerate the experience of feeling anxiety, or sadness, or self-hate until we could talk about it. The stability of her psychological world was poised between depression and psychosis, between personal *and* racialized melancholia, and the disavowal of the pain of this double consciousness.

In working to disentangle Maggie from her mother's misplaced aspirations for her, Maggie discovered that when she acts on her own ambitions, she gets anxious. When she finally allowed herself to explore these feelings, she realized that she fears that making herself happy by doing what *she* wants will make someone else envious and angry with her. That someone else is usually her mother. This is one way that the dynamics of race/gender melancholia turn the original good object/mother into a bad–persecutory object/mother.

One interesting aspect of Maggie's reformulated career is that she has become interested in the topic of race performance, such as blackface and yellowface but in general the phenomenon within theater in which an actor of one race portrays – mimics? – a character of another race. Part of her interest is in the racism implied by such practices, along with subtler aspects of what societal needs are served by this. This was an interest of hers that emerged during therapy before there could have been any possibility that she was taking her cue from anything I might have said explicitly about the theory I described earlier. But I believe that it expresses a self-recognition of her own race performance, as both a black woman mimicking a white woman and a black woman mimicking a black woman. Both are masquerades because racial identities are illusions. It also constituted a creative reworking of the conflict represented in her own forms of double consciousness.

Over the years Maggie has made astonishing progress in many ways. She has created a new career for herself, different from but related to her previous one. She maintains a close relationship with her mother, albeit one in which conflict is more openly expressed, and in which Maggie often has to enforce her boundaries and fend off her mother's attempts to be controlling, or to undermine her with expressions of disappointment or criticism. She has taught at the college level, and last year was awarded tenure, one of the first (racialized as) black women to do so at her institution. While she still suffers the occasional return of hallucinations, usually in the form of critical voices, they are less severe, and she is able to resolve them through self-reflection and talking about them in session. She no longer takes neuroleptic medication, and takes only a tiny dose of antidepressant. She works hard to maintain close friends, and does not allow herself to withdraw socially in order to avoid anxiety. Recently, after much exploration in therapy, she has become the foster mother of a ten-month-old bi-racial child, a girl whom she hopes one day to adopt.

Even after ten years, there are significant mysteries we have yet to unravel. For some reason, the onset of psychotic symptoms, on the rare occasions now when they recur, is signaled by an increase in intensity of Maggie's religious feelings. Her sexual feelings, which she has explored in many ways, continue to be too disturbing for her to risk expressing in an intimate relationship, male or female. And in some way that we have yet to pin down, her sexual feelings are mixed up with religious feelings, with cosmic feelings of good and evil.

I think that conceptualizing Maggie's life in the more relational and societal terms of Du Bois's double consciousness and Eng and Han's racial melancholia is helpful in many ways, not the least of which is that it takes the burden of responsibility off Maggie, and emphasizes the role played by societal forces beyond her control, but from which she could not escape. It also implies that racial melancholia cannot be treated solely by attending to individual casualties, but must be addressed through social and political change. In this way, the pathology is properly attributed to societal mores and institutions rather than individuals. In this model, helping the individual no longer entails blaming and stigmatizing the victims of racial oppression.

References

Dalal, F. (2002) *Race, Colour and the Processes of Racialization.* New York: Brunner-Routledge.

Du Bois, W. E. B. (1903) *The Souls of Black Folk.* New York: Bantam, 1989.

Eng, D. and Han, S. (2000) A dialogue on racial melancholia. *Psychoanalytic Dialogues*, 10:667–700.

Geertz, C. (1973) *The Interpretation of Cultures.* New York: Basic Books.

Chapter 10

The beheading of America

Reclaiming our minds

Maureen Katz

The week of the beheading of Nicholas Berg, the first publicly posted internet beheading from the Iraqi–US conflict, no fewer than three of my patients came to treatment agitated, in states of great anxiety. Each had seen pictures of the beheading; none had viewed the video. Each associated the terror s/he was experiencing with images of the World Trade Center explosions some two and a half years earlier. While I had heard these patients speak of distress over the intervening years, none had made reference in some time to the specific spectacle of the World Trade Center destruction. As a result of the beheading images, the symbolic significance of those events several years earlier seemed to shift and coalesce in ways that created panic of a very personal, violent and threatening nature. Patients felt certain of imminent destruction.

The week before the beheading of Nicholas Berg, the perverse, violent and horrific images of Abu Ghraib prisoners being tortured had been posted on internet sites, in newspapers and in television broadcasts. While these photos caused distress among many of our patients and ourselves as well, the panic of the beheading was, as I believe it was intended to be, felt to be much more viscerally dangerous to us. The image of the literal head, cut from the actual body of an American man, became associated in my patients' minds with the symbolic beheading of the World Trade Center, an American center of global capital and financial domination. These images are now linked temporally, politically, and psychically in our consciousness.

In the past three years, our government has explicitly told us to feel more afraid. Homeland Security officials tell us to "be afraid, be very afraid" (though we should still "go and shop"), and they feel the best way to create this sense of fear – dare I say, terror – is to have a visual code. Color codes change due to phantasmic information that we aren't allowed to know about. We are told that if the government tells the truth it will put us in danger! We can even believe for a moment in the Attorney General when he tells us that duct taping ourselves inside an airless room will protect us from imminent biological destruction. At the end of the day, we find ourselves awash in a sea of confusion, where mental tyranny and psychological terror take hold against thinking.

Several months after 9/11/01, I was running by the San Francisco Bay in the late afternoon. The government had just announced another code orange. I was stopped at a particularly picturesque spot by four Arab men who asked if I would take their photo with the Golden Gate Bridge behind them. As I framed the picture, noting the orange color of the bridge, I had a fantasy of the picture being held up by the mother of one of these men after he had died in some suicide attack destroying the bridge. This outrageous, paranoid, and racist thought made me laugh ruefully at myself, at what all this had come down to on a lovely December day. Two years later, as I started to write down patients' associations, the memory and accompanying fantasy came back to me. The scenario in my mind had been altered by intervening historical events. Now, as I saw myself taking the picture, the image shifted and rather than witnessing the destruction of the bridge, I saw one of the four men hooded, kneeling on cement, a second in the position of one of the tortured men at Abu Ghraib, and a third holding a sword in his arm raised above my head.

Here, the questions I wish to address are: How does witnessing these spectacles create terror and affect our ability to think and fashion our own identities as spectator or participant, perpetrator or victim? What are the social and political environments that contribute to our psychological defenses, and how can we see evidence of those defenses and their breakdowns?

The intrusive imagery of the spectacle

My patients' reactions to the images of beheadings draw our attention to the intrusive nature of violent spectacles in our daily lives and psyches. Historian Martin Jay (2003) refers to these commonly displayed images as a "visuality of violence," which most definitely has an observable relationship to our increased sense of anxiety and fragmentation of thinking.

Within psychoanalysis, we are used to talking about images in dreams, in fantasies, in art. However, the role of images as a conduit of ideology and its impact on our psychology, while less commonly discussed, cannot be denied. Ideology is the frame placed over reality, through which we interpret that reality. It is a means by which individuals understand their relationship to society. Images are crucial for the delivery of ideology and primary to modes of psychological processing (and we are inside of it even as we try to describe it).

It is a feature of contemporary life that we are bombarded by an immense accumulation of spectacles and images distant from their original context. The French Situationist movement in the mid-twentieth century wrote about the modern spectacle as a tyranny of images, detached from life, apart from lived experience, preventing dialogue, destroying memory (Jay 1993). John Berger has discussed the way in which "the spectacle creates an eternal present of immediate expectation: memory ceases to be necessary or desirable. With the loss of memory, the continuities of meaning and judgment are also lost to us. The camera relieves us of the burden of memory" (Berger 2001b:290).

Who produces the spectacle remains of the greatest importance in understanding its ideological and psychological effects. Our current spectacles are brought to us by the folks down at our not-so-neighborhood web link, monopoly-owned newspaper or consolidated global television network.

The intrusive immediacy of visuals that invade our personal, individual spaces, while intended for the "mass," creates an experience of alienation. The way in which images are communicated to us, the techniques that create that imagery, and the way in which we receive those images perpetuate an ideology where relations between people are confused with relationships between things; humans are degraded into abstractions. This alienation and confusion create defensive structures that make it more difficult to be aware of the manner in which we are treated by others, especially by those transmitting the images, and we suffer from the absence of social spaces within which we can think together and create alternative meanings.

In a recent article in the *New York Times* about the death of war photography, Pete Hamill (2004) noted that professional photographs taken in the Vietnam war had come to define that conflict: the shooting in the head of a Vietcong prisoner; the girl, Phan Phuc, running naked seared by napalm; the photo of the dead at My Lai. In contrast, the first Gulf War was photographed and transmitted to us through images looking like a video game, the current war from embedded journalists rigidly censored: no soldiers bleeding in the sand, no body bags, no coffins. Yet, as Hamill writes, "The unsettling truth is that, so far, the defining photographic images of Iraq were taken by amateurs in the prison at Abu Ghraib."

Who were the photographers, the creators of the images at Abu Ghraib, and who were the images produced for? Some of that we cannot answer, but we can begin to address how they expressed something hidden in the current ideology and cultural consciousness of Americans. In order to investigate this, we need to return to what was revealed in patients' associations to the World Trade Center (WTC) at the time of Berg's beheading.

"The uncanny" and images of beheading

In 1919, in his paper on "The uncanny," Freud referred to certain phenomena that are frightening, that arouse dread and horror. He writes that the uncanny is something that is secretly familiar, which has undergone repression and then returned from it. It ought to have remained secret and hidden, but it has come to light. He attributes the experience to the fear of being robbed of one's eyes. Freud relates the fears about the loss of one's eyes to fears of castration. The uncanny creates a terrible sense of dread. The uncanny is the class of frightening things in which the frightening element can be shown to be something repressed that recurs. We might make the interpretation that the beheading of Berg/WTC symbolically represented a form of castration. In this equation, castration does not mean that a man becomes a woman, but in fact, the man is destroyed. As in the Bible and the Koran, the serpent has been destroyed when his head is cut off. The beheading of a man caught on video, the association with the symbolic castration of American global hegemony in the destruction of the WTC, were at least triggers of the sense of the uncanny. But what if the something that came to light that we wanted to remain hidden were the contradictions and complexities of the American way of life leading up to the attacks? Perhaps, then, images of Iraqi prisoners being tortured to the seemingly sadistic glee of US military forces made us vulnerable to that anxiety and dread. Freud writes:

> An uncanny effect is often and easily produced when the distinction between imagination and reality is effaced, as when something that we have hitherto regarded as imaginary appears before us in reality, or when a symbol takes over the full functions of the thing it symbolizes . . . it is the over-accentuation of the psychical reality in comparison with material reality – a feature closely allied to the belief in the omnipotence of thoughts.
>
> (Freud 1919:244)

Following this line of inquiry, we might propose investigating a chain of events:

1 The trauma of the WTC explosion, which occurred at a particular historical moment within a social context, symbolized a loss for the American public, necessitating a collective mourning process and working through. Mourning the loss of our historic sense of invulnerability was, at best, attenuated.
2 In an environment with continued threats of danger and actual experiences of politically repressive policies, along with failed mourning, our capacities to think, for creative imagination, were profoundly affected.
3 Under these pressures, mental mechanisms employed for some time to defend against unpleasant contemporary political and social realities failed. Alongside the disquieting sense of uprooted, anxious states of mind, symptoms can be seen in phenomena as disparate as the 2003 California gubernatorial recall election and in the outbreak of sadism and its photographing by torturers at Abu Ghraib.

Political repression, mourning and cynicism

Psychological trauma results when events disrupt the smooth running of a symbolic order. The idea of a catastrophic terrorist attack by foreign, usually Arabic, nationals was something depicted in numerous films prior to the events on September 11th. In his book *Welcome to the Desert of the Real* (2002), the psychoanalytic philosopher Slavoj Žižek refers to the events of the attack as the image entering and shattering our reality, a reality where Third World horrors didn't happen in the USA, but only in our imaginations and our nightmares. With the WTC destruction, our historic sense of invulnerability, of safety and relative prosperity, was lost. But to find a continuity with our past from before the WTC destruction, we need to understand together how that smooth-running symbolic order actually contained some very unpleasant political realities.

The fall of the Soviet Union and Communist bloc countries changed the balance of global powers. Living in the United States, middle- and upper-class people could not be unaware of our singular good fortunes, as stock portfolios and housing values increased against a more or less vague background of disintegrating countries and ethnic massacres. Of course, within the same United States, as a result of an accelerating globalization of the economy, many working people and families were descending rapidly into poverty, with less access to meaningful work or a safety net to catch them.

While global capitalism allows for the free circulation of commodities, the movements of people are more and more restricted. There is an increasingly rigid divide between economic prosperity and those who will never benefit from it. There is a divide between those accorded human rights and those who are not protected. There is increasing racism within and outside of our borders. We know these things and yet we don't change our activities. We might know that driving SUVs consumes enormous amounts of fossil fuels and releases truck-like gas emissions into the environment, but we feel "safer in them." We might understand that public education is the foundation of democracy, but nevertheless feel compelled to send our children to private schools and systematically underfund public education. Before 9/11, we might easily have condemned torture and rape, while ignoring these practices in every prison in America – a system in which one in three adult black men will spend some time in his life. On many social and political fronts, actions taken by the present US government resulted in losses of human rights and environmental protection, and worsening lives for people here and around the world.

In 1966, Alexander and Margarete Mitscherlich, two German psychoanalysts, published *The Inability to Mourn: Principles of Collective Behavior*, an extensive study on the social–psychological behaviors of people living in what became West Germany during and after the Nazi regime. In his 1975 preface to this seminal book, Robert Jay Lifton emphasized the necessity and yet inability to mourn certain political tragedies (Lifton 1975).

There is no love without loss. And there is no moving beyond loss without some experience of mourning. But what if one discovers evil in what one has lost – and by implication, in oneself? How does one reconcile that evil with the sense of nobility one had originally associated with one's love? Is it then possible to mourn? If so, for whom and what? What is the relationship of guilt and responsibility to mourning, or not mourning? What are the collective consequences of the inability to mourn?

In postwar Germany, the Mitscherlichs found that "intensive defense against guilt, shame and anxiety" rendered mourning impossible (Mitscherlich and Mitscherlich 1975). In bypassing mourning, the Germans, by the mid-1960s, had eliminated from memory events of the past, rejecting any inner involvement or internal processing of one's own behavior. The result of this effort was a "psychic immobilization" in the face of acute problems confronting German society. A persistent autistic attitude led to a majority of citizens of the democratic West Germany being unable to identify themselves with any activity of the country beyond its economic system, an inability to tackle the problems of present-day society in a socially progressive fashion. Lifton's studies of returning Vietnam veterans showed a similar phenomenon of impaired mourning due to guilt, shame, and anxiety.

Our experiences of the alienating, violent, terrifying spectacles meet up with the guilt and shame due to actual social losses. Together these forces collude to disrupt psychological processes, especially collective mourning, which might lead to collective memory, assessment, insight, and judgment.

In our current context, trauma and loss did not stop with the destruction of the World Trade Center and only re-emerge with the beheading of Nicholas Berg. While some Americans might have felt uncomfortable with what the WTC represented before the attack, the possibilities and promises of future attacks and the US government's so-called "war on terror" created (some might say intentionally, for purposes of control) additional mental anguish, chaos, and confusion.

Within the United States, the Patriot Act and subsequent legislative and administrative rulings have threatened basic constitutional rights and liberties. Actions have been taken that mirror actions taken in societies of state terror: threats of constant surveillance and restriction of free movement – at times comical, as with Ted Kennedy being placed on the No Fly List, to tragic, as in the case of numerous immigrants being detained on grounds of unknown or misinformed suspicions. Intrusions into our private lives and our public sphere have proliferated, from libraries, travel arrangements, and phone conversations, to arrests and detentions of dissenters from government policy.

This was a *San Francisco Chronicle* report from the Republican National Convention:

> Amid renewed threats of terrorist attacks and concerns that some protests may turn violent, city and federal security authorities have turned midtown Manhattan into an armed camp, sealing off major streets with barricades of concrete and steel, in an unprecedented show of force, assembling the largest army in city history. "This doesn't look like America anymore," said Adrian Salvoni, a taxi driver. "It's safe, but it's really unpleasant to look at."
>
> (Badkhen 2004)

Whether one agrees that the ominous signs of an increasingly militaristic, policed society are a source of anxiety, there is ample evidence of the government misleading us. The authority whose purpose is to protect us becomes authoritarian and antidemocratic as the government deliberately confuses what is known and truthful with what is unknown or false. We can recall together the facts revealed about weapons of mass destruction and so on. The "prison house of language" is a term cultural critic Fredric Jameson (1972), following Nietzsche, used to refer to the transmission of ideology through language. The assault on language and truth by the present US administration makes speech resemble more a funhouse of mirrors than a prison: the literary images of 1984 arrive 20 years later (let alone what we might say about the assault on our psyches brought about by religious fundamentalism at the highest levels of the US government). In the face of these continuing psychological violations, many of us retreat to states of mind in which we can avoid otherwise overwhelming depressive and persecutory anxieties.

Disavowal is the mechanism by which we disregard acknowledging the reality of our traumatic perceptions. Disavowal involves a splitting of the ego where the attitude of the disavowal of perception is always accompanied by the opposite attitude, knowing but ignoring it. Slavoj Žižek (2001) extends this description to include the term "fetishistic disavowal." The term "fetishism" psychoanalytically refers to a specific avoidance of anxiety associated with castration. As Žižek explains, fetishistic disavowal is "an expression of the will to halt one's view just prior to hitting the traumatic spot that discloses the Other's castration" (2001:13). Extended into the realm of the social, this state of individual and collective functioning involves the perverse pleasure of knowing about reality, and knowing that you know, yet continuing to act and ignore it.

We might note the way in which, increasingly, we will talk on a cell phone in front of others. We know those around us can hear all aspects of what is said and yet continue as though we are having a private conversation. There is a casual, almost obscene disregard for those around us who in the social space are made lifeless in the moment we are so animatedly talking to another on the phone.

Cynicism is a profound aspect of this attitude. Diamonds are mined in Third World countries through horribly exploitative means and used in an exchange for guns that aid genocide and social destruction in areas of Africa. We may know this and also that the corporate diamond mine giant De Beers advertises to create desire for us to buy more diamonds. Despite being hip to manipulative advertising and oppressive social practices of obtaining diamonds, we still exchange them as tokens of love to each other. The fetishized aspect of the disavowal involves ignoring social relations between humans that material objects represent. We all know about the ways our actions perpetuate destructive social relations and yet continue to enjoy what we do, necessarily stopping our gaze before encountering what we would otherwise see. The anxiety of castration is mitigated through the creation of fetishes – surrogates for what is perceived as missing.

After the WTC, such forms of disavowal and cynicism paled before arguments about the need for torture. Prisoners in Guantanamo Bay were called "enemy combatants" and, for three years before the Supreme Court ruled otherwise in the Spring of 2004, these prisoners were subjected to detentions and torture without representation or even charges against them. Despite the evidence of pictures of hooded men kneeling on concrete in tiny cells, we were told by our highest officials that they were not being tortured. At the same time, government officials, as well as liberal and conservative columnists, argued that perhaps we needed torture for our safety – if not at our own hands, contracted out. Those of us who have worked in communities with victims of political torture are well aware that US military and intelligence forces have long been engaged in covert practices of torture. That the American government and public figures would argue for the need for torture is heart-wrenching.

There has been an acquiescence to the false representation of the social reality in which we live. Third World violence, for which US policies are in part responsible, is termed minor in comparison with the "absolute evils" of an Iraq or Afghanistan or suicide bombers. Rumsfeld said that Abu Ghraib torture may have been a bad thing, but it was nothing compared to the horror and evil of the beheading of Nicholas Berg. The fetishistic disavowal embodies a lie that enables us to endure the unbearable truth.

In this atmosphere, persecutory and depressive anxieties leach through our defenses. British analyst Donald Meltzer (1973, 1988) referred to a class of defenses against these anxieties as states of mindlessness, where the personality is unable to symbolize and think about emotional experience. In these states, where there is a constantly felt violation of the space of privacy, both from the outside and from the anxieties that are felt to be too painful to bear, internal objects and values slide into what Meltzer calls a psychic degradation. In these states, emotional experience is available only for evacuation. Attention and inquiry, as preludes to judgment, decision, and action, are impossible. The individual aligns himself or herself with tyrannical, destructive aspects of the self in order to seek protection from the perceived assaults and violation. Mental tyranny is a state where no sensuality can be lusted after but only perversion, a world built on lifelessness, avoiding the anxieties of the living, time-bound. The emotive quality is of sadistic, perverse states of mind in which the sense of identity has been invested in or captured by the destructive part of the self (Meltzer 2001:92–97, 99–106, 143–150).

Tyranny, then, is not just an expression of "mere will and cruelty of unbridled undisciplined feeling" (Meltzer 2001:144), but is also a social perversion in defense against depressive anxieties. In an atmosphere of intolerance, of disavowal of external realities, signification, meaning, and an acknowledgment of the existence of otherness are severely compromised. These defenses are notorious in preventing the psyche from developing workable strategies to tolerate anxiety. If we can't control the object of terror, we align with it. For the social context, this takes the form of believing that reality can be defended against by aligning with measures that support state terror or with authoritarian figures that are imagined terminators of terror.

In the California gubernatorial recall election of 2003, Arnold Schwarzenegger, a movie actor who had never held a political office, and who had only recently taken on any active political campaigns, defeated Cruz Bustamante, then Lt Governor, who had had a long career in public service, and many other candidates as well. Schwarzenegger's brief campaign relied heavily on his identification with his fictional movie roles. These roles were about invulnerable characters, part man, part machine, who terminated all who got in their way. In the world of post 9/11, post-Iraq war, Schwarzenegger used lines from these movies to the cheers of voters. He said he would terminate the opposition. His ads played on a racist and sadistic triumphing over the ineffectual little Mexican opponent. Latino voters split their votes between these candidates. Regardless of his capabilities, it was the fictional, fetishized, hard-bodied character Schwarzenegger whom the voters made into an actual governor: the carefully constructed image, endlessly replayed, that, in a particular historical moment, becomes an "über-reality."

The pictures taken at Abu Ghraib subverted what Americans understood the mission in Iraq to be. Regardless of the logic that democracy cannot be brought about by conquering and occupying another country, these images, as broadcast and used, were irrefutable evidence of a visual violence, a perverse sexualizing of American activity, which created enormous anxiety, shame, and guilt. The amateur photographers of Abu Ghraib were forced into our consciousness. These weren't dispassionate documentarians. In a grotesque imitation of "what I did on my summer vacation," their pictures captured a moment in time that showed people manically engrossed in their activities, ostensibly for viewing by friends and family. In part, we are caught by the photos, identifying with the familiar faces of military personnel, torturing Iraqi prisoners. That's the function of tourist photos: we are to imagine ourselves in their place, enjoying ourselves. Perhaps we can also see this through the lens of the cultural phenomenon of the perversely named "reality TV shows" – the real pretend! It is as though the people in the photos are asking us to pretend with them that they are only acting as though they were real prison guards, pretend with them that they are really torturing Iraqi prisoners, which they indeed are. These soldiers in states of chaos and degradation cannot tolerate knowing they are indeed real and real-ly present. In these states, they might indeed not feel real, as they then capture themselves in their photos. It is as though the culture that spawned the pretend real of TV has prepped them well to do the humanly inhuman and to make other humans into things. (We do know that several of these soldiers were well trained in the homeland fields of prisons and menial degrading labor before their turn in Iraq.)

Once these photos are shown as public images, no longer for private viewing, we also see them from a distance and we are horrified by the moments captured. The contradiction between the function of the photos, to share in a moment rather than document it, and the image they show us, documenting torture and murder, is irreconcilable to us. That contradiction, and the chaos and degradation that it represents, breaks through defensive structures and leaves us with more intense anxieties. For those of us who go one step further and understand that the chain of command that leads to degradation and torture does not stop with those photographed but extends throughout our government, in our name, there is more shame and anxiety.

A clinical vignette

It is essential for the analyst to be aware of her own feelings and acknowledge external social reality at certain critical moments in the consulting room. As described earlier, "mindlessness," as Meltzer uses the term, is a defense against mounting psychotic pressures that causes a retreat from engagement with realities that create intolerable anxieties. The analyst's presence and ability to acknowledge a tolerance of confusion and dangers of internal and external realities allow the possibility of employing a different strategy when facing danger; when the analyst acknowledges the existence of danger, it allows for an opening in the analytic dyad to explore these different strategies.

Shortly after the Berg beheading, a 54-year-old professor noticed that she was increasingly irritable, testy and withdrawn at home and with her children. She found herself withdrawing from activities at her children's school, feeling that there was no longer any contribution she could make to the school community. She associated the malaise with a sense of helplessness similar to what she felt about the spiraling chaos in Iraq. As we explored the actual situation at the school, she revealed that the principal, much to the dismay of teachers and parents, had started to rigorously pursue improving test scores for students. We began to explore what it was that made her feel she couldn't participate in organizing with parents and teachers to assert their shared priorities. She then started to discuss her doubts about the war. She had vigorously supported the war in Iraq and any measures the US government might need to take to keep her family safe. She had become increasingly uncomfortable with what she was learning as time went on and with her identification with US forces in Iraq. She felt acutely ashamed at the photos of prisoners in Abu Ghraib, and yet found herself returning time and again to internet sites to view the photos. As she talked about the sense of contamination she felt from the identification with the US activities in the war, she also began to talk about her sense of helplessness and fear in the aftermath of the World Trade Center destruction. She was able to respond to the analyst's interpretations that she had not felt protected by the analyst either. She assumed the analyst was against the war, judging from the magazine selection in the waiting room, and felt that the analyst had refused to engage in an actual discussion of whether invading Iraq would indeed make the patient safer. She felt the lack of such a discussion had abandoned her, the patient, to fantasies of danger that might or might not be real, but either way could not be discussed in the analysis. We discussed what she had perceived as an analytic failure to talk about what was happening in the external world, which created a great deal of anxiety and dismay for her. We spoke about the contradictions in her perceptions and what she was hearing and reading in the mainstream news. We began to identify the specific instances of news and information sources that she sought out and to identify responses she would have to them: where she felt she could think and make judgments and where she felt overwhelmed and at sea. Her sense of malaise and irritability lessened noticeably. She began to take an increasing role in parent–teacher discussions with the school administration about priorities in the classroom. The recognition of helplessness in the face of viewing the WTC destruction and government warnings, and her sense of shame at falling in with the US government's response in attacking Iraq, could be talked about and tolerated. She felt less threatened and compelled by the beheading and the Abu Ghraib photos, though no less outraged by the incidents. In turn, she felt able to use her skills to negotiate discussions between differing interests at the school. No longer a bystander or hostage to fear and shame, she was able to reclaim status as a willing and creative participant in a socially progressive activity. While there were obvious transference meanings to this expression of her conflicts, this was not the primary focus in the treatment during these discussions.

Conclusion

The spectacle of the beheading of Nicholas Berg, with its attendant sense of the uncanny for my patients, draws our attention to the many ways in which Americans collectively have lost their heads and minds in the years prior to and after the destruction of the World Trade Center. However, the failures of our disavowal, the pain of our symptoms, allow for a second look at what have been the illusory accepted realities.

Traumatic events that cause unbearable anxiety can be responded to in ways other than disavowal and losing our heads. There is also the possibility of the ethical action: to track and take inspiration from others who are also acting ethically, allowing for a culture that can tolerate mourning and reparation. Rather than relinquish our ability to think about alternatives to destructive human social relations, we need to accept that there is a complexity of circumstances and not remove ourselves from the obligation to act.

Spectacles and images are powerful conduits of ideology. As we collectively think about the sources of these images, we can break through the ideological fog that asserts that this is the way our society must be organized. Thinking collectively about globalization, about alternatives to modes of production that lead to vast inequalities, hunger, global ecological degradation, war – these discussions can allow for a reclaiming of our subjectivity: we do not have to be alienated, fetishized objects for terrorist or government fantasies. We can know about our own destructive illusions, tolerate our guilt and anxieties, imagine and act differently. Fredric Jameson writes, "It seems to be easier for us today to imagine the thoroughgoing deterioration of the earth and of nature than the breakdown of late capitalism; perhaps that is due to some weakness in our imagination" (1994:xii).

There are moments when we have a sense of disorientation, moments when we are able to reclaim social and political memory. These memories must encompass images of the past, no matter how tragic, however guilt-inducing, in order to make our own history from a continuity of our experiences. To paraphrase John Berger, if we are horrified by what we are shown, by what is being done or fought for "in our name" (Berger 1978:290), then we need to confront our own lack of political freedom, and in doing so confront those responsible, including ourselves. To think and act, keeping memory in mind, is the only way to reclaim the world against perversion and terror, to put our heads back together again.

References

Badkhen, A. (2004) Republican convention security: Manhattan under the gun with cops on corners and 250,000 protesters ready. *San Francisco Chronicle*, 29 August, A1.

Berger, J. (2001a) *Selected Essays*. New York: Vintage Books.
Berger, J. (2001b; orig. 1978) Uses of photography. *Selected Essays*. New York: Vintage Books, pp. 286–293.
Freud, S. (1919) The uncanny. *Standard Edition of the Complete Psychological Works of Sigmund Freud*, Vol. XVII (1917–1919). London: Hogarth Press, pp. 217–252.
Hamill, P. (2004) When the shooting stopped. *New York Times*, 25 September, A15.
Jameson, F. (1972) *The Prison House of Language*. Princeton, NJ: Princeton University Press.
Jameson, F. (1994) *The Seeds of Time*. New York: Columbia University Press.
Jay, M. (1993) *Downcast Eyes*. Berkeley, CA: University of California Press.
Jay, M. (2003) *Refractions of Violence*. New York: Routledge.
Lifton, R. J. (1975) Introduction. In A. Mitscherlich and M. Mitscherlich, *The Inability to Mourn: Principles of Collective Behavior*. New York: Grove Press.
Meltzer, D. (1973) *Sexual States of Mind*. Strath Tay, UK: Clunie Press.
Meltzer, D. (1988) *The Apprehension of Beauty*. Worcester, UK: Clunie Press.
Mitscherlich, A. and Mitscherlich, M. (1975) *The Inability to Mourn: Principles of Collective Behavior*. New York: Grove Press.
Žižek, S. (2001) *The Fright of Real Tears, Krzysztof Kieslowski Between Theory and Post-Theory*. London: British Film Institute.
Žižek, S. (2002) *Welcome to the Desert of the Real*. London: Verso.

Chapter 11

Psychoanalysis and the problem of the bystander in times of terror

Nancy Caro Hollander

> We are all guilty, in one form or another.
> (Argentine President Raul Alfonsín)

> Silence is the real crime
> (Hannah Segal)

For the past 30 years, I have been writing about the psychological effects on Latin American citizens who have been forced to live in the cultures of fear constructed by terrorist states. I have been particularly interested in exploring how extreme political repression can produce a bystander population that inadvertently, through low-level acceptance or active complicity, plays a supportive role in a government's perpetration of all kinds of human rights abuses of its own citizens. In this context, I have studied the response of the psychoanalytic community in Argentina to the difficult challenge of their patients' and their own psychological negotiation of the impingements of a terrifying social reality constructed by the military dictatorship's Dirty War against its own citizens carried out between 1976 and 1983. I believe this experience has significance for psychoanalysts and citizens living in the USA under our present social and political circumstances.

Since 9/11, I have thought a good deal about how the dynamics of life under state terror might illuminate aspects of our own experience in another time of terror. As citizens, we have been forced to negotiate profound anxieties that are being stimulated by our contemporary culture of fear, and as psychoanalytic practitioners, we are encountering a growing challenge to think about what, beyond the familiar conflicts related to the private sphere of family and work, might constitute legitimate topics to be included within the psychoanalytic project.

By doing so, we become part of a radical tradition within psychoanalysis that has been interested in the relationship between the individual and the larger social group. Many psychoanalytic theorists have explored from a variety of perspectives the conscious and unconscious experience of the subject who from the beginning of life is inserted within a sociosymbolic order characterized by asymmetrical relations of power and force (Chapter 6, this volume). I want to argue that the relationship of the subject to the social and political world and one's role as citizen is so central to identity that it ought to be a legitimate part of psychoanalytic theory and practice.

Let us briefly explore this theme in the context of what happened to citizens who lived in the extreme situation of Argentine state terror. There, as in other Latin American authoritarian regimes, the military violently assumed guardianship over unjust social and economic institutions whose legitimacy had been challenged by a variety of progressive political movements seeking to reform or replace them (Hollander 1997). The possibility that this struggle between contending political forces might take place within a democratic process was foreclosed by the military coup, whose ideological justification was the military's assertion that it was preserving Western Christian civilization against a vast network of "subversives" who had taken over every aspect of Argentine life. This persecutory vision energized a massive assault by the military on the entire body politic, the goal of which was to silence critical consciousness and paralyze civic engagement. A complicit media provided a continual disinformation campaign, turning reality on its head by depicting the military as peace-keeping guardians of citizens' security and their saviors from the violence it was itself responsible for perpetrating.

The discourse and policies of the military reflected a psychology whose symbols and rituals were the ideological and institutional manifestation of the following primitive defenses: splitting of the world into good and evil (Western civilization vs "subversion") and the projection of everything bad onto a hated object (the so-called subversive), with the consequent need to control it, for fear of being controlled by it. Their omnipotent stance, with its incapacity for empathy, promoted an all-out attack on free inquiry and political difference. As the military put it, "Argentina has three main enemies: Karl Marx, because he tried to destroy the Christian concept of society; Sigmund Freud, because he tried to destroy the Christian concept of the family; and Albert Einstein, because he tried to destroy the Christian concept of time and space" (Timmerman 1982:130).

Although some among the elite classes, in whose interest the Dirty War was carried out, were perpetrators themselves and active collaborators with the military regime, others took on the role of bystander, employing defenses of denial and disavowal that served to protect them from having to bear witness to the price paid by civil society for the violent maintenance of their society's economic and political inequities. The majority of citizens whose interests were antithetical to the military project became victims of the military's doctrine of "collective guilt." The armed forces and paramilitary organizations attacked groups and individuals they labeled as "subversive," but they also indiscriminately and randomly detained and secretly kidnapped apolitical citizens in their homes, their workplaces, and on the streets in order to impose a terrifying and unpredictable social reality and to splinter public ties.

Most citizens knew about the "secret" prisons and concentration camps, awoke to see or hear about the disfigured cadavers of torture victims rotting in the streets or floating in the rivers, knew someone whose relative or friend had been "disappeared". Even while the terrorist state officially denied the accusations that it illegally imprisoned and tortured citizens, its release of selected torture victims was purposefully orchestrated for the important political function of intimidating those who witnessed their testimonies. Their stories were a warning about what could happen to anyone at anytime. Their very existence drove others into isolation and silence, creating a "fractured society" (Viñar and Viñar 1993).

The terrorist state's culture of fear and the threat of annihilation it imposed on the psyche required a variety of conscious and unconscious maneuvers to manage the sense of ongoing threat. Adaptation to authoritarian rule produced extreme personal vigilance, and the ability to distinguish between internal and external sources of persecutory anxiety was profoundly compromised (Hollander 1999). Those who occupied the position of bystander lived with constant anticipatory anxiety that suddenly and without warning they could be thrust into the victim position. Primitive defenses were revitalized, such as splitting, dissociation, and projective identification in response to the violence and uncontained aggression unleashed by the assaultive cultural symbols and rituals of state terror. For example, in an effort to protect themselves against annihilation anxiety inherent in an empathic identification with the victims of the military, citizen-bystanders could identify with the aggressor instead. Their own violent impulses, which increased in every domain of daily life within the generally militarized environment, could be projected onto the socially created scapegoat, who could contain the projected aggression and then be destroyed. *Habra hecho algo* (he/she must have been up to something) became the metaphor for people's predictable responses when they observed or heard about the apprehension of a neighbor, co-worker or stranger on the street. This reaction represented the impulse to dissociate themselves from the persecutory symbol of the disappeared, or to identify with the aggressor by convincing themselves of the rationality or just actions on the part of the repressive state.

Moreover, individuals often unconsciously dissociated significant aspects of the self as a means of dealing with persecutory anxiety. In the highly politicized cultures of Latin America, under such repressive conditions, many citizens abandoned their former passions for political discussion and debate, withdrawing into a highly personalized and individualistic lifestyle. Intimidated progressive activists were driven to disavow their deeply held belief systems and political commitments in the wish to escape the persecutory fantasies induced by the threatening external environment. In this instance, the disavowal of any connection between oneself and the victims – the disappeared – of state terror also signified a profound mechanism of dissociation of a part of one's own personality, a part that threatened personal annihilation because of its identification with the politics and values of the unfortunate victims of repression.

As has been documented in other extreme situations, especially the Holocaust, because of the psychological states induced by state terror, the majority of citizens during Argentina's Dirty War could not bring themselves to join the courageous individuals and groups that resisted state terror until almost the end of the regime's reign, when for a multitude of reasons the military were forced back to the barracks. They thus played a pivotal bystander role – representing what Ervin Staub (1993) has called a "deathly silence" – in sustaining the oppressive relationship between the perpetrator and its victims.

The practice of psychoanalysis was deeply affected by state terror. It is interesting that despite some prominent exceptions in the history of psychoanalysis, the tendency within the profession has been to pay attention to the intrapsychic and intersubjective relations within the limited domains of family and work. In Argentina, this orientation had predominated within mainstream psychoanalysis since its inception in the early 1940s, but during the Dirty War it functioned to a degree as a defensive use of a professional stance that could justify assuming a position of neutrality with respect to the political world. This public posture existed in spite of the fact that psychoanalysts and other mental health professionals were specific targets of the military dictatorship. They were viewed as containers of their patients' secrets and thus an important source of potential information on the "subversive" opposition to the social order. Within this general environment of intimidation, many psychoanalysts, like the citizenry in general, withdrew defensively into an isolated social and professional life. They supported the leadership of their psychoanalytic associations, which refused to take a publicly critical position against the extreme human rights violations of the state. This stance was justified on the grounds of "professional neutrality." It was argued that psychoanalysis was a scientific enterprise, a profession whose study and treatment of psychic reality needed to be separate from social and political activities and pressures. It was also argued that the avoidance of taking a critical stand protected institutional psychoanalysis and individual psychoanalysts from political repression.

The idea of neutrality when referring to the analytic posture required of the psychoanalyst with respect to the various agencies of the patient's mind (id, ego, superego) could function to justify a focus on exclusively etiological and transference interpretations of the patient's material to the exclusion of social reality – in this case an extraordinarily persecutory one

– as a source of anxiety, depression, dissociation, paranoia, and so forth. Interpretations that centered exclusively on transference, projection, unconscious conflict, symbolic use of social reality for inner world experience and so forth, often paradoxically led to an alliance on the part of the analyst with the patient's unconscious defenses, including splitting, infantile omnipotence, dissociation, and disavowal of the threatening social reality. By not providing a space in which patients could reflect about the social world and its impact on them, the psychoanalytic frame could in some cases end up failing to protect either patient or analyst or both from an external reality that represented a potentially serious, even fatal, threat to their lives. Further, this psychoanalytic approach ran the risk of reproducing the isolation from which patients suffered that reinforced paranoid-schizoid anxieties.

However, a minority of psychoanalysts took the position that it was essential to deal within the analytic relationship with the real events that were affecting their patients. They chose to practice a psychoanalysis that addressed the dialectical relationship between subjectivity and social reality. They held that it was necessary to recognize and work with their own anxieties and symptoms of ongoing trauma related to the external world so that they could be more effective in understanding and interpreting those of their patients. They tried to responsibly balance the professional mandate to focus on the patient's perspective and subjective reality rather than on external events, on the one hand, with the need on the other to provide at times a pivotal source of reality testing to patients whose denial of external danger put them at risk (Volnovich 1994). They believed that the psychoanalytic space was a crucial matrix in which patient(s) and analyst(s) could use their minds together to reflect, to symbolize, what was taking place in society that profoundly affected them. A collaborative exploration of internal experience stimulated by the culture of fear was seen as an important factor in overcoming the sense of dread born of isolation and in potentially containing psychotic anxieties mobilized by a terrifying social order. As time went by and the opposition to military rule grew, this psychoanalytic approach was especially salient for those patients whose courageous participation in the struggle for democracy exposed them to increased levels of danger and thus anxieties and fears for their own and their families' safety.

Among psychoanalysts who treated the direct victims of state terror – survivors of torture and families of the disappeared – many came to the conclusion that in conditions of such extreme political polarization, they could function effectively as mental care providers only if they conveyed to their patients their alliance with an oppositional position toward the perpetrators responsible for their pain and loss. Increasingly, these analysts became associated with a network of human rights activists who were aiding poor and working-class communities, the most vulnerable populations in

Argentina whose members had suffered extensively at the hands of the military (Hollander 1997). Under such conditions, assuming a position of neutrality would contravene the possibility of securing the trust and alliance of one's patients. These psychoanalysts thus embraced a therapeutic perspective they termed "ethical nonneutrality." In the context of working with victims of state terror, there was no room to be a bystander, even within the psychoanalytic frame.

From my perspective, as psychoanalysts practicing in the contemporary United States, we may take advantage of the various reactions among our Argentine colleagues to stimulate our own thinking about what we do as citizens and as psychoanalytic practitioners. Relevant to this point was a study done by Andrew Samuels in the early 1990s, which he based on a detailed inquiry of psychoanalysts in many countries as to what they considered the legitimate domain of psychoanalytic work. I would like to mention two important observations Samuels made. First, many more analysts than he had assumed actually deal with political reality in the clinical setting; and second, the group of analysts who do this most is from the USA. Samuels writes that a total of 83% of respondents from the USA say they deal with political reality, though most express "distinct preference for regarding political material on the level of symbolism, intrapsychic process and transference [rather] than in terms of personal relevance or hermeneutical significance for the patient" (Samuels 1993:Chapter 10). I am encouraged by how many colleagues consider the political concerns of their patients, but I am also struck by the proclivity to put limited interpretive parameters around the material. It seems to me that our profession needs to consider political life as a significant aspect of our own and our patients' psychic experience, worthy of being a legitimate part of any treatment in terms, to use Samuels' words, of its "personal relevance or hermeneutical significance for the patient." Samuels noted that those psychoanalysts who do not do so reported that their disinclination stems from a conviction that they do not know or understand much about the social and political world or that it would be an ethical violation of what they presume to constitute the psychoanalytic frame. I would suggest that, perhaps more than ever, we professionals, like all other citizens of the USA, are presented with the challenge to think more seriously about and even study what we call social reality so that we feel more capable of providing our patients with a space to explore their own thoughts and feelings.

The time of terror in which we now live, while different from the dynamics of the Argentine military dictatorship, is nonetheless also characterized by a complex and multifaceted assault on citizens' collective sense of safety and well-being. We live in a traumatogenic environment whose multiple threats to our security, and perhaps even to our very survival, originate not only from potential terrorist threats from abroad but from the policies of our own government as well. Since the tragic events on 9/11, the Bush administration has developed a course of action that, while being depicted as a justifiable *defense* against aggression, represents an escalation of a tradition of US global reach and aggressive diplomatic, military, and corporate policies toward countries throughout Asia, Africa, and Latin America. There are many studies that document the history of US violations of the national integrity of countries around the world (Johnson 2004) and a growing literature that analyzes the Bush administration's faithful implementation of a strategy worked out long before 9/11 to sustain the US as the only superpower in the twenty-first century (Project for the New American Century 1997). To the misfortune of the citizens of the USA, it was almost certain that the Bush administration's response to the horrendous terrorist attacks on the World Trade Center and the Pentagon would escalate unilateral US military and economic policies abroad. Government priorities foreclosed the possibility that in the traumatic aftermath of the unprecedented attack on the country citizens would experience a leader(ship) capable of modeling restraint and the capacity to tolerate psychic states of anxiety, fear, and rage in a crisis situation. US leaders were not prepared to provide, in Winnicottian terms, a new potential space, or, from a Bionian perspective, a containing environment so as to permit the considered exploration of important questions, the honest answers to which might have expanded the options of the USA in the direction of diminishing the cycles of violence in the world. There is no doubt that the neoconservative agenda has been able to take hold of the country on a broad range of social, political, and economic priorities as a result of the psychological atmosphere since 9/11. Although the political decisions and economic policies of the Bush administration have constituted a redistribution of the wealth of the USA from the majority upward to a small elite, it has been able to secure consensual support from a significant percentage of the population suffering from a sense of vulnerability and fear and thus not predisposed to question and analyze the general impact of its government's policies. At first, the government's bellicose actions fulfilled citizens' fantasies of being rescued by a strong leader who would enact wishes for revenge. The government's simplistic discourse, which bifurcated the world into good and bad, civilization vs barbarism, the Christian world vs Evil, provided citizens with the means by which they could identify with an all-powerful goodness, while all that was bad was projected onto a demonized other. In a fashion similar to the reaction of citizens during the Argentine Dirty War, many people in the USA, by virtue of their need to ward off feelings of extreme helplessness, had recourse to unconscious defenses that merged easily with prevailing themes in the patriotic ideology of the mass media and government discourse that inhibited their ability to recognize the multifaceted assault on their safety and welfare.

In the months that followed 9/11, the corporate-controlled mass media played a complicit role through campaigns of disinformation that confused and obfuscated, labeling any critical perspective on US policy as non-patriotic. In the initial climate of intimidation that was produced by the Patriot Act and its attack on civil liberties, freedom of speech was compromised and self-censorship more widely employed. A traumatized people shielded themselves from what Robert Lifton calls collective "death anxiety" (Caruth 1995) via an identification with an aggressor government that was projecting death and dying onto others through its unilateral right to declare war, occupy other countries, and threaten those that have attempted to acquire nuclear capacity. All the while, this government is simultaneously initiating plans to develop a new generation of "baby" nuclear bombs and to militarize outer space. The superpower seems unable or unwilling to recognize its role in further polarizing the world and contributing to an intensification of paranoid-schizoid states and defensive splitting already extant among other peoples and their governments as well as within the USA itself.

However, in the past year, the sociopolitical environment has begun to shift. In spite of the initial responses of most US citizens to our aggression-saturated social reality, more and more people have developed a capacity for rebellious separation/differentiation from public authority, intensified by indignation and rage at growing evidence of economic and social inequities and political corruption perpetrated by the government. Increasingly, a transitional space within the public sphere is widening, and more people are choosing to act in concert in a reparative impulse toward the construction of foreign and domestic policies that have the potential to diminish violence in the world and to increase social and economic justice. These developments represent a positive step in the dismantling of the psychodynamics that sustain a bystander population.

I would like to end this exploration by addressing how the current political situation in the USA is viewed from Latin America, given its historical experience with state terror. Five months ago I returned to Buenos Aires to continue a research project based in part on interviews of psychoanalysts and other participants in the spontaneous popular movements that arose in December 2001, when Argentina experienced a complete economic meltdown. Up until that time, the country had been the poster child of the US-sponsored free market globalization model that had dominated since the 1980s throughout the hemisphere. However, Argentina's economic collapse called into question the viability of corporate globalization as a strategy for economic development and the fulfillment of human needs. I went to Rio de Janeiro, as well, where for the second time I participated in an international psychoanalytic congress called The Estates General of Psychoanalysis, the first meeting of which had been held at the Sorbonne in Paris in 2000.

In Buenos Aires and Rio I had an opportunity to share my understanding of the complex meanings of what has transpired in the USA since

September 11 and to learn about their views of the current political culture in the USA. Several specific experiences will serve by way of illustration. In Buenos Aires, I was invited by psychoanalytic colleagues to speak about what is happening in the USA to a diverse group of professionals, intellectuals, psychoanalysts, and workers in the cultural center of a factory called Grissinopoli. This factory, which produces breads, biscuits, and crackers, is one of about 200 "liberated factories" in and around Buenos Aires that were taken over by the workers when, following the economic meltdown in December 2001, the bosses fled the country, absconding with their capital and leaving indebted businesses and workers who had not been paid for months. The Grissinopoli workers, like thousands of their counterparts, occupied the factory and began to run it themselves. Many were women and they constituted themselves into a cooperative called The New Hope. A group of psychoanalysts interested in working with people engaged in social struggles have facilitated this progressive departure from the customary place of workers in society both psychologically and socially. They have undergone a shift from a passive and submissive psychic and ideological relationship to authority to one of assertion of their right to take control over their lives on their own and their families' behalf. At Grissinopoli, the psychoanalysts have played a pivotal role in the development of a mutually supportive and creative relationship between the workers and the community surrounding the factory and helped to establish a cultural center within the factory that has functioned to bring together Buenos Aires' intellectuals, professionals, artists, and working-class people associated with the factory. It was in this environment that I presented a paper on the psychological meanings of the current political culture in the USA. In the very intense discussion that followed, what most stands out in the context of my comments on the bystander phenomenon was the repeated expression of surprise and appreciation that someone from the United States was thinking in a critical fashion similar to their own about the psychosocial aspects of the response of the USA to 9/11. While they all recognized that the USA has every right to find and prosecute those responsible for the terrorist attacks, they believe that the world's only superpower must deal with the growing resentment of its global reach. Many pointed out that with more than 700 US military bases throughout the world and aggressive policies aimed at controlling most of the earth's energy resources regardless of whose country they happen to be located in, the USA has contributed to the growing tensions throughout the world that threaten international stability. They were surprised to hear that I held similar views. In spite of the sophistication and international contacts characteristic of the literati in the audience, as of November 2003, few were aware of the dissident voices in the USA, attributable perhaps to the success of the corporate media that until recently has successfully kept rather invisible the growing divergence from consensus politics in the USA.

My experience in Rio was similar, quite dramatically so. There, at the Estates General of Psychoanalysis congress, over 400 participants from Latin America and Europe gathered for four days to address the problems of the malaise of our time. Only two psychoanalysts – my colleague and husband Stephen Portuges and I – had come from the United States to participate in the congress. The central themes focused on how psychoanalysis can continue to be relevant to the various contemporary discontents from which human beings suffer throughout the world. Unlike the majority of psychoanalytic meetings, the Estates General is concerned with social and political issues and how a psychoanalytic appreciation of the convergence between social and psychic reality can shed light on the psychological effects of living in an increasingly decentering and terrifying world. Indicative of this interest were two of the scheduled keynote speakers: the Italian philosopher, Antonio Negri, whose work on empire has made him an international authority and critical voice among intellectuals and political activists associated with the global justice movement; and Pakistani-born, London-based journalist, broadcaster, playwright, and novelist, Tariq Ali, whose latest books are *The Clash of Fundamentalisms: Crusades, Jihads and Modernity* (2003) and *Bush in Babylon: The Recolonization of Iraq* (2004). The themes of their presentations and the discussions that followed centered around the emergence of empire in the contemporary world and the dangerous contradictions that are being played out in response, especially in South Asia and the Middle East. In these exchanges, psychoanalysts and radical social theorists struggled together to understand the psychological and social implications of the major crises that face human beings today. The rest of the dialogue during the congress was organized around the following areas: vicissitudes of subjectivity in the postmodern world; psychoanalysis, politics and the state; psychoanalytic experience and contemporary culture; and the mass media's production of new subjectivities and the social imaginary. Throughout, colleagues articulated a shared critical perspective on the prevailing international social order, corporate globalization, terrorism as a strategy for political change, and the international role of the US government in escalating the cycles of violence in today's world.

Brazilian journalists were covering the plenaries and interviewing participants daily. One journalist interviewed Dr Portuges and me, prefacing her interest in our views by gently inquiring how it felt to be the only two North Americans in such an anti-US political and intellectual climate. Our responses, which indicated our agreement with the participants' views regarding US global reach, were apparently so discrepant with Brazilian assumptions that the majority of people in the USA provide consensual support for the government's policies and priorities, that they made the front page of a major Rio newspaper the following day. During my presentation in the plenary on the mass media's production of new subjectivities and the social imaginary, I began by noting the appropriateness of my inclusion in this plenary because, as I explained, I am from California, where people clearly have a difficult time distinguishing between fantasy and reality, given their recent election of the Terminator as the governor of the state. I then went on to talk about the current political culture in the post-9/11 environment and its psychological meanings. However, I noted, alongside those whose subjectivity is profoundly affected by the corporate-created definitions of legitimate leadership, many dissident voices and movements are arising in the USA that demonstrate the psychological capacity to separate and individuate from social authority. I suggested that the deepening polarization in that country, while problematic in many ways, represents a positive step in the dismantling of the psychodynamics that sustain a bystander population whose government implements unacceptable policies in their name. To my surprise and embarrassment, I received a standing ovation. The reason I describe this experience is that it highlights the fears experienced by people in other countries who assume that there is no diversity of opinion in the USA and no countervailing influence that can impact on the direction of US policy in the world. Such anxieties are due in large part to the lack of coverage by the international corporate print and electronic media, which thus successfully "disappear" oppositional movements from view, a lamentable situation that fuels anti-Americanism internationally. Later, as I chatted privately with colleagues, they explained that the enthusiastic reception to my presentation had represented a spontaneous expression of relief and appreciation that the US population is not only composed of those who uncritically endorse or "stand by" their government, but of people as well who constitute an oppositional perspective to the prevailing policies that people in other countries find so threatening.

I believe that, as citizens of the most powerful nation in the world, and especially perhaps as psychoanalysts, it is our social responsibility to understand the complex nature of subjectivity as it is formed in relation to a sociosymbolic order composed of asymmetrical relations of power and force and, like our Argentine dissident colleagues, to hone our skills to take it into account in the clinical setting. Perhaps it is important to clarify that while I do not advocate my analysis as the only viable one to explain the factors responsible for the creation of our traumatogenic environment, I do believe that as psychoanalysts it is essential that we commit ourselves to the important task of independently making sense for ourselves – mindful of the ideological function of government and media discourse – of what today constitutes our time of terror. Neither do I advocate that we impose whatever views we have of social reality on our patients. Rather, I am suggesting that we acknowledge the significance of our patients' as well as our own experience in the social/political world, so as to permit our mutual and reciprocal exploration within the psychoanalytic frame of the objective aspects of our patients' subjectivity. I am suggesting that the psychoanalytic space is a crucial matrix in which our patients and we can use our minds together to reflect on how the impingements of social reality profoundly affect us. A collaborative psychoanalytic exploration of subjectivity that overcomes the reductionism of an exclusive focus on psychic reality, especially during a period of multiple escalating social, economic, and political dangers, can help to diminish the isolation of the bystander. It can help, as well, to develop psychological strategies that realistically contain anxieties stimulated by multiple threats in this time of terror. Individuals who have such an opportunity may be more able to become thoughtful citizens actively engaged in civic life. Without a critical mass of such citizens, we run the risk of living in a democracy in name only.

References

Ali, T. (2003) *The Clash of Fundamentalisms: Crusades, Jihads and Modernity*. New York: Verso.

Ali, T. (2004) *Bush in Babylon: The Recolonization of Iraq*. London: Verso.

Caruth, C. (1995) An interview with Robert Jay Lifton. *Trauma: Explorations in Memory*. Baltimore, MD: Johns Hopkins University Press.

Diaz, J. P. (1993) The silences of culture. In S. Sosnowski and L. B. Popkin (eds), *Repression, Exile, and Democracy*. Durham, NC: Duke University Press.

Hollander, N. (1997) *Love in a Time of Hate: Liberation Psychology in Latin America*. New York: Other Press.

Hollander, N. (1999) The individual and the transitional space of authoritarian society. *Mind and Human Interaction*, 10(2):98–109.

Johnson, C. (2004) *The Sorrows of Empire: Militarism, Secrecy and the End of the Republic*. New York: Henry Holt and Co.

Project for the New American Century (1997) Website: http://www.newamericancentury.org/statementofprinciples.htm

Samuels, A. (1993) *The Political Psyche*. London: Routledge.

Staub, E. (1989) *The Roots of Evil: The Origins of Genocide and Other Group Violence*. Cambridge, UK: Cambridge University Press.

Timmerman, J. (1982) *Prisoner without a Name, Cell without a Number*. New York: Vintage Books.

Viñar, M. and Viñar, M. (1993) *Fracturas de Memoria: Crónicas para una Memoria por Venir*. Montevideo, Uruguay: Ediciones Trilce.

Volnovich, J. C. (August 1994) Personal communication, Buenos Aires.

Chapter 12

Is politics the last taboo in psychoanalysis?[1]

A roundtable discussion with Neil Altman, Jessica Benjamin, Ted Jacobs and Paul Wachtel. Moderated by Amanda Hirsch Geffner

Introduction

On a warm spring evening in early May 2004, four prominent Manhattan psychoanalysts (Neil Altman, Jessica Benjamin, Ted Jacobs, and Paul Wachtel) got together at the invitation of *Psychoanalytic Perspectives* to talk about politics and psychoanalysis. Each participant in the discussion had been provided with a list of questions, composed by the journal's editorial board, to reflect upon in advance. Some of the questions were later selected by the group as foci for the evening's conversation, while others, although not directly asked, helped serve as a shared ideational context, and remained accessible as reference points for the hovering attention of those involved.

The process of formulating these questions is a story in itself, to be told, perhaps, at a later date (see also Chapter 16, this volume). Suffice it to say that in this post-9/11, post-invasion-of-Iraq, pre-presidential-election time period, a number of us have found ourselves more moved by things political than we have been in many, many years. This sentiment has come to infuse our lives, our patients' lives, and our in-session lives with patients. Emotions (fear, sadness, anger, even excitement) about things beyond the immediate, familial–social sphere are running high, finding resonance with – and magnifying – many of our more personal concerns in the process. The consequences of political action or inaction have become, it seems, more vivid, more tangible. In many cases, we find ourselves entering into unfamiliar and often volatile territory with family, with friends, with colleagues and (dare it be said out loud?) with our patients, as well.

It had been our desire to provide an intimate, collegial setting for the discussion – perhaps oxymoronically, one in which the participants would feel relatively contained and sheltered from the very public and political forces they were convening to discuss (see below, Neil Altman's and Paul Wachtel's related comments on, respectively, a tension between the "real-life" dangers often faced by patients and the constructed "safety" of the analytic frame, and the wish to find alternatives to the dualistic concepts of "inner" and "outer" worlds). Accordingly, other than the panelists themselves, only a small circle of those who had a role in moderating, hosting, and taping the event were present: *Perspectives* editors Kenneth Frank, Judith Becker Greenwald, Amanda Hirsch Geffner, Sheldon Itzkowitz, and Mary Sussillo, and the audiographer Michael Geffner.

In the interests of creating a lively and spontaneous experience (for participants and readers alike), we asked that the panelists not prepare written statements or papers, and editing of the transcript of the discussion (for publication purposes) was kept to a minimum. By virtue of this less formal approach, the panelists, each an experienced scholar/clinician in his or her own right, are in addition presented here in a vital, in-the-moment, rawer way, as complex individuals, as citizens. As the questions were many and the time and word-space limited, responses and ensuing discussions were, in places, halted, left dangling and under construction, in order not to have left unturned the next ideational stone. Despite the multiple mini-cliffhangers this stone-skipping, ripple-making method may have produced, we hope that the accompanying frustration for the reader will be optimal, and inspiring of the impulse to embellish or to fill in the blanks with thoughts (reactions, protestations, provocations, speculations) of his or her own.

Amanda Hirsch Geffner, July 2004

Welcoming remarks

Amanda Hirsch Geffner: Thank you for being here tonight to participate in this roundtable discussion on the topic of psychoanalysis and politics. We hope for you to explore the relationship between these two spheres of action and interaction, the one typically private, intimate, dyadic; the other basically public, utilizing group energies, and broadcast via mass media. We will be asking you for your thoughts on if, where, and how the two processes of mutual influence and change overlap and interact (or have the potential to), and if, where, and how they do not. This discussion is, of course, being held in the context of an upcoming national presidential election in a post-9/11 world, a world "presenting," so to speak, with powerful international and political tensions.

Such tensions take their toll – manifestly and in ways unrecognized – on both analysts and analysands, as well as on psychoanalytic relationships. We invite you tonight to jointly grapple with several questions that *Psychoanalytic Perspectives* has developed on politics and psychoanalysis, with an eye to deepening and extending our understanding of the impact of the current political climate on our work (and vice versa – of the potential impact of our work on our politics and on the current political climate). We especially hope that tonight's discussion will stimulate and begin to advance new ways of thinking about working with patients under these intense conditions. In recognition of a historical and ongoing sense of controversy and ambivalence regarding the intermingling of these two experiences, we have named (or set) this roundtable with the descriptive question: "Is politics the last taboo in psychoanalysis?"

The questions

I: Psychotherapy and social action

AHG: The first question is: how do the experiences of conducting psychotherapy and engaging in social action have an impact upon each other? Is it appropriate, and is it possible, to engage in an exploration of politics in psychoanalytic treatment without closing down the analytic space and/or falling into binary patterns of dominance and submission? What other dyadic problems might come up? What about neutrality/anonymity/self-disclosure considerations?

Neil Altman: I'll address part of this question. I think that the way that the two experiences impact on each other or influence each other in my mind has to do with the experience of impasses. Getting into impasses and trying to find a way out of impasses in psychoanalysis or psychotherapy seems to have a lot of relevance to how one thinks about how political disputes get engaged and then either get stuck or unstuck. So, experiences of – and here I draw on Jessica's work a lot – the experience of getting into what she calls a split complementarity, wherein there is a kind of a splitting going on, where there's an inability to see the other person's point of view. For example, in a situation where you charged for a missed appointment and the other person, the patient, feels that that's unfair. So, my point of view is that I'm entitled to be paid for the time and their point of view is they shouldn't have to pay for services not rendered; both entirely valid perspectives, and the only way that that can be resolved is if each person can find a way to take account of the other person's point of view.

To me, this is an analogue for the Israeli–Palestinian situation, for example, where, from my point of view, there are two perspectives, both of which are entirely valid, and it's a split complementarity; neither side can see beyond their own point of view to the other side. And the question is, how do you work with that? How do you both get beyond that? You know, there's the vicious-circle phenomenon. As Jessica points out in *The Bonds of Love* [1988], dominant–submissive relationships and violence are the ultimate result of needing to assert one's point of view at the expense of the other person's point of view. The alternative is to find within oneself some resonance with the other person's point of view, even as you retain your own point of view. And that's the tricky thing that I think we, as psychoanalysts, get a lot of experience in doing – not giving up our own point of view, but at the same time finding a way to resonate with the other person's point of view, so that they feel understood. And if they feel understood, then they're more likely to feel free to resonate with your point of view.

We have a lot of advantages as psychoanalysts; we have a certain protection that political actors don't have, and we also have the rituals of our work, which have to do with exploration of the other person's experience, and so that's a setup for being able to transcend these kind of splitting situations that don't necessarily happen, that are very hard to make happen in a political kind of discussion. But I think that's something that one learns as a psychotherapist that is very valuable for social action.

Paul Wachtel: I agree with that very much, but also I think we need to think about what are the limits that impede the extension from the analytic dyad to the group phenomenon. And what I'm thinking of particularly is: as you were talking, it brought back an experience I had back in 1969 when I visited the Soviet Union at a time when the Vietnam War was still going on, and I went with a group where we had lots of opportunities to discuss things with Soviet citizens – everyday citizens and people in somewhat official positions – and I sort of took a position (which was easy for me, because I was opposed to the war and I was critical of my own country in many ways) – and I took a position like what Neil is describing of conveying my appreciation of their point of view, but expecting at some point some reciprocation, which was totally not forthcoming, I think not because of the properties of them as individuals, but because they were part of a system that didn't allow for that kind of reciprocation. So that I think that part of what happens is that when group mores reinforce a certain position, that's part of why it becomes locked in much more tightly. So, I agree very much in principle, but it may be worth our thinking about what the obstacles are to kind of getting the spark to leap over from the individual to the group situation.

Jessica Benjamin: What I found myself thinking about was this – recently, I did go on a trip to Israel and the Palestinian Territories – how when talking with people, I found that something that I had suspected from my analytic work on the issue of recognition actually seemed to be very much the case: that acknowledgment of the other person's suffering that we may not have directly caused, but in which we participate as Americans, and in which I participate, in some sense, as a Jew, was enormously important. I found that because this is being done in my name, regardless of the political background of the oppression carried out in the Territories by the Israeli Army, I need to acknowledge responsibility. My identification of responsibility for, first, not really being able to know or understand the suffering of the Palestinians, and secondly, being in some way allied with those who cause it, was important to me, and had a huge effect for people there. In many cases, they were less interested in political details in many ways than they were in having this acknowledgment. That is to say that this was the first step in any political process. And this came in the context of my rather openly espoused view that nonviolence would be a very helpful strategy for them and make it possible for there to be more conflict resolution and also more sympathy for their cause in America.

And, in my view, this stance toward acknowledgment comes directly out of my psychoanalytic practice, where I feel that it's necessary, at times, to apologize for suffering, regardless of whether you're truly the instigator – no, you're not, you're just the activator of old traumas, old pain – but you acknowledge that you have, you know, bumped into the person's bruise, and you acknowledge that there is hurt and pain and that you may have some responsibility for that, and in doing this, you alleviate a whole level of tension that makes it possible, then, to talk about, to explore. So, for me, even though this is not going to extend to all of politics, there are specific parts of politics where what we learn in the clinic is extremely germane.

Ted Jacobs: I just want to respond to a different part of this question, which I think was implied – anyway, to me – which has to do with the exploration of politics *in* the psychoanalytic treatment itself. And, as I was thinking about this, I was really surprised myself to realize that in over 40 years of practice, very rarely have I entered into a political discussion with a patient. In fact, I would say that this is an area that is, consciously or unconsciously, avoided by both therapists and patients quite regularly. Even in major events in the world, sometimes it's surprising how little it comes up in the treatment. I mean, this is partly understandable from the point of view where the patient is concerned about their inner world and their own particular issues, but I think there's something else that goes on, and that is that both people may be wary of entering into a situation in which very strong and sometimes quite irrational feelings will enter into it, so that one can easily lose one's stance as a therapist, because of one's own passions or feelings with regard to a particular issue. And patients, too, will sense that their views may not be in accord with yours, and they too may avoid that. So there may be here a kind of collusion to avoid a particularly important topic – one, however, that I think always has to be looked at not only in its overt, manifest form, but also with an eye to what its particular meaning is to the patient, so that we don't speak of it [politics] quite the same way as we would with others, but rather understand the unconscious or the less unconscious meaning to the patient. It's a tricky area, I think one that is very well labeled as a "last taboo," and one that we really should explore more in detail.

PW: To amplify in some way what Ted is referring to, I remembered one of the classic observations that calls the idea of neutrality into question. In

Ralph Greenson's book (1967), he describes a patient who, at a certain point, refers to Greenson's politically liberal positions and the challenge to the patient's conservative views, and Greenson didn't think he had said anything about it, and asked, "On what basis do you say that?" And the patient said something like (I guess this must have taken place back in the forties, this actual session of analysis), "Whenever I say something negative about Roosevelt, you ask for my associations . . . [*group laughter*] and when I say something positive, you don't say anything" [*group laughter*]. So, I think it comes through sort of in unconscious ways, but we don't really tend to pick it up.

JB: My patients talk about their political views with me constantly, and they know what my political views are, whether I tell them or not, and that has to do with my style, my reputation, my writings – I don't know, what else? All kinds of things, so that only people who are extremely outside my cultural world (and there are some people) don't know what my politics are. Anybody who's inside my cultural world can tell what my politics are. I'm totally legible to them, within a certain framework, though, of course, they don't know the specifics. And I think that that has everything to do with how they then use politics with me, because they are using it on the assumption that we have certain fundamental agreements. Whereas, if they thought that we didn't, they would use the politics very differently, and maybe they wouldn't talk about it, but this way it gets used a lot.

NA: The way that Ted was putting things before made it sound like politics maybe *is* the last taboo in psychoanalysis, that it's actually the place one should go for, or at least one should be aware of the anxieties organizing not talking about it. But then I was also thinking about the issue of what's manifest and what's latent, and I was thinking it could go either way; that a political discussion – a manifestly political discussion – could have latent meaning at some psychological level, but it could be the other way around, too, whereas something that's not manifestly political could be latently political. And, to me, that's where I'm very confused about how to engage, if I think of something as latently political – for example, I think the area that's best explored in this respect has been brought to light by feminism; you know, people can talk about self-denigrating activities that they engage in and you can hear in that a reflection of their position in society as women. It brings up the issue of the sociocultural unconscious, the way that the psyche is organized by sociocultural factors, and how to engage that in a treatment without doing something didactic. That's the place where I get stuck.

TJ: Just to share a clinical vignette: I was working with a patient who was an extremely right-wing Republican woman who was about as far right as one could get, and hated all the things that I valued, but I felt – whether I was right or wrong, I don't know, but I felt that it was a kind of dangerous area to enter into directly. But, through talking about it – some of her identifications with her father, who was very much a hero, just as Bush and Cheney were heroes to her – one was able to get at some of the roots of the particular view that she had, which really, I think, had a lot to do with these kind of unconscious actors, not so much with the more manifest and, I think, in her mind, not really as important issues of the values or the social policies of these people, but rather with their connection unconsciously with a loved and rather ambivalently held figure. So, one way that I found, at least with her, of dealing with the issue was more by dealing with its underlying underpinnings, rather than to speak directly about that. Now, that might have been a mistake. It might have been due to my anxiety more than anything else, but I think it does cause a challenge clinically that we haven't really addressed, or at least I haven't addressed, very well.

AHG: Well, each of you has made interesting points, and I'm also wondering if there are ways that you might approach it differently, based on what school of analytic thought you come from. That may come up further as we go along. And I was also curious about what you said, Jessica, about being in Israel and speaking with the Palestinians and them feeling empathized with and being able to respond. As you said, it works in many cases, but I was wondering about examples of where that doesn't work, about the limits of that –

JB: You want me to be more specific about when it doesn't work? There are times when you can't really acknowledge or accept another person's hatred, for instance, and that hatred really makes you too uncomfortable and anxious, and you're giving lip service to acknowledgment, but you're not really acknowledging. A friend of mine describes a group of Buddhist peace workers going to an Arab village, and then when they actually had to hear about the people from the village who'd been killed, they fell apart, they became defensive, they lost all their nonreactivity. And so, I guess that's what we're talking about. We're talking about the fact that, first of all, we're all human, and we fall apart in the face of hatred and aggression or too much pain, or we dissociate, or we become unable to really think in these situations. The second thing is that we don't know yet how we can translate this into the larger political arena. We haven't found really good ways of translating this into the larger political arena, except that certain nonviolent movements have clearly used this and channeled this kind of approach, but we're not doing that. We [therapists] maybe need to [collectively] think about it.

II: Polarization

AHG: The next question is also one you [Jessica] wanted to address: what group psychological processes (such as trends of extreme and emotional polarization and mutual demonization of the political sides – liberals versus conservatives, Democrats versus Republicans, etc.) do you see playing a significant role in current public discourse and/or group dynamics? How do you psychologically understand these phenomena? (Are we, for example, seeing a process related to intrapsychic splitting played out on the American sociopolitical level, and if so, what function might it serve, adaptive or otherwise?) If possible, in answering this question, please try to address blind spots or other problematic dynamics of the groups towards which you feel the strongest affinity.

JB: Well, before I get to my self-criticism of the Left, I'll start by saying that I don't think that what you call "mutual demonization" is really equal. I actually strenuously object to this – that is to say, we're right and they're wrong. No, seriously [*group laughter*], they're demonizing us and we're correct about them [*more laughter*]. The problem is the following: that if we think about the opposition that's occurring right now in terms of fundamentalism versus liberalism, then clearly one of the contradictions that we have to deal with is that the fundamentalist position is by definition intolerant and we [liberals] are by definition tolerant, and yet we can't really tolerate their intolerance. So we come into this very difficult place.

It's easy to see their intolerance at work; it's easy to see that they don't want to give space to our point of view. It's also equally easy to see that our organizations are at least nominally committed to giving space to their point of view. The American Civil Liberties Union famously defended the Nazis' right to demonstrate in Skokie. We don't say that everyone *has* to have an abortion. So, nominally we have this position where we are on the side of the basic American values of tolerance and freedom of speech, etc., and yet we are continually portrayed as being sort of anti-American and in the wrong by the fundamentalist camp, which actually uses the term "freedom" constantly; [President] Bush constantly talks about freedom.

So, we're in a very peculiar world, where to be liberal is to be against freedom and to be a fundamentalist is to be for freedom. And, given this fact, I think that it is wholly comprehensible that our [liberal] side would tend to be extremely frustrated and to react the way that clinically you react when you're dealing with someone who's very paranoid. This is not to say that all fundamentalists are paranoid, although I think their politics are definably paranoid – without question – and they involve projection and so forth. I'm not saying that all people who espouse that are more paranoid than people on our side – quite the contrary; that doesn't have to be the case, but that's another issue we'll get into – but what I am saying is that we face that particular piece of frustration.

Now, the way that I would want to deal with that is actually to break down a little bit more what I see as a sort of fundamental psychodynamic of the opposition between Right and Left, which is what I call the guilt/shame axis. I see the Left as being driven by guilt – guilt about having too much power or guilt about having too much, period – whereas I see the Right as being driven fundamentally by shame, that is, shame about being weak. So, the right-wing position is, in my view, organized around defending against weakness, vulnerability, dependency, femininity – as it's projectively identified as weakness – and so forth. If the Left responds to this via the guilt position, they simply confirm the paranoia of the Right, which is, you see, "Here are these people who really kind of embrace their weakness." They don't understand that we're driven by a sense that, actually, we have too much power and privilege and the rest of the world has too little. They see our guilt as a sign of our masochism, our willingness to take on the blame for something that we didn't do.

What impresses me about that, in part, is that we then end up not recognizing the fear that drives that [right-wing] position. That is to say, it's probably more difficult for people who assume our [liberal] position to actually get in touch with the fears and anxieties that drive the right-wing position and [we] instead resort to moralism about their position. For instance, we might say, "These people are so obviously selfish, or they are so obviously externalizing and projective, or they are so obviously engaging in splitting with regard to the degradation of the feminine, or they are so obviously racist with regard to the degradation of the other." So, it's so easy for us to be moralistic even in our psychoanalytic positioning about that viewpoint that they assume.[2]

Judith Becker Greenwald: I was curious, Jessica, if you think the fundamentalists are in a sadistic position, since you described the liberals to be in a masochistic position?

JB: Oh yeah, I think that they are. They are fundamentally embracing their sadism with a sense of righteousness. They feel entitled to be in a retaliatory position – I mean, they feel entitled to be in a position in which the other deserves our retaliatory action, because paradoxically, they are always acting out of a position of presumed victimization. And the problem is that, actually, each side has its own version of victimization, which I think makes for the underlying symmetry. In that sense, what I am trying to describe in relation to political difference has to do with different responses to victimization, and I think the right-wing response to victimization is to become sadistic. But then again, I think that our response to victimization is to, in a sense, have a reaction formation against sadism.[3]

NA: I think the analysis that Jessica laid out is so helpful, and I think the Democrats, every Democratic candidate should be, it should be required reading [*group laughter*]. It explains so much in terms of the Dukakis syndrome, the Jimmy Carter syndrome. And it also is very hopeful, I think, because the intolerance of fundamentalists can make them seem like an immovable, sort of monolithic force, and to see it in terms of shame opens it up, puts it in terms of dynamics that we can all identify with. I would just propose one amendment to the way Jessica laid that out, which is, I think liberal guilt is not basically about having too much; it's about wanting too much.

JB: OK, I'll go with that, but could you say a little bit more? Why do you say that?

NA: Because liberals, despite their guilt about having too much, don't give it up, the hypocrisy in –

JB: OK, so maybe it's not having versus wanting. It's about the fact that they don't renounce.

NA: It's the fact that they don't *want* to renounce.

JB: And they don't renounce.

NA: And they don't, but the knowledge that despite my sense of misgiving about having all the things that I have and the inequities that are associated with that, I won't give them up. It would have to be torn away from me. And I just feel that that's more fundamentally what I feel guilty about – which is important, by the way, because it links us to the Right [*group agreement*].

AHG: It sort of takes away from some of that polarization.

NA: Yeah.

AHG: I think what you're saying also relates to the question about working with conflicts between self-interest and the public good, which I hope we'll also get to.[4]

PW: I want to add something. It doesn't contradict anything that's been said so far, but I think it gives a somewhat different angle on it. When I think about fundamentalism, which we've been talking about now for a while, it seems to me that there's another way to look at both the problems of fundamentalism and the potential for addressing the phenomenon, because I think we are, for example, equating fundamentalism with sort of hard Right attitudes. Certainly it's true that that is often the case, but I think one of the things that from our non-fundamentalist point of view is very obvious is that scripture is inherently ambiguous. It doesn't *necessarily* point to right-wing values. In other words, any particular value may not be [liberal], but you can make a case for very liberal positions from scriptural foundations. You know, you might not call Martin Luther King a fundamentalist, but he certainly rooted his work in scripture.

I think there's another potential problem with fundamentalism that is important to bear in mind, which is the preemptive quality of it, in the sense that, if I look at the group dynamic dimension – which is sort of how the question was, in part, phrased – it seems to me that where we get into frightening and aggressive deadlocks politically is when one identification, one identity, one commitment becomes utterly preeminent, and then that becomes "us" and "them." In many ways, the potential resolution to this is crisscrossing identifications. That is, the way that we can begin to resolve "us"–"them" is when I have a connection with somebody who is like me in three respects and different from me in three others and, as a result, there isn't a clear or sharp answer to whether the other person is "like me" (one of "us") or "different from me" (one of "them"). Fundamentalism makes that harder, because one identification becomes utterly preeminent, and then the question really becomes, how can we work within that to, for example, highlight that there may be humane potentials in a biblical emphasis?[5]

AHG: We're discussing this mostly in terms of "fundamentalism" versus "liberalism," but as you [Paul] I think may have alluded to, there are also far-Right points of view that don't describe themselves as fundamentalist. Would anyone else like to respond to the topic or to each other?

TJ: I think that sometimes we get caught up in trying to maintain certain self-representations as ideal selves in one way or another, or as standing for certain values, and we want to see ourselves and want others to see us in a particular way, so that fraternizing with the "enemy," in a way, becomes something unacceptable. And yet, in the practical world, one has to get elected, one has to pass legislation, and that is always dealing with others in a way that allows the process to move forward, and if one maintains too ideal a stance, you cannot do that. So some people who we don't always like so well may be more effective in reaching some of the goals that we endorse.[6]

III: Core beliefs

AHG: Due to the time, we need to move on to the next question, which you showed interest in, Paul: how do you view the complex connection (if, in fact, you believe there is one) between the core psychodynamic underpinnings of an individual's identity, his or her view of the human condition, and the stances he or she takes *vis-à-vis* political issues? And then, on a related note, what do you believe is the connection (if any) between a psychoanalyst's various theories about what helps people to change and grow and the political beliefs he or she espouses?

PW: Well, I think I was interested in that question because of an apparent contradiction that has interested me for a long time, which is that it seems to me that as far back at least as I've been a member of the profession, psychoanalysis has clearly been a liberal profession politically, and that there are relatively few conservative psychoanalysts, at least as I – look, I'm sure there are, but, you know, relatively few. And yet, at the same time, the profession has seemed to be very conservative in at least two different respects. One is it changes very slowly. It, for many years, was organized around an iconic figure. It was organized very hierarchically. There was kind of an enforcement (implicitly, at least) of a discipline, and the possibility of excommunication, and so on. And the other is that psychoanalytic technique, for many, many years was – and in its more conservative forms, still is – conservative, not just in the sense of retaining a tradition and sticking to an orthodoxy of sorts, but in the very content of it.

And one of the things that has illuminated this for me a little bit more, with the opportunity for me to explicate what I mean by that, is I've been very interested recently in the work of George Lakoff (2002), who's a linguistic cognitive scientist, who has been looking at some of the psychological foundations of liberal and conservative outlooks, and he suggests a distinction that in some way parallels and intersects in interesting ways with what Jessica was talking about around the guilt/shame axis. He talks about two visions of the family that impact upon individual personalities, but also upon an individual's vision of the body politic as a family; what he calls the "strict father" model, which is associated with a conservative outlook, and the "nurturant parent" model – and it's not a coincidence that one says "father," and one says "parent" – which he associates more with the liberal outlook.

And when I read his description, the "strict father" model includes a kind of vision of people as needing to be disciplined, as inherently in some way unbridled in their aggression or their self, trying to grab for themselves and so on, needing to be disciplined, but also needing to learn to work hard in order to accomplish, and so on. And it seems to me that the more traditional psychoanalytic model is very much rooted in that vision – the instincts, you know, *Civilization and Its Discontents*, and a vision of our basic nature being antisocial, the notions of acting out and trying to keep the patient from gaining too much gratification, from manipulating for gratification; all of that very much fits the "strict father" model. In some way, the relational models fit more the "nurturant parent" model.

I think that in all our psychoanalytic patients, we often misconstrue character as singular. We talk about people as being fixated at a certain developmental level. We talk about someone who's pre-oedipal or oedipal, and so on, and actually, we have a great multiplicity. And I think in some way what happened in the evolution of psychoanalytic technique is that the "nurturant parent" part of analysts was being extended to society and the "strict father" part of them was being expressed in sessions in some ways, and that that is part of how these two seemingly contradictory visions were getting expressed. And in that sense, the "nurturant parent" vision of therapy may be a more internally consistent vision for analysts who are also politically more liberal, and may, in part, reflect the shift that has begun to occur in psychoanalytic technique.

JB: Well, I see a couple of things immediately when you talk about this. First of all, what Lakoff says goes back to what Adorno, Horkheimer, and the Frankfurt people already said in the *Authoritarian Personality* studies (Adorno 1969). That goes back a long way. And the vision of the Right as having this view of human nature, that we are greedy and grasping, is also well known, that is to say, goes back to conservative thought and the whole debate between conservatism and liberalism in the late modern era. But it also seems to me that, at the same time, there is something new, and something specific to psychoanalysis, that is not only about nurturing, but about ambiguity, contradiction, and lack of moralism. This is not just associated with nurturance, it's associated with a more postmodern position, where it doesn't matter whether people are greedy and grasping or not. It doesn't matter whether their nature is to be punitive or not. That is to say, we can embrace this idea – and this is what I hear you saying – we can embrace the idea that people have such impulses, if we like. That is to say, we can have a fairly Freudian view or we can have a more object-relational view, in which we see things in terms of needs; in either case, we can still – with each of these positions – come to fairly radical or left-wing, liberal views, as the history of psychoanalysis has shown.

So this really raises a problem for me, in terms of the fact that if, you know, Fenichel and I can have fairly similar politics – in fact, all of the old Viennese leftists basically accepted what Freud said – how do you explain the fact that we have something in common? And I think that, as I said, I find it to be related to something about our belief in – that rather than accepting a sort of a moralistic, ideal-driven stance (and this relates to what Ted said before, actually), that we have a notion that it is possible for us to tolerate all kinds of things that we find out about ourselves and (now, here, I think I see the post-Freudian addition from my side of the fence) we can also tolerate finding out all of those things about the father, or the mother. So our belief, our commitment, is that we can stand to find out things about ourselves and about the other that are inherently painful and disappointing. And how we can do that is by having some kind of faith, either in the strength of self-reflection or the connection between ourselves and an other, who is committed to truth. Either way, there is some truth commitment. There is some commitment to facing what's going on underneath the surface that I think unites all analysts and causes them to move to a socially critical dimension that rejects authority, that insists we have to face what is unpleasant, either in human nature or society.

NA: I've been struggling with this a lot, too, because I've been wondering if there's anything inherent – it's been very clear to me that psychodynamics could be appropriated by any political position, like, say, the idea that right-wing people are disavowing weakness, let's say, could be countered by the idea that left-wing people are disavowing strength. You know, you could turn these things around. So if you talk about particular psychodynamics, psychoanalysis can be appropriated by any political position. But I've been grappling with maybe the same thing you are, with what – there's something inherent in psychoanalysis that – I won't give up the idea that there's something in psychoanalysis that is more consistent with, with what?

JB: A critical position.

NA: A critical, more tolerant position. On the other hand, there's also something about the destabilizing potential of psychoanalysis that may predispose toward authoritarianism, actually, like the kind of phenomenon that you were describing [Paul]. Orthodoxy within psychoanalysis may be precisely a reaction to the destabilizing potential. And in the same way that many fundamentalists have sometimes gone through chaotic periods in their lives, which they then end up resolving by being fundamentalists, there may be some kind of way in which psychoanalysis actually predisposes to an uncritical orthodoxy as well as undermining it.

IV: The last taboo?

AHG: This is a question that's not exactly on the list, but it's the title, and we were just wondering, why is it such a taboo, as both Ted and Neil mentioned? It does seem that everyone agrees there are a lot of mixed feelings about actually "doing" politics in the consulting room. So maybe we could talk about that a little bit.

NA: Well, whatever's taboo in psychoanalysis tends to be seen as a slippery slope, right? There's sex: sex is taboo, because it's a slippery slope. Anger isn't so taboo, because it's *not* such a slippery slope. I think you can conceive of being angry in a contained way a little bit better. The "uncontainability" of a topic makes it taboo. And politics feels like a slippery slope. I was just thinking about my temple. I was very uncomfortable with the fact that there was very little discussion about Israel and Palestine in our temple. We have a relatively new rabbi who's more to the right than had been traditional to that temple. So, I went to the rabbi and I told him I was uncomfortable with the fact that there was so little discussion, that I was having a lot of anguish as a Jew, because of the Middle East, and that I wanted more opportunity to process that in my shul. And he was open to that, and we kind of agreed, and we talked about how to set up something that wouldn't be a setup for people to be at each other's throats from the get-go, and how to frame the idea. And then, he forgot all about it, and I had to e-mail him after a month.

He had said he was going to send out a notice to the congregation; he forgot to do it. He said he was truly sorry, and he would get right to it, and then about a month later, he called me and he said, "I'm really sorry, but it's just fallen by the wayside, and I'm going to get to it right away," and again he didn't. And, finally, he said, "Let's get to it in the fall, anyway," you know, "we'll get to it in the fall." I just couldn't deal with that anymore, and I'm going to see another rabbi tomorrow about changing congregations. I've just had it, and I feel like that sort of thing can happen so easily when you get into politics with people. I started out trying to create a space in which there could be different points of view about the Middle East. That was what I wanted to do – where things could be talked about across points of view – and I ran into something that made me shut down, and I'm leaving. I'm furious.

PW: It's interesting, because I understand that completely. When I think of the clinical situation, what strikes me is that it almost works for me in the opposite direction – and I'm curious if it's true for the other panelists – in the sense that I find it relatively, surprisingly easy, in a way, to work with people who are to the right of me, whose political views are very troubling to me. And this is partly because I feel like I find it easier to maintain what is usually called neutrality. I think what's really going on is that I know there is such a potential for clash, I sort of keep reminding myself that my job here isn't to convert him, my job is to understand him and help him, and so on, and I find it relatively untroubling.

Where I have a tremendous difficulty is with patients who are to the left of me. And the difficulty there is that in many ways they are closer to my own ideal than I am, and I can feel guilty, even sometimes just about – I've worked with a couple of people, for example, who had relatively little money, because they were living lives that my superego approves of, so to speak. And then, the issue of my taking money from them when they're, you know, living out my ideals, and so on. Or just generally, their lives as a kind of threat to my self-representations, whereas my right-wing patients don't threaten my self-representations, because I'm secure as to which side I feel I identify with. But with those other patients it really becomes more troublesome. I'm curious if that's the case for others.

JB: Well, I see a couple of things as being very central to the taboo on dealing with politics, and I don't think it's the same as sexuality, actually, Neil. I think that, first of all, there's a kind of fury around nonrecognition that people can feel in relation to politics. And politics is where we project certain dissociated identifications with, say, victimhood that are very powerful, that we tend not to examine. And we also project certain traumatized parts of the self, so that I think that where the political is similar to sexuality is that it can hold certain kinds of trauma, but where I think it's different is the fury of nonrecognition.

NA: Mm-hmm, mm-hmm.

JB: If I may, I will tell you as quickly as I can an anecdote of the most powerful experience I had of dissociation and trauma around politics, which is when I supervised a case at a conference in a city in Germany, where the case began to reveal itself to me as being about the patient's Nazi father's murderous activities during the war. And there were dreams about this, and the analyst could not wait to give me these dreams. She gave them to me the night before, written out. She hadn't been able to get them contained, apparently, in her supervision (she was a candidate). The entire audience denied the obvious references to National Socialism. I had to be the one to bring it up. Even after I brought it up, the people in the audience continued to engage in a kind of blanketing denial, with the exception of one very young person.

I ended up feeling very much as though I, myself (well, first of all, I felt very conscious of being a Jew, obviously), were in a room full of Nazis who were in denial about attacking me, the way that you might feel in some kind of very peculiar family system, where certain people have been, if not killed, have died inexplicably, which was what was happening in the dream. And it took me until I left there to realize what happened. Coincidentally, I happened to be that night with somebody who was describing going to a meeting of people from the East (parts of Germany given back to Poland), where she came from originally, with other people who were originally refugees from the East. Those others were talking about how they were mourning the loss of their land in the East, and she said [to them], "What do you mean? What we lost were the Jews, a whole part of our people. That's what you're not talking about here." And when she said that, the whole thing clicked into place, and I became able to understand what had happened to me earlier that day, which I had been completely fogged over about.

Now the thing about that for me was that, I mean, I do not have any history in regard to this particular trauma. The family [that I have] that may have been killed in the Holocaust are so distant from me. It is not a legend that I grew up with, it's not personal to me, but I became this very peculiar person. I became, first of all, completely identified with the victim and, secondly, I became the Jew from New York who was going to come and somehow solve the problem that was created by the extermination of the Jews, at least for this individual. And all of this is going on at a completely symbolic level that is part of what, I think, Neil was describing as this kind of collective unconscious setup – when you were talking before about women – that we carry an awful lot of things that are not individual, that are what you might call "trans-personal" in our political unconscious.

And I found myself being just in the grip of this, completely in the grip of it in the most powerful emotional way of almost any experience I could possibly think of. And it's not personal, and I think that's part of why we really have trouble with it. It's very emotional. It's very psychological. It's not personal, and you may not have analyzed it, because you didn't tap into it before. It's like stepping into a hole in a road where you haven't walked on that road before, but you're going to fall into that hole. And I feel that there really are these group processes that seize us, in a sense, where our subjectivity is suddenly transformed by something from the outside. Why it's taboo, therefore, in psychoanalysis is because it's *really* about the outside. It's *really* about something outside the consulting room, and, for so long, psychoanalysis denied this.

I'm going to go on for one second longer, because it's really important. Part of why psychoanalysis denied this – and I think Russell Jacoby (*Social Amnesia: A Critique of Contemporary Psychology from Adler to Laing* 1975) tried to talk about this is precisely *because* of the trauma of National Socialism, because there was a *very* strong commitment to understanding society and implementing psychoanalysis practically in the thirties, in Vienna, and that went totally underground. And in the effort to save the psychoanalytic movement, people like Anna Freud and Ernest Jones scotomized entirely what was going on politically to such an extent – you can read this – that when Edith Jacobson was arrested by the Gestapo for underground activities, all they could think about was that this was not going to be good for the psychoanalytic movement that she was implicated in opposing the Nazis. So, the denial of historical forces is very much embedded in our early history, and the way that we failed to reorganize ourselves around that has had a very powerful influence, even for those of us who departed from Freudian tradition.

TJ: I'll say a word about what Jessica said, because today many psychoanalytic institutions remain extremely conservative with regard to entering into public discourse about even the most blatant kinds of biases and prejudices. For example, the meeting in Durban, in which Israel and the Jews were roundly attacked, and unfairly, as you know, in the Durban meeting, and the representatives of the International Psychoanalytic Association who were sitting there raised no objection whatsoever, and did not in any way stand up for the very things that are so important, that we all as individuals would feel were values that we would hold, but as a group, they remained very passive. And that was true also in a situation in Brazil, in which, essentially, a Nazi was practicing psychoanalysis. It took them twenty-five years to take any active role in this. Now, you could say this is sort of some perverse extension of the concept of neutrality, but it's more than that. It's a fear, it's a certain timidity, a fear of alienation, of alienating others and of taking a stand, which would offend certain other groups, so we've remained paralyzed as an organization. I think it's a very important problem.

Now, in the clinical situation, there is, at least for me, and it may be for others, too, some question about, not only is it a taboo, but is it appropriate to enter into this arena? Are we serving the patient's best interest by doing that, especially with regard to areas which can so easily touch on our own countertransference feelings and our powerful personal feelings? For example, I'd be very interested in Jessica's experience with regard to the fact that people know of her politics. I came from a training in which one was very careful about any self-disclosure of any kind, especially of a personal nature. I mean, you might talk about something that you've experienced in the session with a patient, and so on, but anything personal, that was not advocated as useful.

And it went to the point of which, for example, Phyllis Greenacre [in a personal communication] made a direct statement that the analyst should *not* be political, because it would expose him or herself to a kind of public scrutiny and a public openness, which she felt was not the role of the analyst. [The role] was to remain anonymous in order to allow for – the old idea – the projection of the patient to exist in a way that would be untrammeled by too much knowledge. So, it resulted in a kind of inhibition, even outside of the clinical situation. Very few traditional analysts have I ever seen as very active, for example, at marches or in rallies, and so on. You never see them. And I think it has something to do with the carrying over of the idea that one should remain relatively in the background, and that whatever one's personal beliefs were, they were personal. They weren't to be shown in public – an idea that, maybe, needs some re-examination.

AHG: [*To Jessica*] Do you want to respond to that?

JB: Well, yes, the reason people know my politics is they know that I wrote a book called *The Bonds of Love: Psychoanalysis, Feminism, and the Problem* *of Domination* (1988). It's not that I bring it up. I mean, there are people who I've never said a political word with, but they know that I wrote this book, so they know that I'm a feminist, and they know, if they've looked at the book for five minutes, that I'm a fairly left-wing one. So, that's the point. It's not that I actually – I don't inject it, but they come to me knowing this.

TJ: But do you discuss it at all, ever?

JB: I think that's another story. Not too often. Every now and then there's somebody who really has a need to bring this stuff into the work. Again, I think because they know who I am and it's a way to try to reach me, or get at me, or find some kind of commonality with me, or create some difference with me. And, clearly, when somebody does that a lot, it's really because they already know this, so now it's a factor that's available for them to comment about. So, I think that that creates a very specific set of conditions that you don't have if you don't have a public persona that's identified with anything politically. Neil has written a book that indicates he has certain politics, so people know that (Altman 1995). So I would picture you [Neil] get some of the same responses.

I would completely differentiate that from somebody who comes in frothing about what they just read in the newspaper about what Bush did. They might do that regardless of who I am. They're just in a rage about the current political situation. I try to see what the latent content of that is, but I don't immediately assume they've brought that in because of me, but when somebody brings in certain kinds of issues, especially related to feminism, I assume that it's related to myself.

And one time in particular, I remember somebody who was describing to me her situation, having these little babies at home and trying to do her work. And she was excoriating herself for not getting enough of her work done while she had these babies at home, and I knew that this was based on some idea that she had of me as a feminist who could do all these things. And I said to her something like, "You know, this is like the nightmare of feminism, the idea that you have to work a 70-hour week. Let me tell you, if you're thinking that this is what I imagined you should be doing or anybody should be doing, this is not what we had in mind when we came up with feminism." So, on occasion, I have said something that – I mean, *that* felt very emotionally important to say that to this person, but that's not my general – I can't even think of another instance where I've done that, and it was a very spontaneous, emotional reaction. But by and large, I think that's quite different from someone bringing up directly political issues that concern them or that they know concern you. This was really much more about me as an ego ideal and that's how we dealt with it. And it just so happened she had this information, so that's the area in which I was the persecutor and the ego ideal.

NA: I also would be interested in Paul's experience here, because he's also written books where his politics are just right out there (e.g. Wachtel 1989), but every once in a while, a patient will say something about me based on my book, and my experience is kind of like, I'm not sure who wrote that book [*general laughter*] and it always feels just like anybody saying anything about me based on their experience of me in the session; that it's kind of interesting, and it sounds like me and it doesn't sound like me, and – so, there's that.

I wanted to say one other thing. It seems to me that the place where politics permeates the session is that it permeates psychoanalytic theory, and that if we're to take account of politics in clinical psychoanalysis, we have to think at a very fundamental level, like, for example, the politics of the Oedipus complex; and when we think oedipally, there's patriarchy that is *infusing* that discourse, and to be aware of that. I'm not exactly sure where that takes you, but it gives you pause. It gives you a critical point of view about your own thought.

There was a situation at the conference that some of us were just at where somebody was presenting a case and was talking about a patient who was afraid of his wishes for closeness with the analyst, and the analyst commented that it brought up anxieties around sexual and aggressive impulses. And I thought, when I heard that, that the taboo against closeness between men – these were both men, patient and analyst – creates a caricature, that the specter of the sexual and aggressive impulse is a reflection of the anxiety around closeness between men – in other words, that what sounds like theory is actually a reflection of a socioculturally conditioned anxiety, and that we should strive to be aware of things like that.

PW: My association to what Neil is saying – in a sense, what it stimulates me to think about – is the way in which the political climate and the sociocultural context change psychoanalytic theory and change psychoanalytic assumptions. And I think that homosexuality is one good example, where until relatively recently, mainstream views about homosexuality were about explaining a pathology, and it was almost entirely about what is the source of the pathology. And it's only as the political climate has changed that that assumption that this behavior is automatically pathological has begun to change, and then *theories* have had to change. And I think the same has been true around issues of mothering – issues of parenting, generally – but there's a whole host of ways in which we often talk as if we're talking about a universal human nature, when we're really talking about the reflections of what it's like to grow up and be human in a particular cultural context. And, in that sense, I think another part of our discussion really has to be about how the politics shape psychoanalysis, as well as what light psychoanalysis can cast on the politics.

AHG: And I'm also hearing the underlying question of what do you do with that as the analyst. Do you work with that awareness in yourself? Or do you make it overt in the discussion between yourself and the patient?

Did everyone address whether or how you talk about politics with your patients? Or self-disclosure?

JB: I think it's not primarily a matter just of self-disclosure. I mean, it's like what Neil was saying: you don't always recognize yourself in the portrayal of yourself that comes back to you politically, and you have to inquire about that the way that you'd do about anything. But what I was trying to say in my earlier anecdote is that I think that the fear that comes up is similar to what both Neil and Paul were saying about homosexuality, which is the fear that something can grip you, or seize you, that really doesn't come from your personal unconscious, or not from your personal unconscious alone, but from some element that seems to be in the collective, that you could suddenly tap into. And yet, it's somewhere in you, but it's not something that you've particularly gone through in your own analysis, or that you even know is hanging around in there.

And that makes me sort of wonder, actually, Ted, about your experience, because it seems to me that, at the very least, you were trained in a time and in an institution where there was a lot of what I would think of as persecution of homosexuality, and also a lot of theorizing of homosexuality as being integral to all people, and I'm kind of curious whether that is something that – for instance, in your work with supervisees over the years – has come up as being political. What happens when that gets raised as a political issue in the analysis?

TJ: Well, I think that many people trained as I was in that tradition have undergone a great deal of change over the years, but originally, the idea of bisexuality was very much accepted as a kind of part of human nature, that human nature had bisexual qualities. Whether you were male or female, you had heterosexual and homosexual impulses. Homosexual behavior was another matter. Homosexual behavior in those days was seen as a pathological compromise formation. That is, it was the result of a lot of interacting forces, but it tilted towards the side of pathology, due, probably, to some arrests in development or to too much of a feminine identification. A variety of factors would be adduced to explain why this outcome could be seen as pathological and, potentially, changeable through analysis – an idea that Charles Socarides (1990; Socarides and Volkan 1991) has held very stubbornly, as one knows. He's very powerful in that point of view.

Over time, it gave way to a very different set of ideas, which are essentially that all of our sexuality is the result of the confluence of many forces, and the outcome could be heterosexuality, could be homosexuality, could be asexuality, whatever, and that it's not pathological. It's just that one tries to understand it, and nor does one try to change it, other than to try to work with whatever the conflicts are – a very different view. But many patients who have come over the years have suffered terribly from this former view, because it implied that they were disturbed and sick and required change, often putting them in a terrible bind, because they couldn't change. It just was not possible, and so they essentially became persecuted by the system. For a while, I myself was in a group in which this older view held forth, and I sometimes – looking back on that – regret having sort of put my weight on the side of heterosexuality, and it usually didn't turn out very well. But now I think things are quite different. Those older views aren't maintained very often. At least, I don't see them anymore.

V: On shared perspectives; to be or not to be political

AHG: You [Ted] were also interested in the next question, which is: what are your thoughts on the various ways that having either a shared political perspective with a patient or an opposing one (or somewhere in between) impact upon the treatment in terms of transference–countertransference or otherwise? Thinking in terms of Greenberg's "interactive matrix" (1995), might it not often be the case that working with patients who have a political stance similar to one's own poses more of a challenge to productive engagement (at least on political explorations) than working with patients whose politics clearly oppose or contrast with one's own?

TJ: I guess I was thinking about that in terms of something that has interested me, which is the problem that occurs when we like a patient too much, or when we find ourselves in agreement with so much that the patient stands for and with their values, and so on. Some people have written about this as the "unobjectionable positive transference," or "unobjectionable positive countertransference," because it is very engaging and pleasing in certain ways and gratifying to work with someone who shares our views and who we like personally, and that often involves political as well as social and other views. And I think that it does, sometimes at least, become a kind of trap in that one enters unconsciously into a collusion with that person, in the sense that we both sort of signal we won't get into the dirty or the difficult, the most painful areas of life, or areas of disagreement, where we may really find ourselves in a certain kind of conflict. So it is easy for us to find ways in which we and the patient agree not to enter into tough areas, and that includes many aspects of our work, but I was thinking about it, because particularly with politics, it would be very easy to avoid the kind of engagement that would really be most helpful, but often most difficult and painful, for both people.

Whether we should have as a goal for the patient to be more interested in the world, be more altruistic, have more of a feeling for society, and so on –

I was discussing this with my brother [also an analyst], who very strongly feels that this is something that should be one of our goals for patients. And I think that, again, it's a tricky area, because in some ways we endorse that, and maybe it is a sign of growth and health for some patients, because it probably means a movement away from narcissistic concern to a kind of feeling for others that represents a real alteration in themselves and their growth. On the other hand, it would be hard for me to make that a standard of health. I'm thinking about some people who need simply to live their lives with a certain kind of privacy, in which they want to sit and write poetry. That's the thing that they want to do. Or someone has a kind of more private world, in which he doesn't want to enter, or cannot feel comfortable entering, into the social network. And we can't describe that as an illness, and I think if we have too much of a bias in favor of the political, the good of the world and society, we may not do justice to our patients. So, it's a difficult balance to find, I think, with our patients.

AHG: I think that's a good point, and I'd be curious if anyone else has feelings about that balance or comments?

PW: Well, thinking about the topic makes me realize that, in general, I tend to keep those questions out of my mind, perhaps more than I should, but I tend to take a position very much like Ted's in thinking about that dimension. As I reflect on that now, what comes to mind is some research that I've been interested in by a number of social psychologists – Tim Kasser and Richard Ryan (1993, 1996) among others – that looks at the differences between people who organize their lives around what they call "intrinsic" versus "extrinsic" motivations, and the "intrinsic" are the sorts of things that we kind of like to see people pursuing. The poetry would pass muster in that, as well as a wide range of other more relational kinds of efforts; social efforts all would, whereas making money, getting ahead, being famous, etc., would fall on the "extrinsic" end.

And what they have found in many, many studies is that people who are "extrinsically" oriented – even when they are very successful – tend to have much more depression, much more anxiety. When there are studies of how they were raised, including interviews with their parents, and so forth, it looks like they had much less nurturant mothering and so forth. So, I realize I haven't brought it into my psychoanalytic work (and this conversation is making me think maybe I should), but looking at that as an interest that I had from outside of my psychoanalytic work for other work I was doing, it suggests that people whose values are more, in a sense, greedy, rapacious, etc., actually, also are less happy, in which case, maybe we do have a psychoanalytic responsibility to interpret it and work with it and so forth [*group laughter*].

NA: When I work with people who are apolitical, I think about people like Albert Einstein, who was very socially responsible and a jerk in his private life. I mean, the things just don't go together at all. Well, I have a patient now who's just trying to tend her own garden. I don't want to say too much, because of confidentiality, but she left a relationship with a person who is very politically active, and it wasn't a good relationship, and she's really turned away from the public world into a very private world, where she's created – she's making her political statement, in a sense, by the kind of life that she's making for herself, and I really can respect that. But I do draw on people like Einstein.

Now, on the other hand, I had another experience at the conference recently that gave me pause about being apolitical, which is a child case. And there was a value expressed by the presenter of making the child feel safe, and that gave me pause, because I wondered, how safe should children feel? And I know there's got to be some kind of a balance or tension between helping children feel safe, in light of their developmental place, but at the same time if you're going to be resonating with their anxieties, you also have to make some room for the fact that children are not safe and they're not safe for a whole lot of reasons, including political reasons, the political world that we live in. And the idea that children should be made to feel safe then lends itself sometimes to a kind of splitting, in which the parents are pathologized for their failure to make the child feel safe enough, whereas the therapist who has the privileged position of seeing the child in a protected situation for a little bit of time a week can then be the wonderful one who makes the child feel safe in this world, this little world where the outside world is excluded. So, in that way, I'm not in favor of being apolitical.

JB: Well, I think it's very complicated, because I think that we all – to one degree or another – take our lead from the patient, and we know where they are in a given moment, and we try not to introduce extraneous concerns, but I think that what does happen goes back to what Ted said about how there are people whom we like and whom we are in agreement with and the question of what we are going to aim for clinically, on the one side – and a patient actually came in today, my last patient, and started talking about her discomfort in a particular work setting, how she didn't feel connected to the people, how she found their chitchat really irritating, and I suggested to her that this might be because she wanted to really connect to them in some way or she had some desire toward them, and she said, no, that was completely wrong. How she felt was irritated, because of their attitude toward the world, and she then went into how she felt politically about our society at the moment. And she basically was saying that she felt alienated from the people at work, as she does from many people in her social environment in the borough where she lives, because they are so uncomprehending of what is wrong and what the ills are of our current government, and so on, and she's become completely obsessed with reading every bit of news about what's going on, she says.

But then, there's this sudden shift toward how she does not want to actually go out and be part of a political group and work on the election campaign or do something like that, which she thinks I think she should do – about which she's not entirely wrong, because I do think that she should have some kind of contact with people, and she knows that (since it's a long treatment), and so we then, of course, have to talk about the whole question of what it means. Is it she or I who thinks she should be more connected to other people? And what does it mean that she's connected to me in a way that she's not connected to other people? And the whole time, part of what is, of course, an underlying substratum of this is that she's saying that she can trust me, because I'm not in denial about some of the really evil, ugly parts of the world, which she's witnessing, I think accurately – this is my belief, I guess – and that she has suffered so much from being the sort of person that saw what was going on when others did not see it.

So, in a way, we keep looking back and forth between the political metaphor and the personal issue of being an outsider. They are both separate and fused in a certain way, and I don't think we can really tease them apart. But certainly what I am *not* doing is I am not saying to myself, "I have to figure out how to make this person politically active." Or, "I have to figure out how to empower her." What I am doing, though, could ultimately lead to that, but the track that I'm on is actually staying very close to what I'm seeing as the material, to what I'm seeing as the questions: What does she need or desire from me in the moment? What is she afraid of? And all those really traditional questions. And if that leads to her taking a position somewhere, if that leads to her feeling more comfortable joining other people and being less alienated, that's, of course, all to the good, but I don't see how we could possibly impose that. Nonetheless, what I am doing is I'm using my identity with her in a way as a kind of substratum of the treatment of the way in which she is relating to me as someone who knows her, even at the very moment that she's saying, "But you don't really know me, because if you knew me, you'd know how alienated I am and how much I can't possibly be with other people."

PW: It strikes me as I'm thinking about this that one of the interesting things about politics in this context is that I think politics is actually the realm in which we tend to find it easiest not to inject ourselves, or at least, maybe if we do, we're fooling ourselves at a deeper level, so that I'm not aware of it. But when I think of my own skepticism about general notions of neutrality and that neutrality is a possibility, I am very aware of ways in which my values, my wishes and desires for people, my image of what's good for someone enters into the work. Even if I'm not being overly aggressive about it or pushing it in any overt way, there are all sorts of subtle ways in which it becomes very clear how I feel about whether somebody should continue to pursue a particular relationship or break off the relationship, should express anger at a parent or not, should change jobs or not.

A whole host of things come through this way, and, at this point, although I try not to push it, and I'm not overt or gross about it, I'm also not uncomfortable about, or unaware of, how pervasive it is in the work. Whereas, politics as one mirror of my very strong values feels like one that I do keep out of the work, at least as I'm aware of. And I think, partly, it's because it doesn't feel as much about what I think is good *for the patient*. I think part of when our values tend to intrude more is whether we, rightly or wrongly, think a particular choice is good for the patient. That is why I was raising, only semi-whimsically, that Kasser and Ryan research, because that research sort of suggests, to put it very loosely, that you're happier as a Democrat than as a Republican, so to speak. I don't mean that literally, but it brings in a dimension that would join the political to our ethic, because we have an ethic that requires us really, as much as we can, to be at the service of the other person in this context.

It also raises the awareness issue of our political views being known to patients, and especially in the age of Google, where so much information about us is known. I mean, I've had patients come in and they've been looking me up on Google and they've heard stuff based on Google, etc., so that it's harder to hide. And then the question becomes, it seems to me, that I feel a real responsibility in the session to be a certain kind of – not literally, and not Freudian – but a certain kind of selfless, to be still trying to not inject myself excessively – because I don't think you can *not* inject yourself, but not excessively. I feel that that selflessness, that responsibility, somehow has to stop at the consulting-room door, in the sense that it can't be my responsibility as a therapist or an analyst to not do things in the public sphere that the patient might find out about and react to, that that's too strong a requirement, and that, rather, our responsibility is simply to be sensitive to the meaning of it to the person who picks that up and to work with that. Whatever your views about anonymity *in* the session, it seems to me too much of an imposition to require us to be anonymous outside the session, too.

AHG: Too much of an imposition and maybe even something that could lead to misdeeds or, at least, failures to act ethically, in the world. We're almost at the end here. I'm not quite sure what a good way to gain closure would be, but I want to ask if anybody is still feeling there is a question or something anybody else has said, that he or she wants to further respond to.

PW: I have, not a response to what anyone said, but a thought about something that feels important to me in this realm that I haven't said in response, and that's that, it seems to me, in thinking about these issues, thinking about how we put together our views from a psychoanalytic perspective and our understanding of the larger social, political, economic, cultural sphere, that one very important tool for bridging that conceptually – not necessarily in practice – for me, is to reconceptualize, retranslate psychoanalytic ideas, such that the concept of the "inner world" is replaced by concepts such as "subjectivity" or "personal and private kind of experience." The metaphor of the "inner world" is, I feel, too much in contrast with an "outer world," and really becomes at most where we're interacting with the other (that is, the "inner" world interacting with the "outer"), whereas I think really they're part and parcel of each other – both in terms of the immediate interpersonal experience of patient and analyst and of the individual with other relationships outside and the larger social sphere.

I think that we need to retain the psychological contents and dynamics, which we have often referred to with the phrase "inner world," but I think that it would be good to create a somewhat different terminology. It's not that the words are magic, but that each of our metaphors has consequences for what we do and don't see and highlight, and I would like to see "inner world" replaced, especially in the effort to make that bridge. I would do so – just to add – without losing any of the phenomena that we usually refer to by that.

JB: I just want to say that I think that we should recall that there's a long tradition of psychoanalysts being social critics, cultural critics, and of psychoanalytic theory – beginning with Freud – being on the side of enlightenment, on the side of tolerance, on the side of certain kinds of rejection of authority or repressiveness, oppression, and that this is something that, like with many other such things, is going to get lost and be recovered and be re-instituted in different ways with each generation, but I think that we could do more. I feel we could do more to bring what we have into a public domain and I think, practically, that's very difficult for us here in New York where we have such a rich psychoanalytic community. It's more difficult because of the ways that psychoanalysis has become a field apart, a world apart from any larger intellectual public world, which is, say, not the case in Argentina, where psychoanalysts are very active. It's not the case in many other places, and I think that's a tragedy of what has befallen us for many different reasons that I won't go into, and I'm very happy that you've done this. It's a tiny thing, but it's an important thing in terms of our reminding ourselves of our goals and our roots.

NA: Hear, hear.

TJ: Well said.

AHG: I thank all of you very much for your willingness to participate in this fascinating discussion.

JB: Thank you for organizing it.

Notes

1 This roundtable and its discussions were originally produced for and appeared in *Psychoanalytic Perspectives: A Journal of Integration and Innovation*, 2(1), Fall 2004, a new publication of the National Institute for the Psychotherapies Training Institute and the NIP Professional Association.

2 Invited to amplify later, Dr Benjamin added: "Of course, I have to modify this by saying that our (I mean left-wing) paranoia, I suppose, can take the form of projecting hateful feelings into those we see as sexist, racist, chauvinist, and even feeling persecuted by their hatred. Likewise, we are willing to see those who have power on the right as "demonic" in manipulating for their own self-aggrandizement the fears of the ordinary people who feel helpless. That's our dilemma. Perhaps we actually have a different kind of defense against vulnerability and helplessness, one in which we try to maintain our sense of power and agency by being in the helper position. This certainly fits with our profession."

3 Dr Benjamin also added later: "It might be better to say, we tend to want to suppress our sadistic, hateful, intolerant, bigoted responses in line with 'depressive' ego ideals, but frequently these hateful feelings can be directed in a covert way toward those we see violating those ideals. It's like the role of the 'good' older sibling who resents the selfish behavior of the younger one, but can also be superior in relation to the younger one. Sometimes this moral superiority position of the Left, which can be very alienating and intimidating, causes quite destructive splits in the Left as each side tries to brand the other as unfaithful to the ideals. This is where the term 'politically correct' came from, in the old days of the Left. In my conceptualization, this misuse of ideals, which we can also see in the history of the psychoanalytic movement, leads to a distortion of the 'third' – the common framework that connects us and that we appeal to in order to productively survive conflict. The distortion of that function is extremely harmful; we mustn't underestimate it."

4 The question referred to was: "How do you work with patients who are struggling with conflicts over self-interest versus the public good with regard to various issues (e.g. the distribution of wealth and resources, or the current seeming conflict of interest between defending against terrorism and protection of individual civil liberties)? How do you help patients to find their own way of defining and balancing each of these categories (self-interest or public good) in any given case?"

5 Dr Wachtel explained later: "What I mean is that the problem isn't with the bible or with a belief in God, even a very *strong* belief. The problem is with what *values* lie behind or animate that belief, what motives (often hidden, even to the person himself) are served through that belief. There is as much in biblical texts about tolerance, empathy, love thy neighbor, care for the poor and needy, etc., as there is of intolerance, 'these people are good and these serve the devil,' etc. The reason that specifically *fundamentalist* religious convictions *are* often right-wing is that it is in the very nature of fundamentalism to deny ambiguity, and that lends itself to

a very moralistic, rejecting, and ultimately non-empathic approach to life. (That is true, by the way, in psychoanalysis too, where we sometimes have our own forms of fundamentalism.) But one can certainly point to biblical text and say, 'It says here, with no ifs, ands, buts, or wiggle room in the eye of the needle, that accumulating wealth is *not* the path to Heaven and that we must love and help the least of us.' What we as psychoanalysts can contribute is an understanding of what kinds of hurts, in childhood or throughout life, lead people to interpret the bible in ways that breed selfishness and intolerance."

6 Dr Jacobs later said: "In other words, in politics, as in many other aspects of life, our wish to maintain self-representations compatible with our ego ideals is often at odds with reality and the achievement of practical political aims. Work in this area with politicians and activists is often important in enhancing their efforts."

References

Adorno, T. W. (with Frenkel-Brunswik, E., Levinson, D. J., and Sanford, R. N.) (1950) *The Authoritarian Personality*. New York: Harper & Row. Reprinted, New York: Norton Library, 1969.

Altman, N. (1995) *The Analyst in the Inner City: Race, Class, and Culture through a Psychoanalytic Lens*. Hillsdale, NJ: The Analytic Press.

Benjamin, J. (1988) *The Bonds of Love: Psychoanalysis, Feminism, and the Problem of Domination*. New York: Pantheon Books.

Greenberg, J. (1995) Psychoanalytic technique and the interactive matrix. *Psychoanalytic Quarterly*, 64:1–22.

Greenson, R. R. (1967) *The Technique and Practice of Psychoanalysis*. New York: International Universities Press.

Jacoby, R. (1975) *Social Amnesia: A Critique of Contemporary Psychology from Adler to Laing*. Boston: Beacon Press.

Kasser, T. and Ryan, R. M. (1993) A dark side of the American dream: correlates of financial success as a central life aspiration. *Journal of Personality & Social Psychology*, 65(2):410–422.

Kasser, T. and Ryan, R. M. (1996) Further examining the American dream: differential correlates of intrinsic and extrinsic goals. *Personality & Social Psychology Bulletin*, 22(3):280–287.

Lakoff, G. (2002) *Moral Politics: How Liberals and Conservatives Think*. Chicago: University of Chicago Press.

Socarides, C. W. (1990) *Homosexuality: Psychoanalytic Therapy*. Northvale, NJ: Jason Aronson.

Socarides, C. W. and Volkan, V. D. (1991) *The Homosexualities and the Therapeutic Process*. Madison, CT: International Press.

Wachtel, P. (1989) *The Poverty of Affluence*. Philadelphia: New Society.

Chapter 13

Response to roundtable

Something's gone missing

Muriel Dimen

I am grateful for the opportunity to discuss this roundtable. At first, I thought I would have nothing to say. The intellectual space provided by my colleagues, however, allowed me to articulate a thought different from theirs but not, I am sure, unknown to them.

I take off from Paul Wachtel's inclination to replace the metaphor of the "inner world" with constructs like "subjectivity" or a "personal and private kind of experience." He wants to reduce the contrast, which he finds too great, between inner and outer, for, in fact, "they're part and parcel of each other both in terms of the immediate interpersonal experience of patient and analyst and of the individual with other relationships outside and the larger social sphere." Now, as for me, I am content with that contrast, and wish in fact to intensify it, even as I agree that inner and outer are intimately, if complicatedly, inter-implicated. As I see it, we need to articulate that dynamic web of meaning between them.

No, the opposition between inner and outer is not where I see the problem – or problematic – in this conversation. The difficulty lies in what drops out when psychoanalysis and politics, or, rather, the psychical and the political, are binarized. This thought came to me as I was reading Jessica Benjamin's account of having supervised a case in a German city and her engagement with the traumata of denial, dissociation, and repression related to the Holocaust. The insight dawned when I read her colleague's saying, in regard to Germans mourning the loss of their eastern lands, "'What do you mean? What we lost were the Jews, a whole part of our people.'" Immediately, I asked myself what we have lost that makes psychoanalysis and politics such peculiar strangers.

In the roundtable, political institutions have gone missing. Found are political principles, values, stance on the Middle East, Iraq, gender, sexuality, psychoanalytic structures and processes. But the social structure of politics? The material conditions? There is a lacuna resulting from a problem that is at once psychical and political, both aspects of which need to be interrogated and the results incorporated into our professional conversations.

In the United States, we lack a left-wing history, with its own agenda, and thus we lack part of ourselves. This institutional absence, which entails also the absence of a sustained left-wing party or parties, constitutes a trauma for progressive people. It is a trauma because it is a gap, a hole, a void, where there might be something that we need or perhaps don't even know we need. It is a trauma because there *was* something; *somethings*, in fact, that were erased, obliterated, rendered unspeakable. In psychoanalysis, this trauma is doubled.

As I was reading the conversation, I had in mind what my British co-commentator, Andrew Samuels, might say: he might, I thought, speak of the internal political citizen. Now, as he knows, I am not as comfortable as he is with such inner personages. Here is how, in a critique of the first version of this discussion – the roundtable – he elaborates his position: "My inner politician is not a full-timer. Rather, it is more the outcome of the political channel for libido, one of many such channels in Jungian energy theory." There is much to interrogate here, and what I am about to say may in fact engage in a debate with Andrew's position, or parallel it in different language. More to the immediate point, however, Andrew inhabits a society endowed with a left-wing history and a left-wing agenda, which have also found their way into electoral politics. The same goes for all of Western Europe, and this institutional presence has something to do, I imagine, with his ability to add to the Jungian canon an imago of a citizen.

In the United States, in contrast, left-wing politics has a patchy history. It starts and it stops, an engine that goes full-steam ahead and then sputters out or gets sabotaged or ruined. Utopian communities, socialist intellectuals of all classes, labor unions, political parties – they have shown up here and there until they fizzled out or were broken or shut up. I do not pretend at all to be a historian of these matters. But I did learn some history in high school at least, as well as in my desultory studies on the New Left. I have learned of various incarnations of progressive, socialist, community, and populist movements and parties in this country; indeed, some ballots still sport more and less fringe-y political parties.

What accounts for this absence of a substantial third political force? The problem lies not exactly in appetite: that our varied left-wing movements and groups and parties draw on a deep and enduring spirit is evident in the success of Michael Moore's movie *Fahrenheit 9/11*. Yet it is true that, for one thing, an understanding of the class system is virtually a black hole in the United States. Not only does the general population not resonate to the problem of class; most people identify themselves as middle class, whether they are the poor students at the public college where I used to teach or well-to-do colleagues from, to put it metaphorically, Park Avenue. But the understanding of class's systematic character – the upper is upper only because the lower is lower, and the middle strata (including the professional–managerial class (Ehrenreich 1989; Ehrenreich and Ehrenreich

1979)) have a very complicated, aiding-and-abetting but also resisting role – is only rarely taught in college, not to mention high school, and is but seldom present in popular media. Class analysis constitutes the nub of progressive movements and parties elsewhere; it is rendered a void on these shores.

Most attempts at a politics addressing the inequities of the class system have been shattered or exhausted by equally pressing crises. Since here I will be repeating many histories of left-wing thought and action, I will, out of respect, be very brief. Just to take recent memory, the Cold War and its inquisition, in the person of Joe McCarthy, made sure that any identification one might have had with the best ideals of communism shivered with terror. Whatever reasoned critique of institutionalized communism existed lost any space free of stigma, persecution, and economic impoverishment. At the same time, many of our own progressive energies went into a battle that Europeans are only now facing in the form of immigration politics: the trauma of slavery and its abolition, of enduring racism and the ceaseless necessity to combat it. I would also point to the problem of the American century, the fabulously successful and destructive New World capitalism that smashed or co-opted most progressive forces, including labor unions and nascent political parties.

Internal realities need representation; without it, a crisis ensues. Such a crisis, a permanent trauma, has been suffered by many: women, Third World people (in the United States as well as abroad), homosexuals, and the disabled, to name a few, experience fragmented identities when they look in the sociolinguistic mirror and find no reflection. So it is with citizens of this country. The disintegration of a left-wing history constitutes a trauma because it deprives internal political experiencing of its necessary, external social truth. Lacking a Left opposition, we lack cultural representation for the left-wing citizen. Instead, the cultural stage offers the image of a Left oppositionalist. However, as we know well from Foucault, from our deployment of Kleinian theory, and our observation of paranoid-schizoid workings in the consulting room, and from the splits on the Left that Jessica recalls, oppositionalism winds up re-creating the problems it seeks to change; we are "bound up through symmetrical opposition in the very ideological system [we] want to" change (Echols 1984:51). Hence the moralism of political correctness on the Left.

I recall that, when Jessica and I were involved in forming a reproductive-rights group in the late 1970s called CARASA (Committee for Abortion Rights and Against Sterilization Abuse), one of our coactivists, the journalist Ellen Willis, was very eager that we get ourselves incorporated, with a bank account and everything else a not-for-profit corporation needs, so that she could then argue against those principles and actions with which she disagreed. The important point was that there be an established institution, and then from within that you can go even further to whatever Left (or

Right) you might choose. A left-wing political party would have a platform, and in that sense it would constitute a systematic, principled opposition to the parties we have now.

In the absence of such a progressive tradition and history, if not a party, it is hard to conjure a relationship between psyche and politics, let alone the political and the psychoanalytical. Certainly we can use our theories of mind to illuminate political praxis – think here of Joel Kovel's work on white racism (1970); or Paul's on race and psychology (Wachtel 1999); or Neil's on analysts, class, and race (Altman 1995); or Jessica's on gender domination, doer/done-to, and reparation (Benjamin 1988). We can, as well, anatomize how politics enters clinical theory and technique in regard to problems of analytic authority and sexuality. We can also consider the varieties of political experience familiar to analysts. Here, analysts have our own trauma, a similar voiding of history by the erasure of analysts' activism, as in the sanctions applied to Edith Jacobson by Anna Freud and Ernest Jones, which turn into a secret that haunts the profession. With Jessica, I would point to Russell Jacoby's work on the political bleaching of psychoanalytic history (Jacoby 1975, 1983; see also Zaretsky 2004).

In the roundtable, two sorts of personal relation to politics emerged. Ted Jacobs described the cautions, if not prohibitions, delivered during his own training against importing the externality of politics to the privacy of the treatment. Now he wonders whether this advice was the best. But for him, it would appear, a psychoanalytic and a political identity were meant to be on opposite sides of a gulf. It is a matter of at least half-generations, I think. The sixties constituted a watershed in certain sectors of the society, and its sequelae show up among psychoanalysts. For myself (and perhaps the panelists share this experience), identity was infused with politics: "the personal is political," we said, and "the political is personal." The New Left and feminist movements lived these ideas, and, for me, they remain strong, intensified by Nancy Chodorow's emendation in regard to the academic Left and feminism (1989:213): the political is personal is theoretical. Each of these categories of experience, life, and thought were supposed to validate the others. As Jessica notes regarding the problem of political correctness, this circle soon became a vicious, prescriptive one, and we have had to loosen the demand that the personal, political, and theoretical be immediately relevant to the other, and work hard to allow them to fulfill their original function of mutual enhancement, a practice which I believe can be engaged in psychoanalysis.

But there's another step that might be taken: imagining a political self-state. These days, relational theory, at least, conceptualizes mind as multiple. We theorize multiple self-states, and articulate clinical theory that addresses and employs this multiplicity in intersubjective and interpersonal experience. Perhaps these clinical and theoretical practices formalize what we have been doing all along – thinking of the many sides of our patients (and others) and of the multiple functions (Waelder 1936) their psychic structures perform. Could we not also imagine that one self-state, or an aspect of a self-state, is a civic being? Such imagination does not require that we conjure an inner politician, someone who goes out and does politics as livelihood or hobby. But it could encompass the likely possibility that there is an aspect of internal experience whose realization is potentiated by civic life.[1] Recognizing this does not require the clinician to make sure that self-state gets actualized: after all, we don't intend our patients to live out their murderous impulses; merely, if we can, to register them and then have whatever sort of relation to this interiority they wish. I am thinking here of a current essay by Sam Gerson (2004) on the relational unconscious in which he argues that "some [unconscious] contents achieve coherence only in acts of communication and recognition." An engagement with an other and, in widening concentric circles, with the world, potentiates self-states: unconsciousness "is a holding area whose contents await birth at a receptive moment in the contingencies of evolving experience" (Gerson 2004:69).

By the same token, I don't agree that sometimes analysts are political and sometimes they are not. We are always political beings, as much as we are all creatures of need, desire, and unconsciousness. We relate to the world. Consider Neil's concern about our responsibility in making children safe in relation to the political world. Jonathan Silin (1995), a developmental psychologist and teacher educator, argues persuasively that children are always already engaged with the political world. "To think of children out of their immediate contexts is to take them out of time, to leave them without possibility. The social and material context is the medium through which we define ourselves." Silin is concerned with the eschewal and silencing of any discussion or even acknowledgment of HIV/AIDS in public schools. "By refusing to view the child-in-the-society, [we refuse] individual biography, the right of every child to tell his or her own story; for our stories cannot be told without reference to the worlds in which they occur." But Silin might well be talking about analysts and patients, as about children growing up around AIDS: "We are all historical beings; time is at the heart of every biography. When we seek relief for ourselves and our students by excluding the world, of which it is so easy to despair, we conspire in denying those whom we claim to help. Hope resides in time and time can only be lived in the world, a world of many unsettling realities" (Silin 1995:50–51). Analysts live in the world and in history, and some of our own history – like that of world history – is, we have seen, relentlessly blinkered.

Given the United States' construction of citizenship and psychoanalytic institutional history, it is no wonder that we suppose we are introducing something extraneous if we bring the political into the psychoanalytical. When, as Jessica pointed out, we follow the patient's lead, we are not likely to be led to politics. But even if a patient doesn't consciously want to talk about dependency or sexual desire, aggression or mourning, we are always listening for those leads to take us to these very important matters, aren't we? Might we do the same for civil life?

I must confess that I find it strange, as a New Leftist, to have been speaking of electoral politics. But personal, professional, and political events incline me in that direction. My respect for the problem comes in part from an ex-partner, who was deeply involved in studying electoral politics. Professionally, I have been influenced by Andrew Samuels' ceaseless focusing on the intimacy of psychoanalysis and politics, and his creative approach to finding and expressing that link. Finally, an old friend, a college roommate who, as she ages, becomes increasingly (not, as for so many, decreasingly) active on the Left, told me, when I was speaking to her about the soon-to-be disastrous 2000 election, that she'd been a member of the Green Party for five years, because a vote for any other party was, in her view, a vote for despair. Chastened by the Supreme Court's pusillanimity, she's only going to vote Green again if it looks as though California, where she resides, won't be going to Kerry. But I respect and resonate with her principled stand. I'm not sure the Green Party is the answer. But we need something like it. How can we make sure that history is erased no more? Can we start with our own profession?

Note

1 Interestingly, the theory of multiple-subject positions serves as a nice match for left-wing political theory. Instead of class reductionism, more recent interpretations of Marxism propose a multiplicity of subject positions (Mouffe 1988:90). Race, gender, sexuality, and other categories now join class in overdetermining (Amariglio *et al.* 1988) individual and social life: having multiple determinants, personal fate, for example, can be understood from a variety of perspectives. But subject positions are discursive as well as economic in character, origin, and effect. "Not a mental act in the usual sense" (Laclau 1988:254), "discourse" designates the unending negotiation of meaning, in which material conditions also play a part. This negotiation can and must happen because meaning itself is multiple: in Lacanian view, "a certain cleft, a certain fissure, misrecognition characterizes the human condition as such" (Žižek 1989:2).

This discontinuity, this reflexive division, founding human subjectivity creates a window for personal and social change. Because one's subject positions have their material base as well as their personal, cultural, and historical meanings, one may, given the right circumstances, rework the subject position endowed at birth, whether based on class or ethnicity or sexuality or whatever. Out of our own psychic decenteredness and plural subject positions, we can make more than has been dreamt of in many philosophies. This is Western democracy's Utopian promise, so often not fulfilled: upward mobility, escaping the poverty track. The system helps you to change, to better yourself.

References

Altman, N. (1995) *The Analyst in the Inner City*. Hillsdale, NJ: The Analytic Press.

Amariglio, J. L., Resnick, S. A., and Wolff, R. D. (1988) Class, power, and culture. In C. Nelson and L. Grossberg (eds), *Marxism and the Interpretation of Culture*. Urbana: University of Illinois Press.

Benjamin, J. (1988) *The Bonds of Love: Psychoanalysis, Feminism, and the Problem of Domination*. New York: Pantheon.

Chodorow, N. (1989) *Feminism and Psychoanalytic Theory*. New Haven, CT: Yale University Press.

Echols, A. (1984) The taming of the id: feminist sexual politics, 1968–83. In C. Vance (ed.), *Pleasure and Danger: Exploring Female Sexuality*. New York: Routledge.

Ehrenreich, B. (1989) *Fear of Falling: The Inner Life of the Middle Class*. New York: Pantheon.

Ehrenreich, B. and Ehrenreich, J. (1979) The professional–managerial class. In P. Walker (ed.), *Between Labor and Capital*. Boston: South End Press.

Gerson, S. (2004) The relational unconscious: a core element of intersubjectivity, thirdness, and clinical process. *Psychoanalytic Quarterly*, 73:63–98.

Jacoby, R. (1975) *Social Amnesia: A Critique of Contemporary Psychology from Adler to Laing*. Boston: Beacon Press.

Jacoby, R. (1983) *The Repression of Psychoanalysis: Otto Fenichel and the Political Freudians*. Chicago: University of Chicago Press.

Kovel, J. (1970) *White Racism: A Psychohistory*. New York: Pantheon.

Laclau, E. (1988) Metaphor and social antagonisms. In C. Nelson and L. Grossberg (eds), *Marxism and the Interpretation of Culture*. Urbana: University of Illinois Press.

Mouffe, C. (1988) Hegemony and new political subjects: toward a new concept of democracy. In C. Nelson and L. Grossberg (eds), *Marxism and the Interpretation of Culture*. Urbana: University of Illinois Press.

Silin, J. (1995) *Sex, Death, and the Education of Children: Our Passion for Ignorance in the Age of AIDS*. New York: Teachers College Press.

Wachtel, P. L. (1999) *Race in the Mind of America: Breaking the Vicious Circle Between Blacks and Whites*. New York: Routledge.

Waelder, R. (1936) The principle of multiple function: observations on over-determination. *Psychoanalytic Quarterly*, 5:45–62.

Zaretsky, E. (2004) *Secrets of the Soul: A Social and Cultural History of Psychoanalysis*. New York: Knopf.

Žižek, S. (1989) *The Sublime Object of Ideology*. London: Verso.

Chapter 14

Response to roundtable

Politics and/or/in/for psychoanalysis

Andrew Samuels

Reading this vital, informed, and inspiring conversation led me to draw up a list of the following closely related and overlapping phenomena:

1 the politics of the professions of psychotherapy and psychoanalysis
2 the application of psychoanalytic ideas in a quest for deeper understandings of political processes and problems
3 the usage by politicians and political groupings of psychoanalytic ideas for furtherance of their own aims and objectives
4 political projects of whatever kind undertaken by organizations of psychoanalysts and psychotherapists
5 psychoanalytic understandings of the growth and development of the political dimensions of the subject-as-citizen
6 the struggle to apperceive the micropolitics of the analytical session itself – the power, vulnerability, and differing experiences in the analysis and in the social world of both participants
7 the devising of responsible ways to engage directly with political, social, and cultural material that appears in the clinical session.

In this response, I will work through this list with the expressed views of the roundtable participants closely in mind. We need to recall that the list's compilation would not be possible without the elasticity of the notion of "politics" that feminism has made possible. And there has also been a general epistemological shift in Western thinking wherein experience is seen as being as valid a source of knowledge as empirical data or pedagogical authority. Psychoanalysis is a prime generator of this shift.

(1) Linking – or relinking – psychoanalysis and politics brings us up against the politics of the profession itself. In particular, assertions from the upper sections of our various hierarchies about what constitutes "good practice" have a huge impact on clinical work. To engage with one's patient on a political matter has long been castigated as "bad practice," and political activity itself sometimes referred to as acting out. Would you want to try actively to become a bad analyst? Let me be the first to state that

inappropriate politicization of psychoanalysis, whether on the macro level of the profession as a whole or the micro level of the session, would still constitute bad practice. And there is a degree of wisdom in many of the cautionary notes that more traditional practitioners sometimes sound when they are considering these matters. But, overall, the kinds of ideas being expressed in the roundtable discussion do constitute a reasoned challenge to an orthodoxy whose day may well have passed.

(2) Turning now to the question of the application of psychoanalytic ideas to politics, there is a general problem that I must say I found occasionally in the roundtable discussion. If one uses cutting-edge psychoanalytic ideas too readily and in too sophisticated a way, there will be an understandable response from the political world that this is just psychobabble, and from the intellectual world that it is reductive. But if one finds a more popular, emotive, and common-sense-related way to express psychoanalytic insights on politics then the response is often that you don't have to be a highly trained psychoanalyst to come up with such obvious formulations. (Sometimes, I've had to field both responses in the same meeting!)

How can we respond to these twin criticisms? I think we *must* respond along the lines of "analyze resistance before content." If we want to be of use in the political arena, then we have to look first at the limitations and even the blocks on our ambitions. Basically, I think that psychoanalysts who seek to engage with the political can be compared (and contrasted) with artists and writers who have the same goal, and also with people from the faith communities (progressive and reactionary alike) who see no contradiction between adherence to spiritual values and commitment to political ideals and goals. All three groups of people – the analysts, the artists, and the spiritually oriented – run the risk of being accused of forgetting what they are on the planet for. We analysts – like the others – have to find ways of explaining that we are seeking only an extension of what we do already (for example, paying attention to the whole person of the patient, in which the social dimensions of experience cannot be overlooked).

But this still might not be enough. Don't we have to say that our contribution to political thinking and acting is not something we can offer alone, or from an on-high, hyper-professional position? Don't we have to make an explicit commitment to a multidisciplinary approach to politics, in which we work alongside other groupings with supposedly expert knowledge? We need, I think, to make alliances with social scientists, environmentalists, feminists, those working for economic justice nationally and internationally, other activists – as well as the abovementioned artists and members of the faith communities. I missed there being much reference to this matter in the roundtable discussion.

My slogan has for many years been: Let's have a psychoanalyst on every government committee or commission – but, please God, not a committee of psychoanalysts! On these committees, there would be a spectrum of skills with the analyst at one end and someone like a statistician at the other end. Neither of these would be the most popular or the most influential member of the committee, but, I would argue, the presence of the psychoanalyst could be regarded as being as essential as the presence of the statistician.

I must end this section with just a brief note in agreement with Paul Wachtel about how hard it will always be to move from the individual perspective to the social perspective in our psychological thinking. This is not a problem that can be addressed by group approaches to organizations and institutions – an issue I have addressed elsewhere (Samuels 1993: 267–286). (The best recent discussion of the role of psychoanalytic concepts deriving from individual work in understanding political phenomena such as racism is, I think, Dalal (2002).)

(3) As far as the usage of psychoanalytic ideas by politicians and political groupings is concerned, we have to remember that the history of psychoanalysis includes a number of regrettable collusions with the powerful. C. G. Jung fell foul of this temptation, and recent historical researches show that much the same was true of Anna Freud and Ernest Jones in the 1930s.

There is a distinction to be made between the taking up of psychological ideas without the participation or presence of the theorist and a situation wherein an analyst offers herself or himself in the service of a particular cause or as part of a job. For example, I have done numerous consultations for politicians and activist groupings in many countries, as have many other analysts. All would agree that it can be a wonderful (and frustrating and humbling) experience. But interesting questions of definition and identity arise. For if one gets involved as an analyst with a politician or a political movement, is one doing it as a psychoanalyst or as a citizen who happens to be a psychoanalyst? Or both? How can this problem be better expressed? I think that if it were better expressed, then the inhibition that many psychoanalysts report about getting as actively involved in politics as they would like might diminish. In the early 1990s, I surveyed 700 psychotherapists in eleven organizations in seven countries about what they did when the patients brought political, social, and cultural material to the clinical setting (Samuels 1993:209–266). I asked the respondents for their political biographies. Given the self-selection involved, it was perhaps not so surprising that a large proportion had been politically active in their youth. Giving up politics, though, seemed not only to be a function of aging and having to pay college fees; there were specific references in the replies of many from all parts of the world to professional embarrassment stemming from the values introjected during training and professional formation about being a politically committed psychoanalyst. (I will return to this survey later.)

(4) I turn now to organizations of psychoanalysts (and/or psychotherapists, psychologists, counselors, mental-health professionals) that seek to

make an impact on the political scene, speaking with a coherent political voice that rests on a degree of professional expertise. For reasons of space, I will focus on two issues only. The first concerns whether or not such organizations are (or should be) inevitably Left-leaning, or "progressive," in whatever ways that might be defined in an age that claims to have gone beyond Left and Right. If being part of the Left is an inevitability, then the organization has to accept that it cannot claim to "represent" a consensual professional view (though it may some of the time) and certainly cannot speak for the profession as a whole. A problematic example would be that of an organization of psychotherapists that spoke out against a candidate in an important election.

My take here is that there is a difference between an overall orientation (for example, a commitment to argue for greater economic equality in the society that was put forward on well-argued psychological grounds) and a specific commitment (for example, to campaign for a candidate). Moreover, it is perfectly possible to make the general attitudes of the membership clear without going into specifics. If this is done without excessive camouflage or falseness, then the organization becomes much more open to and inclusive of a range of opinions.

In fact, from my point of view, it is rather important not to neglect some of the intuitions about politics that more right-wing commentators have developed. In particular, the Right was the first to assert that there is more to what people desire from their social lives than can be expressed in material terms alone. Improvement of conditions would then mean things additional to money, housing, education, and so forth. In many Western countries, notably the United States, the areas of "spirituality," "values," or "meaning" have been co-opted by conservative politicians and groupings. Politically oriented organizations of psychoanalysts might (ambivalently) want to see themselves as part of "the rise of the religious Left"!

The second aspect of organization I want to consider is that it is necessary to get a balance between investment in the traditional "psychological" areas ("soft" areas), such as family policy, education, and so forth, and less traditional areas ("hard" areas), such as economics, violence in society, leadership, and foreign policy. The environment has often turned out to be a linking area of interest because ecological concern is (rightly, in my opinion) both a soft- and a hard-policy area. From the "soft" angle, I have become convinced that environmental despoliation and species depletion is one of the nonpersonal sources of psychological disturbances such as depression that has the greatest impact. Something beautiful and valuable is being destroyed via our own (the patient's own) destructiveness. A perfect psychodynamic account of depression!

An example of a move by a therapists' organization into a "hard" policy area has been the discussions in the UK within Psychotherapists and Counsellors for Social Responsibility (PCSR) over the "models of human nature" that underpin economic policy. (For an account of the history of PCSR in the UK, see Samuels (2003:150–153).)

(5) We are gradually moving from the nonclinical to the clinical aspects of the roundtable discussion. In this section, I want to raise why it is that psychoanalysis (as opposed to social psychology) has had so little to say in recent years about topics such as "political selfhood," political development," even, to use a tag of mine that I am still somewhat embarrassed by, "the inner politician." Don't we need to know more about where we (the analyst and the client) got our politics from, of the relative importance of the politics of father and mother, of the ways in which social class operates at an unconscious level, of how ethnic, national, and religious factors transmogrify into political attitudes and behaviors, and – in an imaginative return to the bedrock of psychoanalytic exploration – how issues of sex, sexuality, and gender play into the formation of the political subject? We need to be careful not to get hooked up on facts here, for much political autobiography is personal myth! As I see it, this work is beginning to appear or reappear – Neil Altman's book (1995) is a great example.

But not everyone functions in the same way, politically speaking. In an insight derived from Kleinian speculation about innate/constitutional levels of aggressivity that vary from person to person, I have come to see that people enjoy different levels of political energy. Some people just hate all that is involved in politics, not because (or not only because) they cannot tolerate conflict – no, they are just constituted that way, and psychoanalytical sensitivity to individual difference is needed here just as much as in other areas. (The idea of political energy is intended to be as metaphorical as all notions involving energy – see Samuels (2001:16–20).)

Continuing to explore how politicality and individuality interweave, I wonder if the roundtable discussants could have said more about politics and self-expression. Citizens operate politically using a variety of differing *political styles*. Some love dispute and conflict, others hate it. Some love to work alone, others can't do anything that isn't backed up by an e-mail list. After some experimentation with more formal ways of expressing these differences, I came up with a more imagistic way of encapsulating the phenomenon. While doing conflict resolution work in Israel–Palestine, I developed the following list of one-word tags for political styles: Warrior, Terrorist, Exhibitionist, Leader, Activist, Parent, Follower, Child, Martyr, Victim, Trickster, Healer, Analyst, Negotiator, Bridge-builder, Diplomat, Philosopher, Mystic, Ostrich.

Readers will have their associations to these styles (or types) and can probably imagine more or less what goes along with each. I invite you to choose one that fits you, if you would like to. Or more than one. Or the ones you are most proficient at being within. Or – and maybe this is what you should do first – identify which ones you are really bad at using. Then consider some conflicts you have had in the recent past – at home, work, or in political discussion. Which style(s) were you in, and which style(s) was your opponent in? (This exercise is written up more fully in Samuels (2001:15–34).)

(6) This section and the next are overtly clinical. Regarding the micropolitics of the session, I would like to suggest that the usual sophisticated, contemporary focus on the analyst's power over the client is insufficient (though certainly not wrong). For if we turn to the traditional idea of the Wounded Healer, we see that it underscores the opposing idea that analysts (like shamans and other healers) are basically very vulnerable people. Such vulnerability may be carried by somatic/physiological factors such as their susceptibility to illness. What we need is a political analysis of the power and the vulnerability of both the analyst and the client and how these evolve over the course of an analysis. In general, I think that many analysts have a problem in realizing that they are both powerful and vulnerable – it is not a case of either powerful or vulnerable. In other words, much thinking about who has the power and who has the vulnerability in the politics of the analytical relationship has been rather schizoid. (Here, I would just add that the paradigm of an iconic familial and cultural figure within whom one can perceive both power and vulnerability is "the father," and that maybe much of our thinking about men and masculinity would benefit if male power and male vulnerability could be more often held together in the same frame.)

(7) Finally, we come to the question of how to work with political, social, and cultural material in clinical sessions. The conversation in the roundtable was absolutely riveting when this theme was prominent, and I felt it both showed why this matter is indeed taboo in psychoanalysis and also that we are now in a liminal situation regarding it. Going back to what I said in my first point, about "bad practice," it is clear to me from the discussion (and also from what I hear as I travel around) that yesterday's bad practice is set to become today's good or good-enough practice. The question will soon cease to be "Why did you get involved in that political discussion?" but "Why did you collude in evading the political discussion that the patient was seeking?" I would like to see this matter of politics being part of clinical material become a rather ordinary, everyday matter, nothing special – in the sense that for an analyst to hear about and engage in dialogue over sexuality, relationships, etc., etc., is nothing special; not nothing special in the sense of no big deal but in the sense of something familiar. We surely don't want to limit political discussion only to those moments of war or attack that make avoidance of the world "out there" impossible (and never was there a binary more in need of deconstruction than "in here" and "out there," as Paul Wachtel pointed out). This is not a high days and holy days project.

Hence, I was so glad that Ted Jacobs used the word "discussion," because that usage engages directly with the taboo. "Discussion" of any kind, I was taught in my training, is simply not analytic, and this is the background to why I use the word all the time these days. What we need to do is to highlight the therapeutic and analytical value of political discussion undertaken in a responsible way that acknowledges the dangers. It is not going to be the same as discussion held in a bar or over dinner or at work. The analytical frame (what the Jungians call the *vas* (alchemical vessel) or *temenos* (temple precinct)) guarantees that even mundane occurrences within it acquire transformative potential. So a political discussion with one's analyst (with the latter in touch with the risks of over-influence and avoidance of other problems) is potentially a quite transformative experience for both partners. Agreement is not the goal of this conversation; nor is a compromise or synthesis of views. Sometimes there will be a goal and sometimes not; it is not knowable in advance. I thought what Neil Altman said about "impasse" was very relevant here. Politics is all about impasses. What I do feel will happen on every occasion political discussion takes place is that an "amplification" of the clinical issues will take place: thin material will become more ample, a low volume that made it hard to hear will get turned up.

In the survey I referred to earlier, it was apparent that patients are bringing up this kind of material more and more frequently these days. It was also clear that, when it comes to political material, it certainly makes a difference to the patient whom he or she sees for analysis. This also came out beautifully in the passages in the roundtable discussion in which Ted Jacobs and Jessica Benjamin eloquently described their very different and equally valid experiences in practice over their own politics and politics in general. (For much fuller accounts of my views on ways of working with political material, see, for example, Samuels (1997:155–182); Chapter 1, this volume.)

Up to now, I have kept to the pathways trodden by the roundtable participants. I'd like to end by throwing out a tentative idea for further discussion. Analyst and patient are nearly always citizens in the same polity. But they will occupy different citizen positions due to economic, cultural, and other differences. Nevertheless, despite such differences, they are linked by social bonds (with the psychological potential for mutual recognition as well as oppression along the lines Jessica Benjamin has mapped out). Would any of us, thinking as psychoanalysts, want to regard the common state of citizenship as it applies to analysts and patients within an exclusively social understanding? Could it be the case that what makes unconscious-to-unconscious communication, transference–countertransference dynamics, and therapeutic dialogue *possible* is this shared experience of citizenship? Could it be the political relationship of analyst and patient that leads to their psychological relationship? If this is the case, then what has been located behind the corral fence of the taboo has been secretly facilitating our work all along. A sobering thought reminding me of a phrase Stephen Mitchell once used while responding to something I had written, that "the political is ontological."

References

Altman, N. (1995) *The Analyst in the Inner City: Race, Class and Culture Through a Psychoanalytic Lens*. Hillsdale, NJ: The Analytic Press.

Dalal, F. (2002) *Race, Colour and the Processes of Racialization: New Perspectives from Group Analysis, Psychoanalysis and Sociology*. Hove, UK: Brunner-Routledge.

Samuels, A. (1993) *The Political Psyche*. London: Routledge.

Samuels, A. (1997) The political psyche: a challenge to therapists and clients to politicize what they do. In J. Reppen (ed.), *More Analysts at Work*. Northvale, NJ: Jason Aronson.

Samuels, A. (2001) *Politics on the Couch: Citizenship and the Internal Life*. New York: Karnac/Other Press; London: Profile Books.

Samuels, A. (2003) Psychotherapists and counsellors (UK). *Journal for the Psychoanalysis of Culture and Society*, 8(1):150–153.

Chapter 15

Response to roundtable

What dare we (not) do? Psychoanalysis: a voice in politics?

Cleonie White

The moderator and panelists of this roundtable discussion have undertaken a sorely needed dialogue regarding the role of psychoanalytic thought and practice in American society, and in the world at large, given rapidly shifting geographic boundaries and sustained levels of anxiety and dread in the world community. Can psychoanalysis be brought into the world of politics and still retain its place as a source of discovery and influence in the lives of individual patients who seek our help? What is our understanding, really, of mind, of the human condition in today's troubled world? What role do we play in shaping a different future than seems now almost inevitable? These are among the vast array of questions addressed by this panel.

We know, certainly, as discussed by members of the panel, that ordinary citizens sharing the same fears and hopes have begun national and international debates aimed at bridging differences and stemming the growing specter of aggression and war. We have begun the process of recognition and apology (e.g., Dr Benjamin in Palestine; Dr Susan Bodnar, 2004, on a Native American Reservation) that we understand are essential to the process of knowing and being known. And, with other like-minded thinkers, some of us have engaged in acts of public protest.

When we question whether psychoanalysts should be politically vocal, we rightly bear in mind the possible impact of our choices on our patients and on our profession in the public eye. The panelists struggle courageously with this issue and present much food for thought. Here are some of my ideas on the matter. To speak, or not to speak openly the language of politics with our patients is a question that, it seems to me, is answerable by our own sense of timing and of place; of mutual influence and of how much, as with any other area of clinical discourse, we analysts are open to engaging the "dialectic between *seeing and being seen*" (Bromberg 1994:523). The same might be said of our public engagement of social and political issues. Interpersonalists argue that it is our very silence on real-life factors affecting our patients' lives that has tarnished our image in the public eye (Lionells 2000). Are we, as a discipline, prepared to be "seen into" (Bromberg 1994:523), to be publicly scrutinized? What does it mean if we are not?

My belief is that, if we are to engage the difficult conflicts and fears that grip the hearts and minds of the world's citizenry, and if we are to be effective in applying our knowledge and our skills to the broader benefit of humanity, then we must first suspend rigid adherence to any particular school of thought and come together, as these panelists have done, to teach and to learn from one another. We must also listen to other interdisciplinary voices, if ever we hope to formulate an effective plan of action with demands for direct, open, public dialogues with our political leaders. And we must begin in our own social and cultural home. We cannot, I submit, successfully address conflict and the potential for change in other cultures until, as professionals, and as private citizens, we have grappled with the turbulence that rattles the culture of our own embeddedness.

Whether or not we choose to act, we cannot lose sight of how membership in a politically driven, capitalist society in which voices of dissent are readily labeled "unpatriotic" strongly influences our profession and the choices we make. This, then, brings me to Harry Stack Sullivan, the Interpersonal theorist whose "conceptions of dynamisms, homeostatic interactive mechanisms instead of fixed states or processes, transformed the psychology of mind from nineteenth century science to that of the twentieth" (Lionells 2000). Most particularly, I wish to visit Sullivan's relevance to the roundtable topic under discussion: politics and psychoanalysis.

Psychoanalysis?! Why?

The year was 1994. I was returning home from a celebration of the winter solstice with some of the most outspoken political activists and feminist writers of the sixties, seventies, and eighties, when they asked that I explain my decision to pursue psychoanalytic training. Always encouraging of my career choices, these women were, nevertheless, confounded by my decision to undertake years of study and to pursue a career in a field that, having lost its relevance in the real world, was on its last leg. This, at least, was their take on a discipline that (they did not hesitate to remind me) had yielded a theory antithetical to women's progress; had excluded large segments of the population not meeting its arbitrary rules of inclusion; had supported, in its language and its practices, politically and socially constructed dialectics of "us" versus "them," and so on. How did I, a woman of color, hailing from a so-called "third world" country, expect to find a place in this field, they questioned.

"But," I protested, "you don't understand. I'm not undertaking *that* kind of training. I'm going to study at an Interpersonal institute. Haven't you heard of Harry Stack Sullivan?"

My friends, of course, knew the theorist of whom I spoke. But as they had been raised, so to speak, on a steady diet of positivist, structuralist theories of classical psychoanalysis, it was to this brand of analytic thought that they targeted their criticisms. Indeed, they seemed little impressed, despite my enthusiastic attempts to convey what I knew to be a rapid and exciting shift in psychoanalytic thinking: that, in the spirit of Sullivan's social and political theories, we were at the "intimate edge" (Ehrenberg 1992) of a new analytic frontier. *That* was the draw for me, I explained. *That* was what made me eager to train at the very psychoanalytic institute that Sullivan himself had founded. My friends wished me luck and imposed a mandate that I report our field's progress at regular intervals (i.e., at future celebrations of the solstices). They nevertheless remained skeptical about my chosen journey.

Why, they questioned, had Sullivan's theories not influenced public thought? It did not bode well for psychoanalysis, they argued, that a theory as potentially encompassing of social constructionist thought as Sullivan's had not gained greater currency, even among the larger analytic community. I didn't then have a full grasp of the "problem" of Harry Stack Sullivan, that "quirky guy who could offend even his most passionate supporters" (Lionells 2000:394). But I believed that, if an analyst such as I, under the "triple jeopardy" of fate (i.e., *thirdworldwomanofcolor*) were ever to find a sense of place professionally, it would be within the context of Interpersonal theory and the progressive thinking it had spawned (Greenberg and Mitchell 1983). It is Sullivan's theory, in fact, that has influenced and broadened our thinking to be as inclusive as we have become, of that ever-present, social and cultural "third" in which we, and psychoanalysis itself, are deeply embedded (Cushman 1994; Lionells *et al.* 1995; Lionells 2000). He was not always so recognized, however.

Sullivan: Interpersonalist and political activist

A product of the cruelties of poverty and of class prejudices, Sullivan knew personally the powerful influence of the social realm on the psyche. Ever curious about the machinations of the social world about him, he was greatly persuaded by the observations of other social scientists, especially by the works of anthropologists Edward Sapir at Harvard and Harold Lasswell of the University of Chicago (Perry 1982). Drawing on their work, Sullivan believed that interdisciplinary collaboration would advance informed knowledge about the interactive forces at play between people and the society in which they lived. For Sullivan, the concept of "participant observation" captured the interrelatedness and mutual influences between patient and therapist, between individuals and their culture. He sought to impress upon his followers the idea of mind as a product of experience; that who we are is inexorably intertwined with our social world;

and that the notion of a unique, bounded self is simply illusory (Stern 1997). Sullivan rejected any notion of an internal, psychic world nourished by conflict and always at risk of suffering spontaneous, uncontrolled, destructive explosions. And therein lay the "problem" with Dr Sullivan. Unlike his classically trained predecessors and contemporary American psychoanalysts, he rejected the concept of the biologically driven self.

It wasn't that these destructive images were unfamiliar to Sullivan. He was witness to the vicissitudes of wars and social turmoil in America and around the world. But to this thinker, these menacing images and sounds were not the rumblings of some imagined, universal, psychic cauldron, filled with menacing fuses. For Sullivan, the menace of our society is society itself, which, in its very political and constructed power structure, creates vast and devastating wastelands of hopelessness that cut sharply along cultural, racial, and socioeconomic lines. It is precisely these inequities, Sullivan proposed, in a social structure that determines the experience of self, that set up the potential for social, powder-keg-like explosions, with worldwide, echoing power. And the haunting images of shattered glass, melting metal, and crackling concrete that have become a permanent fixture in our own psychic backyards serve as potent validation of what Sullivan knew and of what he told.

Of course, other psychotherapists in Sullivan's circle, notably Erich Fromm, also attempted to link the psychological with the social and political. Like Sullivan, Fromm knew well the ravages of war, having himself escaped Hitler's Nazi Germany. He believed strongly in the human potential to engage in and further humanistic causes, held this to be the hope of humanity, and became disillusioned with the growing emphasis in American society on materialism and consumerism (Ortmeyer 1995). Fromm, Ortmeyer writes, was of the opinion that "if one lives in a pathological culture, one should leave it" (p. 20). Influenced by socialist and Marxist ideology, Fromm collaborated with Sullivan in attempting to define the interconnectedness between culture and the psyche. Unlike Sullivan, however, who "tried to describe a constructionist, interpretive, critical field theory . . . Fromm positioned himself more within the humanist tradition, favoring a somewhat individualistic, essentialist vision" (Cushman 1994:801, footnote). Thus ended the collaboration between the two.

Sullivan was never simply satisfied with having constructed a theory of self. As he was radical in his thinking, so, too, was he radical in his call to action. He demanded more, in the form of political activity, from practitioners of psychotherapy. He believed it the moral responsibility of psychotherapists to address, actively, those factors in our culture and social structures that negatively affect the lives of our patients and of citizens at large. In this regard, Sullivan appealed to his colleagues' social sensibilities when he asked that they join him in waging a "cultural revolution" against war (Cushman 1994) and other social ills. Needless to say, this psychiatrist incurred the wrath of the analytic establishment. His insistence on locating the self in the context of the social structures within which it is embedded was experienced as a veritable slap in the essentialist face.

Yet one need only examine the current state of affairs in our field to find that Sullivan was, in fact (without shallow reliance on the overstated), well ahead of his time. In a 1994 paper, Philip Cushman discusses what he believes to have been a moment missed by psychoanalysis to be of greater social relevance. This was a crossroads moment in our discipline's history, Cushman proposes, when Sullivan's Interpersonal theory was rejected in favor of Winnicott's object-relations concept of the "true self" and Kohut's "self-psychology," both reflecting Melanie Klein's theory of inherent, internalized objects influencing experience. Cushman proposes that, lacking focus on the historical influences on their theorizing, Winnicott and Kohut inadvertently created "a new consumer language . . . focused on the emptiness, lack of cohesion, and general 'falseness' that came to be characteristic of the new [consumerist] post war self" (p. 823); language that in turn has been co-opted and exploited in the furtherance of sociopolitical agendas. Cushman writes:

> The process by which "the other" is constructed, defined and used is the face of war in our time. The constructed content of "the self" and the determination of that which is split off, disavowed, and then relocated into the unconscious and onto "the other" goes a long way toward legitimizing political decisions regarding the identity of the enemy, the content of major political issues, the distinctions between male/female and white/black, the understandings of right and wrong.
> (Cushman 1994:807)

The projection of unwanted aspects of self into another is generally thought to be a Kleinian concept, based on her notion of implicit, internalized structures. In Sullivan's terms, however, these "not me" experiences are selectively inattended, or split off from consciousness (O'Leary and Watson 1995). They are organized into dissociated "self-states" (Bromberg 1998), still very much a part of that individual, even if they remain out of awareness. What is perceived to be negative, bad, or evil in the other is determined by parallel experiences in the self as a function of one's engagement with the other.

In other words, in a continuing process begun in infancy, "adult experience of others and oneself continues, outside awareness, in this all-or-none bifurcated mode of good and evil me and good and evil others" (Fiscalini 1995:345). Even in the case of paranoid perceptions of "the other," Sullivan distinguished between projection in the Kleinian sense, and the paranoid's capacity to transfer blame (O'Leary and Watson 1995). Interpersonalists, then, embrace difference, and "commonly reject any form of distancing based on an *implicit* 'we–they' split" (Hegeman 1995:835; emphasis added).

Interpersonal theory: its relevance today?

Were Sullivan with us today, he would, I believe, simply continue where he left off. This brilliant psychoanalyst developed a theory not simply applicable to analysts and patients in the consulting room. Sullivan had a vision for our discipline. He saw its potential, embedded in our knowledge of mind as a social construct, to convey a very clear, commanding message of change to the powers that be. So, for Sullivan, whether to link psychoanalysis with politics would not be a question. For him, it could not be otherwise. Note the following observation by Lionells (2000):

> Beyond the tragedy of individual lives, interpersonal analysts can understand the uncanny experience of living in a violent culture, of experiencing disaster or chronic deprivation, constrained by a social order that prohibits self-expression or expansion . . . As heirs to the rich legacy of Harry Stack Sullivan, we have the responsibility to do something about them.
>
> (Lionells 2000:409)

Panelists in this roundtable discussion may, possibly, not regard themselves as Interpersonalists. But the very act of assembling as they have done to question the relationship between psychoanalysis and politics in today's world begins to fulfill Sullivan's dream of intradisciplinary and interdisciplinary dialogs to further the cause of humanity. He would be very pleased indeed.

References

Bodnar, S. (2004) Remembering where you came from: dissociative process in multicultural individuals. *Psychoanalytic Dialogues*, 14(5):581–603.

Bromberg, P. (1994) "Speak! that I may see you": some reflections on dissociation, reality and psychoanalytic listening. *Psychoanalytic Dialogues*, 4:517–547.

Bromberg, P. (1998) *Standing in the Spaces: Essays on Clinical Process, Trauma, and Dissociation*. Hillsdale, NJ: The Analytic Press.

Cushman, P. (1994) Confronting Sullivan's spider: hermeneutics and the politics of therapy. *Contemporary Psychoanalysis*, 30:800–844.

Ehrenberg, D. B. (1992) *The Intimate Edge: Extending the Reach of Psychoanalytic Interaction*. New York: W. W. Norton.

Fiscalini, J. (1995) Narcissism and self-disorder. In M. Lionells, J. Fiscalini, C. Mann, and D. Stern (eds), *Handbook of Interpersonal Psychoanalysis*. Hillsdale, NJ: The Analytic Press, pp. 333–374.

Greenberg, J. R. and Mitchell, S. A. (1983) *Object Relations in Psychoanalytic Theory*. Cambridge, MA: Harvard University Press.

Hegeman, E. (1995) Cross cultural issues in interpersonal psychoanalysis. In M. Lionells, J. Fiscalini, C. Mann, and D. Stern (eds), *Handbook of Interpersonal Psychoanalysis*. Hillsdale, NJ: The Analytic Press, pp. 823–846.

Lionells, M. (2000) Sullivan's anticipation of the postmodern turn in psychoanalysis. *Contemporary Psychoanalysis*, 36:393–410.

Lionells, M., Fiscalini, J., Mann, C. and Stern, D. (eds) (1995) *Handbook of Interpersonal Psychoanalysis*. Hillsdale, NJ: The Analytic Press.

O'Leary, J. V. and Watson, R. I., Jr (1995) Paranoia. In M. Lionells, J. Fiscalini, C. Mann, and D. Stern (eds), *Handbook of Interpersonal Psychoanalysis*. Hillsdale, NJ: The Analytic Press, pp. 397–417.

Ortmeyer, D. H. (1995) History of the founders of Interpersonal psychoanalysis. In M. Lionells, J. Fiscalini, C. Mann, and D. Stern (eds), *Handbook of Interpersonal Psychoanalysis*. Hillsdale, NJ: The Analytic Press, pp. 11–27.

Perry, H. S. (1982) *Psychiatrist of America: The Life of Harry Stack Sullivan*. Cambridge, MA: Harvard University Press.

Stern, D. (1997) *Unformulated Experience: From Dissociation to Imagination in Psychoanalysis*. Hillsdale, NJ: The Analytic Press.

Chapter 16

Political identity

A personal postscript[1]

Amanda Hirsch Geffner

A word about recurrent themes, unfinished thoughts, and questions opened up in the above discussion, along with my associations to certain points of personal preoccupation. (The personal *is*, after all, political, and vice versa, as has been mentioned by the preceding discussants.) In writing what follows, I have necessarily removed my moderator/editor's hat, as I endeavor to convey aspects of the bidirectional impact of preparing for and participating in this roundtable discussion and the process of sorting out my own personal politics. In making explicit this process, I hope to provide an illustration of the complex intertwining of the personal, the clinical, and the political to be found, I believe, in many of our lives.

Along with the panelists, I have grappled (as analysand, and then also, inevitably, as analyst) with the issue, raised by Neil Altman, "of the socio-cultural unconscious." It is a two-way street: society molds the psyche, gives birth to "the family," while the family romance (in its many forms) engenders the civic persona. Endless negotiations with my particularly polarized familial introjects inform both who I am as citizen and who I am as psychoanalyst. The effort to find a livable balance between such personally shaded, yet socially constructed dualisms as empathy/self-interest, tenderness/firmness, and openness/having boundaries largely determines who I am politically. And it is also a co-construction of the time and place (the political milieu) in which the story of my life has happened to unfold.

Paul Wachtel addressed this point when he said, "There's a whole host of ways in which we often talk as if we're talking about a universal human nature, when we're really talking about the reflections of what it's like to grow up and be human in a particular cultural context." A desire to come to terms with these various personal issues and to live in relative peace with myself and others is also what drives my wish to better understand and, perhaps, to find my place (where I position myself, how, how much, and at what pace I choose to act) in the larger political picture.[2]

To return to the most compelling question of the roundtable, connoted by its title, what makes open political discussion – both in and out of the consulting room – so radioactively untouchable, so tricky, so taboo? The panelists richly engaged this topic from many angles: considering political discussion to be a "slippery slope" (NA) and neglecting to deal with politics as a "kind of collusion to avoid a particularly important topic" (TJ).[3] Ted Jacobs links this wariness of "entering into a situation in which very strong and sometimes quite irrational feelings" exist to a fear of losing "one's stance as a therapist." And one might imagine the latter, in turn, resulting in destructive explosion, treatment impasse, or abrupt termination. Introducing politics into the conversation sometimes stirs up a disturbingly intrusive awareness of difference and sometimes threatens, from the other direction, to plunge us back into a sea of non-differentiation. We feel ourselves swept up and overwhelmed by forces larger than, unformulated by, and indistinctly known to our personal selves (JB, PW).

My own thoughts on "the taboo" are that it has to do with just how inextricably, how implicitly woven into the fabric of our personal identities political convictions are. Much like religious convictions, they are housed, it seems, not in the cerebrum's "rational" left side, but rather in its primordial, nonverbal crevices. To a certain extent, we inherit our political dispositions; we are born into them, in a sense, as products of temperament. They adhere inseparably to the strands of our earliest memories, and are intersubjectively and interpersonally constructed as part of our most basic organizing principles. They are deeply rooted (almost feeling "hard-wired"); obdurate, although not totally impervious to the forces of change; like any personality structure, slow to alter; and guarded against external influence. Stockpiles of statistics have minimal, if any, impact in political discussions. And well-researched facts and figures may be taken in as interesting, but at the end of the day, with few exceptions, we tend to remain in our guts, politically, who we are.

Just think: when have you ever changed someone's mind politically? And perhaps this is precisely the point; that a reasonable aim of political debate is not so much all-or-nothing change of the other as the achievement of some degree of mutual tolerance, which, in the best of circumstances, might lead to harmonious and perhaps even fruitful coexistence (NA, JB). One might also, of course, draw parallels here with the reasonable aim of psychoanalysis, i.e., the achievement of mutual recognition, a tolerance for the other's separate subjectivity, and the successful negotiation of difference (Benjamin 1988; Aron 1996; Slavin and Kriegman 1992).

Clinically, patients' political beliefs are often placed in the category of assumptions we dare (not) question, to borrow a phrase from discussant Cleonie White. We often tread lightly in their presence, due to our sense that to challenge them would traumatically disrupt a needed self-object relatedness on the patient's part – or is it our own? And we are, with good reason, wary of the destabilizing – and therefore polarizing – potential (TJ, NA) of delving too precipitously into core beliefs, core self and self-with-other experiences. On the other hand, politics is, at times, experienced benevolently, as a cultivating medium or tacit substratum of the therapeutic alliance (JB) (an aspect of the "unobjectionable positive transference–countertransference" (TJ)) – this mainly applying to cases of assumed political concordance between analyst and analysand. (And one can only imagine the drastic change in analytic ambience that likely would occur were a patient to be abruptly, or even gradually, disabused of such assumptions.)

In fact, it seems to me (to amplify upon what Ted Jacobs said) that analysts and patients often tacitly collude to preserve the idea of political concordance, even when both participants are aware on some level that this implied agreement is illusory. On the one hand, illusions factor into all transference; we often find it hard to recognize ourselves in what is reflected back to us through the lens of our patients' subjectivity (NA). On the other hand, when psychic pressures to keep political difference under cover are intense, more than a wish to avoid foreclosing analytic imagination may be at play; a reluctance to confront political assumptions may be similar to, and at times a re-enactment of, the keeping of shameful family secrets.

Even when patient and analyst hold relatively similar political opinions (as, for example, in Paul Wachtel's comments on issues raised for him when working with people who are "living lives that [his] superego approves of"), a choice not to analytically examine or to foreground this aspect of the therapy relationship has significance. Since politics concerns itself with how power is distributed and exercised, it stands to reason that politics is ever present in the consultation room in the form of the built-in power differential between analyst and patient. Analysts (to varying degrees) present themselves as, and are experienced to be, authorities, although over the course of a successful treatment, a deconstruction of this authority (JB) and a process of de-idealizing the analyst (gradually transforming him or her in the eyes of the patient from idealized parent to fallible co-human) occurs.[4]

Given these factors (i.e., the analyst's perceived authority, power, and idealized status), unanalyzed implications of shared political attitudes may unintentionally give an analysand the message that her analyst's is the "right" or "only" way of viewing the world, and lead either to unquestioning adoption by the patient of her analyst's views or to the submergence of the patient's true views in order to keep them safely hidden from her analyst, upon whom she depends, as well as from herself. In the roundtable, only brief attention was given to the topic of politics and power in the analytic hour. The panelists did, however, visit a number of variations on this theme. In listening and re-listening to the tape of the discussion, a simultaneous, mutually influencing play of these concerns at the level of intimate pairing (be it lover–lover, parent–child, or patient–analyst) and of collective discourse became discernible.

In proposing a way of working with "the Israeli–Palestinian situation," for example, Neil Altman imported theory pertaining to relational conflict, impasse, and abuse into the land of politics. To extend the metaphor, I believe that, much in the same way that an understanding of the dynamics of difference in couples (i.e., the various kinds of "intermarriage") has been helpful, an understanding of dynamics in the "interpolitical" relationship – a kind of interrelationship yet to be theorized or clinically explored, by psychoanalysts, at least – might give us a better sense of how we relate to each other and to ourselves politically.

Now is probably the time to disclose (or to make explicit what may already have become implicitly clear) that I, along with all four panelists and three discussants, locate myself politically on the Left. I might also mention – make of it what you will – that my editorial colleagues and I could not locate a politically conservative analyst to participate in the discussion. Of course, we might have balanced things more by including one or two *less* left-of-center liberals, but the most impassioned and politically active analysts we knew were first to come to mind, and – to our good fortune – were more than willing to sign on. To consider for a moment this difficulty in finding a right-wing psychoanalyst, the possibility of geographical skewing (this being a US East-Coast project) notwithstanding, the question does arise as to whether there might be some connection between a liberal progressive stance and the life experiences, values, traits, and worldviews behind the making (painting here with broad, somewhat distorting strokes) of a "typical" psychoanalyst.

In tossing around this question, the panelists creatively reached for words to articulate what seemed to be an ineffable, yet nonetheless real, common psychic cause of psychoanalysts. What they had time that evening to develop was the notion of "a critical, more tolerant position" (NA) comprising (among other things) a refusal to accept a "sort of moralistic, ideal-driven stance," the idea "that we can stand to find out things about ourselves and about the other that are inherently painful and disappointing," and an insistence that "we have to face what is unpleasant, either in human nature or society" (JB).

These descriptions, infused as they are with a sobering, open-eyed, post-modern sensibility, led me to muse about the distinction between having ideals (perhaps even being unabashedly idealistic) and being ideal-driven. Perhaps the difference is to be found in the degree to which one recognizes that an ideal is just that; an ideal, abstract and never realizable in time and space. Critical thinkers are, for good reason, suspicious of embodied ideals (their own included), as they can represent a pseudo-wholeness, a hypomanic effort to cover over lack and brokenness (both aspects of the human condition), along with related, dissociated, and unmourned losses. (See, for example, Mitscherlich and Mitscherlich's *The Inability to Mourn* (1975).) And yet, idealism was clearly a feature of political and therapeutic attitudes of the sixties – i.e., the civil rights and antiwar movements (see Chapter 13, as well as P. Wachtel's references to Martin Luther King, Jr, and left-wing spiritual values) and humanistic trends in psychoanalysis and psychotherapy (Loew 2003). It also seems that efforts by the Left to unseat the current President are fueled to some extent by a sense of anger at ideals betrayed.

The dilemma I am presenting is that ideals are both a basic necessity and a potential danger for humans of either political persuasion. The panelists noted that liberals and psychoanalysts are, in their own ways, prone to the seductive power of overbearing ideals, which tempt us, for example, to hold ourselves above the fray of political negotiation and compromise for fear of dirtying our hands or (as Ted Jacobs aptly stated), of "fraternizing with the 'enemy,'" and of, thereby, tarnishing our idealized self-representations. From the other direction, ego ideals sometimes come back to bite us even more fiercely when we are among our own political "kind," as we see in Paul Wachtel's refreshingly frank description of the countertransferential difficulties he sometimes faced when "working with patients who are to the left of [himself, and who,] in many ways are closer to [his] own ideal than [he is]." In a similar vein are Jessica Benjamin's comments on "destructive splits in the Left," originating in the "covert" expression of suppressed "sadism" and other "hateful feelings" unacceptable to our "'depressive' ego ideals."

In Kohut's self-psychological terms, we have a lifelong need for selfobject-relatedness, including opportunities to be mirrored by, and to idealize, admired others. One thing that paradoxically might lead to being uncritically swept up by one's idealism is an overly strenuous effort to outgrow (prove oneself too sophisticated, too mature for) it. And perhaps a mass denial (on both sides) of one's own group's idealizing trends is a factor in the current political polarization of Left and Right. Ultimately, I am not entirely convinced that either liberal progressives or psychoanalysts lack an ideal-driven stance. I do, however, think that a tolerance for our own imperfection and that of others – an intention to be nonjudgmental and accepting, as we attempt to observe ourselves and others, without attachment to any particular outcome – is the model (or ideal, if you will) of a postmodern psychoanalytic (if not also Buddhist, for that matter) stance. And it is a stance that seems to parallel the socially tolerant open-mindedness of a liberal, progressive position or ideal.

To now step out on what feels, in present imagined company, like a rather shaky limb, I will venture again to make the implicit explicit by disclosing that some of my "best friends" are conservatives. (And I ask of myself and of the reader why it is that I sense such strong resistance from the collective analytic field to making such an acknowledgment. Is some transgression of a tacit professional agreement to preserve a comforting sameness through partisanship in this one area, perhaps, involved?[5]) To be specific, one of my closest friends has, in recent years, most vexingly, crossed over the political divide. Thus, ours has become an "interpolitical" friendship. It is out of the tension of struggling to reconcile my deep affection and respect for this friend with my profound, nearly visceral distaste for those whom my friend now considers to be his fellow travelers – and in some cases, his guides through the murky terrain of "new normal" – that the idea for this political roundtable was conceived.

I am therefore motivated upon multiple levels to ask myself, as we have asked the panelists, about the degree to which forms of projection enable us (on both sides of the political fence) to externalize and to critically reject our own inner "demons" – much as married couples or the partners in any kind of dyad often do – while at the same time splitting off core (if ego-ideal alien) energies. Here I believe myself to be in accord with the Interpersonalist view that dissociated self-states (Bromberg 1998) are still very much part of the dissociating individual, and not to be thought of as literally projectable onto inherently receptive "others." Cleonie White's account (Chapter 15) of the politics of psychoanalytic theorizing (i.e., the privileging of Klein *et al.*, and the marginalizing of Sullivan), and its historical impact upon sociocultural realities, brings home just how concretely relevant the making of such distinctions can be. In rigidly adhering to idealized representations of ourselves, Ted Jacobs remarks, we hinder "the achievement of practical political aims." And, I feel, we also – to use a currently "conservatively" valenced word (see Chapter 14, and also roundtable comments by P. Wachtel) – "morally" deplete ourselves and weaken our own integrity.[6]

I had hoped to ponder this systemic splitting in more detail. However, since "our space" is almost up, I will need to be content with presenting a number of questions, which I plan to take up at a later date in the hopes that the reader will do so as well: Can dyadic principles such as splitting and projection be applied to political group phenomena? If so, what is it that people on both sides of the political divide are psychically "holding" for each other? (See, for example, Jessica Benjamin's comments on the "guilt/shame" axis.) Further, is internal political integration (i.e., a blending of Right and Left) desirable, as a marker of health, on the individual level? Are there parallel forms of psychic integration to be identified, or striven for, on the political-party, or even the national level? Does psychic integration (of the individual or group) lead to a greater capacity for tolerance? Is tolerance the most adaptive stance or the better, more moral approach to every situation? Is there a place for morality in critical thought, and if so, what is it? And where does passion fit in? We value it (e.g., having the "courage of one's convictions" and "standing up for what we believe"). Yet, how does, or can, being passionate about one's political beliefs (with the implication of being willing to "fight for" them) mesh with an equally compelling value of being tolerant (even of those whose beliefs or interests and ours seem mutually exclusive)?

To just begin to touch upon my answers to these questions, on a psychological level, what the Left seems to "hold" for both political sides is "depressive" ego ideals, while the Right's ideals (also "held" for both sides) may be described as "paranoid-schizoid." Thomas Ogden suggests that a more or less fluid access to both psychic positions is needed by the individual to function under life's continuously varying circumstances (Ogden 1989). One might ask, is fluid access to both of these psychic states by individuals on both the Right and the Left also a requisite of political health? Or does it make more sense to view the body politic as a cohering organism (or as an amalgamation of multiple, political self-states), analogous to the individual? In this case, one might argue that political entities (both regional and global), when taken as a whole, do, in fact, have fluid (or perhaps more accurately, dialectic) access to a multitude of stances.

My inclination is to believe that, in the best of scenarios, both liberals and conservatives would have an ability to more consciously enjoy and utilize the strength of paranoid-schizoid, unconflicted self-states, while at the same time fully feeling and tolerating depressive guilt about our more selfish or self-protective impulses. (And being more consciously in touch with these "ugly" truths about ourselves, ironically, we might be freed to choose to pay their beckoning less heed – and also to be less paralyzed by guilt over them (JB, NA).) This brings to mind Donnell Stern's comments in a recent paper about "finding it possible to experience guilt and pleasure simultaneously, even if it was not comfortable" (Stern 2004). "Not comfortable" is also a fitting way to describe the state most likely to emerge when the topic of politics is engaged in psychoanalysis, by psychoanalysts (in treatment and beyond). And, given the pervasive saturation of our lives with things political, how crucial it is for us to feel just that!?

Notes

1 Much of this essay is the product of an ongoing, at times unsettling conversation with Ken Frank, to whom I am grateful for his unflappable emotional poise and many useful insights. My thanks also to Judy Greenwald for her sharp sense of clarity and insistence upon understandability.

2 Of course, I am far from the first to take an interest in such researches, this having been a mainstay of early Interpersonalist theory and practice (one might even call it "ideology" or "mission") (see Chapter 15). And I also owe a considerable debt of gratitude to Andrew Samuels and his writings for validating and providing a model for embarking upon this sort of exploration.

3 Here, and throughout this chapter, I cross-reference panelists' related ideas from the roundtable discussion, using their initials.

4 While analysis of the idealizing transference is a theoretical goal, the human inclination to idealize is also made use of in treatment, easing patients – through the imparting of procedural knowledge and implicit learning – into the acquisition of new relational patterns and expectations (Lichtenberg *et al.* 2002). Thus, there is a tension in analysis between the therapeutic use of idealization and the aim of working to dissolve the same.

5 Andrew Samuels, for one, has recognized, and taken steps to remedy, such tacit exclusionary practices of our profession in explicitly voicing openness to

participation of those on the Right, as well as the Left, in his grassroots organization, Psychotherapists and Counsellors for Social Responsibility.

6 Interestingly, the panelists noted the workings of splitting in other permutations as well; for example, a historical tendency of some psychoanalysts to adhere to a "strict father" model professionally, while shifting to a "nurturant-parent" style in their dealings with society (PW), and the Albert Einstein phenomenon (NA), in which an individual may behave as if, to paraphrase Charlie Brown, they love mankind; it's people they can't stand.

References

Aron, L. (1996) *A Meeting of the Minds: Mutuality in Psychoanalysis.* Hillsdale, NJ: The Analytic Press.

Benjamin, J. (1988) *The Bonds of Love: Psychoanalysis, Feminism, and the Problem of Domination.* New York: Pantheon Books.

Bromberg, P. (1998) *Standing in the Spaces: Essays on Clinical Process, Trauma, and Dissociation.* Hillsdale, NJ: The Analytic Press.

Lichtenberg, J., Lachmann, F. and Fosshage, J. (2002) *The Spirit of Inquiry: Communication in Psychoanalysis.* Hillsdale, NJ: The Analytic Press.

Loew, C. (2003) The evolution of N.I.P. in a historical perspective: a founder's reflections. *Psychoanalytic Perspectives*, 1:7–10.

Mitscherlich, A. and Mitscherlich, M. (1975) *The Inability to Mourn: Principles of Collective Behavior.* New York: Grove Press.

Ogden, T. (1989) *The Primitive Edge of Experience.* Northvale, NJ: Jason Aronson.

Slavin, M. O. and Kriegman, D. (1992) *The Adaptive Design of the Human Psyche: Psychoanalysis, Evolutionary Biology, and the Therapeutic Process.* New York: Guilford Press.

Stern, D. B. (2004) The eye sees itself: dissociation, enactment, and the achievement of conflict. *Contemporary Psychoanalysis*, 40:197–237.

Index

For Product Safety Concerns and Information please contact our EU representative GPSR@taylorandfrancis.com Taylor & Francis Verlag GmbH, Kaufingerstraße 24, 80331 München, Germany

Batch number: 10725798

Printed by Printforce, the Netherlands